The Resilience Game Plan

The Tween Playbook for Developing Cognitive, Communication, and Mindfulness Life Skills

Middle School Student Edition

by

Colleen Carter Ster, A.L.M.

THIS PLAYBOOK BELONGS TO:

_____

DATE:

_____

Published by Reflections Publishing LLC
© 2023, 2024 Reflections Publishing LLC. All rights reserved.

No part of this book may be used or reproduced in any manner whatsoever without the prior written permission of the publisher, except for brief quotations embodied in critical articles and reviews.

Disclaimer of Warranties/Limitation of Liability: The publisher and the author make no representations or warranties, express or implied, with respect to this book, including without limitation the accuracy or completeness of the content thereof, and the publisher and the author each specifically disclaim any and all such representations or warranties, including without limitation any warranty of title, merchantability, non-infringement, and/or fitness for a particular purpose. No warranty may be created or extended by any sales or promotional materials. The advice and strategies contained in this book may not be suitable for every person and/or every situation. This book is sold with the understanding that the publisher and the author are not engaged in rendering medical, legal, or other professional advice or services. If professional assistance is required, the services of a competent professional should be sought. Neither the publisher nor the author shall be liable for any damages or losses arising in any way from this book and/or the content thereof. The fact that an individual, organization, or website is referred to in this book as a citation and/or potential source of further information does not mean that the publisher or the author endorses any information or recommendation that the individual, organization, or the website may provide. In addition, readers should be aware that any website listed in this book may have changed or disappeared between when this work was written/published and when it is read. While the author has made every effort to provide accurate telephone numbers and/or internet addresses at the time of publication, neither the publisher nor the author assume any responsibility for errors or for changes that occur after publication. The publisher and the author do not have any control over and do not assume any responsibility for third-party websites or their content.

Neither the publisher nor the author is engaged in rendering professional medical advice or services, including without limitation to any individual reader. The ideas, information, and/or suggestions contained in this book are not intended as a substitute for consulting with your physician and/or other professional service provider. All matters regarding your health require medical supervision. Neither the author nor the publisher shall be liable or responsible for any damages or losses allegedly arising from any ideas, information, suggestions, and/or other content in this book.

Names, characters, businesses, organizations, places, events, and incidents included in this book either are the product of the author's imagination or are used fictitiously. Any resemblance to actual persons, living or dead, events, or locales is entirely coincidental.

First Edition. Published in the United States of America.

Paperback ISBN: 978-1-61660-019-8

Visit our website at www.reflectionspublishing.com for more information or inquiries

* * *

The photograph on the cover was taken at Torrey Pines State Park in San Diego, California.

APA Formatting and Style Guide (7th Edition) was utilized for citations.

The fonts used in this playbook are **Ad Lib** (section headers and page headers), Times New Roman (body copy), and Futura Condensed (Appendix body copy).

• About the Author •

Colleen Carter Ster earned her Master of Liberal Arts from Harvard University's Division of Continuing Education in Psychology in 2023 out of concern for the self-harm cases among youth worldwide. Ster created *The Resilience Game Plan: The Playbook for Developing Cognitive, Communication, and Mindfulness Skills* to provide a curriculum for middle schools, high schools, and colleges to help adolescents and emerging adults build resilience by giving them tools to understand how the brain works and help them deal with difficult life situations.

In the mid to late 1990s, Ster served as Executive Vice President for The Electronic Bookshelf (EBS). During her time at EBS, she created curriculum questions for K-12th grade students and developed continuing education credit materials for EBS Reading Power Seminars. Ster conducted training seminars to administrators, library media specialists, and teachers around the United States for several years. In 1998, EBS was acquired by Scholastic, Inc., and Ster became the Director of Marketing Services for Scholastic Reading Counts! in the Learning Ventures Division of Scholastic in New York, New York.

During Ster's years traveling around the United States conducting "Reading Power" training seminars for EBS, she listened to what types of books educators were looking to purchase for their students. Time and again, the answer was to find literature to help students when they were struggling with difficult life scenarios. In 2008, Ster addressed this need by founding a children's publishing business, Reflections Publishing LLC. *ALA Booklist* called the first Reflections Publishing LLC book series "a unique series by children, for children." This special collection by Reflections Publishing LLC is a book series called "Kids Helping Kids Through Books."

As a Girl Scout leader, Ster consulted with her troop members and developed the Reflections Publishing Communication Assessment. Since 2008, this assessment has been a useful tool for K-12 students and their caregivers (parents/guardians), emerging young adults, and adults. The purpose of the assessment is to help individuals understand how their communication skills play a role and affect the way they communicate with others. Ster wants children, tweens, teens, and emerging adults to understand that communication skills are valuable interpersonal tools for them to learn at a young age so they can use these skills during their academic years, when entering into personal relationships, and navigating professional work environments. The Reflections Publishing Communication Assessment and its concepts are incorporated throughout *The Resilience Game Plan* playbook.

Ster is vested in continuing her education to keep *The Resilience Game Plan* an up-to-date and valuable tool for elementary, middle, and high schools and colleges. As a postgraduate student in the University of Oxford's Department for Continuing Education, Ster developed in-person and HyFlex training materials that best support users of *The Resilience Game Plan* intervention program.

With a focus on taking neuroscience, neurobiology, self-harm, and cognitive behavior therapy courses, Ster is determined to try to reduce self-harm cases among youth around the world. Ster wants to get *The Resilience Game Plan* into the hands of every student—providing students their best chance to obtain strong, short- and long-term developmental and well-being outcomes.

Proudly born and raised in Indiana, Ster has called San Diego home for more than 20 years, and is married with three daughters and a son-in-law.

• Acknowledgments •

Professional Mentors and Professors:
- **Jan-Emmanuel De Neve, Ph.D.,** University of Oxford: Director of the Wellbeing Research Centre, Professor of Economics and Behavioural Science; Editor of *World Happiness Report*; Co-founder of the World Wellbeing Movement
- **S. Barak Caine, Ph.D.,** Harvard Medical School Director: Associate Professor of Psychology, McLean Hospital: Neuroscience and Behavioral Pharmacology Laboratory
- **Steven Boomhower, Ph.D.,** Harvard Instructor: Psychopharmacology, Gradient Corporation: Associate Toxicologist
- **Karyn Gunnet-Shoval, Ph.D.**, Harvard University: Department of Psychology- PhD in Counseling Psychology, Yale University: Clinical Psychology, Post-Doctoral Fellowships at Harvard University (Research) and Dartmouth-Hitchcock (Clinical), Dartmouth: Assistant Professor of Psychiatry, Columbia Coaching Certification Program
- **Katie Heikkinen, Ed.D.,** A.B., Harvard College: Psychology, M.A., Harvard Graduate School of Education: Mind, Brain, and Education, Ed.D., Harvard Graduate School of Education: Human Development
- **Stephanie Maddox, Ph.D.,** Yale University: The Jackson Laboratory, Harvard Medical School: Depression & Anxiety Disorders Division, McLean Hospital: Asst. Neuroscientist, Neurobiology of Fear Lab: Director, Brains Matter
- **Melinda Nevins, D. O.,** Scripps Health: Family Medicine
- **Denise Pope, Ph.D.,** Stanford Graduate School of Education: Co-founder of Challenge Success
- **Alexandra Sedlovskaya, M.S., M.Phil., and Ph.D.,** Associate Director at Harvard Business School
- **Jesse Snedeker, Ph.D.,** Harvard University Instructor: Developmental Psychology
- **Dante Spetter, Ph.D.,** Harvard University Instructor: Adolescent and Young Adult Development
- **Jacqueline Sperling, Ph.D.,** Harvard Medical School: Instructor, McLean Hospital: Co-Program Director of Anxiety Mastery Program, Clinical Psychologist
- **Kelly Zuromski, Ph.D.,** Harvard University: Department of Psychology, Research Associate in Nock Lab

Peer Reviewers:
- **Kristen Miller Bilkey, Ed.S., M.S.Ed.,** Northwestern School Corporation: Superintendent
- **Andrea Clark, M.A.Ed.: Administration,** San Dieguito Union High School District
- **William S. Eggert, A.L.M.: Psychology,** Harvard Extension School, AP Psychology/Chemistry Teacher Jesuit High School
- **Staci Emerson, Ph.D.,** Clinical and Organizational Psychologist
- **Naomi Ferrel, B.A.: Psychology, M.A.Ed.,** Tri-Central Community Schools
- **Mythily Herz, A.L.M.: Psychology,** Harvard Extension School, **J.D.,** University of Chicago
- **Cheryl James-Ward, Ed.D.,** Former Superintendent, high school charter school CEO/principal
- **Josh Larsh, B.F.Ed.,** Co-Athletic Director, Zionsville School District
- **Ana María Perez Uribe, A.L.M.: Psychology,** Harvard Extension School, Asst Directress, Alexander Montessori School
- **Kellie Rodkey, M.A.Ed.: Administration and Supervision,** Simon Youth Academy
- **Dr. Randolph Ward, Ed.D.,** retired San Diego County Superintendent of Schools, Exec. Dir. of Teaching for America
- **Julie Watts, Ph.D.,** Rhoades School, 6th & 8th Grade Social Studies, Humanities
- **Paula Yohe, B.S.Ed., M.A.Ed., M.L.I.S.,** Director of Technology and Information Systems, Dillon School District IV

Beta Test Schools:
- **Canyon Crest Academy • San Diego, CA**
  - Many thanks to Zachary Brown and Timothy Stiven and the Humanities Conservatory Students.
- **The Rhoades School • Encinitas, CA**
  - Many thanks to 8th grade educator Dr. Julie Watts and principal Dr. Regina McDuffie and the eighth grade class.

My Cheerleaders:
- **Family -** Much love and grateful to Patty Barry, Liz Crocker, Chad Freeman, Tanja Freeman, Jenn Kaufman, Alexandra Ster, Brian T. Ster, Caroline Ster Weeks, Izzy Ster, and Blain Weeks.
- **Friends -** Thank you for your brainstorming sessions and support: Kandace Baron, Terri Carter, Judy Cours, Cynthia D'Luna, Erin Eaves, Judy Enns, Fred and Lucia Franke, Doreen Hutton, Micki Jones, Mica Martín, Jamie and Sara Nelson, Jennifer Neff-Powell, Kimberly Robbins, André and Molly Rocha, Janette Shelton, Mike and Nancy Stansbury, Mindy Suarez, Larry Warner, Emma Webb, and Heidi Zhang.
- **Reflections Publishing Interns:** Lily Freeman, Kiran Herz, Mursal Obaid, Nargis Obaid, Miriam Obaid, and Caroline Yao. Many thanks to Shinhae Kang for the illustrations in the playbook.

• •

In Loving Memory of Cody Banks Jones

Table of Contents

Foreward	1
Introduction	3
Section One: *The Resilience Game Plan* Pre-Assessment	5
• Pre-Assessment	6-7
Section Two: Reflections Publishing Communication Assessment	9
Section Three: How *The Resilience Game Plan* Will Benefit You	11
Section Four: How to Become a Resilent Global Changemaker	15
Section Five: How to Use *The Resilience Game Plan*	17
• Six Strategies for Success	18
• Creating Your "Personalized Game Plan"	18-19
• How to Use *The Resilience Game Plan*	20-42
4114U Life Topic Pages	20
Playbook Strategy #1: Understanding Brain Power	20
Playbook Strategy #2: Learning Cognitive Skills	22
• Step One: Expressive Writing	22-24
• Step Two: Gauging Your Emotions - Subjective Units of Distress Scale	25
• Step Three: Overcoming Obstacles - Fear and Avoidance Hierarchy Ladder	26
Playbook Strategy #3: Learning Communication Skills	27
• Compliments and Praise	27
• Feeling Respected	27
• Friendliness and Caring	28
• Helping Hand	28
• Hugs	28
• Spending Time Together	28
• Token of Friendship/Gift-Giving	28
• Unconditional Love	29
Playbook Strategy #4: Learning Mindfulness Skills	30
Playbook Strategy #5: Developing New Habits	31
• **Well-Being Game Plan • Well-Being Habit Tracker:**	33
- Sleep	34
- Exercise	35
- Mindfulness	36
- Nature	37
- Hydration	38
- Nutrition	39
- Social Fitness	39
- Caring	40
- Gratitude	40
- Happiness	40
- Laugh	41
- Smile	41
- Music	41
Playbook Strategy #6: Setting Goals and Reducing Anxiety	42

Section Six: What's Your Game Plan? • Warm-up — **43**
- Academic Pressures — 44
- Habit Formation: Forming New Habits and Breaking Old Habits — 50
- What is Your Legacy? - Core Values — 56
- Who Are Your Mentors/Coaches? — 62

Section Seven: What's Your Game Plan? • Life Choices — **69**
- Self and Identity — 70
- Social Media - Setting Boundaries — 76
- Time Management - Life Balance — 82

Section Eight: What's Your Game Plan? • Life Crises — **89**
- Abuse - Domestic, Physical, and Verbal — 90
- Anxiety — 96
- Depression — 102
- Self-Harm — 108
- Substance Abuse - Alcohol and Drugs — 114

Section Nine: What's Your Game Plan? • Relationships — **121**
- Bullying/Cyberbullying — 122
- Caregiver (Parent or Guardian) — 128
- Friendship — 134
- Peer Pressure — 140

Section Ten: *The Resilience Game Plan* Post-Assessment — **147**
- Post-Assessment — 148-149

Section Eleven: 4114U - Appendix — **151**
- Depression Game Plan — 152
- Nutrition Game Plan — 153
- Brain Power Color Chart — 154

Section Twelve: 4114U - Notes — **155**

Section Thirteen: 4114U - Glossary of Terms — **169**

Section Fourteen: 4114U - Resources — **171**

Section Fifteen: 4114U - References — **175**

Create-Your-Own Life Topic — **188-193**

Space to Download and Process Your Thoughts — **194**

***The Resilience Game Plan* Certificate of Completion** — **195**

• Foreward •

Dear Reader,

    Until a few years ago, admitting students had mental health challenges such as depression, suicidal ideation, anxiety, or eating disorders was seen as taboo. The challenges and others related to students' social and emotional wellness were only to be discussed with pediatricians, therapists, and maybe school counselors. Students lucky enough to have the family resources or districts with dedicated therapists, like Licensed Marriage and Family Therapists (LMFTs), were generally provided the invaluable care that may have saved their lives and/or provided them with the skills to be successful students.

    The U.S. Surgeon General, Dr. Vivek Murthy shared that teen mental health has reached crisis and endemic levels (US Surgeon General Advisory Report, 2021). He said that mental health challenges are the leading cause of disability and poor life outcomes in young people. He further reported that in recent years, we have seen a significant increase in certain mental health disorders in youth—noting the aforementioned: depression, anxiety, and suicidal ideation.

    In a partnership with Challenge Success, Donahue (2021) with NBC News reported on their research study highlighting three key findings:

- Students, especially females and students of color, continue to experience high levels of stress and pressure.
- Student engagement with learning, which is always a challenge, is especially low.
- Students' relationships with adults and peers are strong, yet appear strained at times.

    This means that many students are struggling to maintain healthy relationships with peers and adults, to perform well in school, and to experience happiness and joy. Strong social and emotional skills are necessary not only to ensure students do well in school, have self efficacy, but are also needed to grow into productive adults. Ensuring that students have resiliency skills, specifically cognitive, communication, and mindfulness skills to develop strong mental, social and emotional wellness, is critical to their overall and future success.

    The OECD 2030 Life Skills Study found the following:

    Achievement at school depends on a number of social and emotional skills, such as perseverance, self-control, responsibility, curiosity, and emotional stability. Some social and emotional skills are a prerequisite for successful participation and performance in academic settings. Moreover, while cognitive skills have long been considered the most important determinants of success in employment, recent studies show that social and emotional skills also directly affect occupational status and income. In fact, in some cases, social and emotional skills are equally, if not more so, as important as cognitive skills in determining future employment.

    Responses to these findings require an "All in Village" effort; hence, ensuring the mental health of our adolescents requires collaboration—schools, policymakers, families, institutions, and individuals—and a commitment to how we view, prioritize, and address mental health.

As a high school principal of mostly first-generation college-bound students with numerous challenges stemming primarily from poverty and the pandemic, I had young folks who could barely find their way to the schoolhouse gates—due to the trauma they had experienced in one form or another. We were lucky at my school though because we had one of the best LMFTs and generally two LMFT interns on staff. Because we were a small school with two entrances, we could look every student in the eye each morning to check their readiness to learn (mental state) and provide real-time support. We were fortunate enough to provide support to not only individual students, but also to their families and our teaching staff.

Being superintendent of an affluent secondary school district gave me a window into the challenges of students who are constantly under pressure to perform and, in some cases, by any means necessary. Sometimes this led to students' self-harm, attempting to take their lives and, unfortunately, in a few cases succeeding. What struck me was that the number one and two districts in the state at the time both had some of the highest suicide rates in the state. The Psychiatric Emergency Response Team (PERT) was called to our high-performing high schools several times a month. Although we cannot pinpoint the exact numbers, we also had a group of students who regularly engaged in self-harm with cutting.

One analysis of self-injury across more than 40 countries discovered (Recovery Village, 2023):

- About 17% of all people will self-harm during their lifetime.
- The average age of the first incident of self-harm is 13.
- 45% of people use cutting as their method of self-injury.
- About 50% of people seek help for their self-harm, but only from friends instead of professionals.

Having LMFTs at every school and/or parents who can afford services for their children is ideal, but unrealistic. Therefore, we need a way to get ahead of the crises by providing students with a systematic means to manage their mental, social and emotional wellness and prevent crises. An effective structured plan promoting self-efficacy and productive ways to address possible mental health crises is needed—before they become a crisis.

The author of *The Resilience Game Plan*, Colleen Ster, understands the challenges facing students and is determined to find a way to address them. *The Resilience Game Plan* is a way to do just that. In fact, adults who reviewed *The Resilience Game Plan* have reported how reading the book was helpful to them and other adults as well, not just students.

Everyone needs a game plan for dealing with life's difficulties, especially adolescents regarding ways to address social, emotional, and even physical challenges in a healthy manner and before reaching crisis levels. Using *The Resilience Game Plan* is a viable solution to building our students' repertoire of such tools.

Wishing you all the best,

Cheryl James-Ward, Ed.D.

Cheryl James-Ward has been a Superintendent of Schools, Schools CEO, Director of Academics and Innovation, elementary school principal, vice principal, math teacher and NASA software engineer.

• Introduction •

Dear Reader,

You were handed this workbook and may be feeling annoyed. Possibly you are thinking, *Great—what must I do now?* LOL—I get it. My husband and I have three children, and we got a daily play-by-play regarding most of their frustrations at school. My goal is not to add to your workload, but to give you a game plan to help you navigate your life ahead and ultimately make your life less complicated. Right now is a key developmental period of time for your brain. Situations you experience from friendship troubles to keeping up with the pressures of social media—all have a critical impact on your developing brain.

After reading about the growing number of self-harm cases among teenagers in our country, I decided to go back to school. I went back to school for YOU to understand the big picture of teen stressors. I went back to school because I felt like you need an advocate to help navigate all of the unrealistic expectations adults have put on YOU that stress YOU out. While you may think there are not any adults who understand what you are going through, that simply is not true. I want you to know that people in your life hear YOU, see YOU, and care about YOU. Please remember that **YOU are not alone**.

If I could, I would bubble-wrap your brain in protection; however, since I cannot do that, I created the next best thing called *The Resilience Game Plan (The RGP)*. In *The RGP,* you will find strategies to help you navigate life with skills that will provide a buffer to help protect your developing brain. After reading mounds of evidence-based research studies, I worked hard to decide what information will give you the best tools to grow and thrive into your ultimate best self.

The reality is that we all have something we are working to overcome—even your classmates you think are popular with no problems in the world. **Everyone has problems**. Nobody's life is perfect, and post-pandemic, we can all benefit from the cognitive, communication, and mindfulness strategies listed in this playbook.

While you may not think that some of these topics relate to your life, they likely will affect someone you know, so please learn these tips and tools...if not for yourself, then for someone else you care about in your life. If you find any information listed in this workbook triggering or upsetting, please talk to your parent/guardian, trusted adult, school counselor, teacher, medical doctor, or trained professional.

In closing, I want to leave you with three simple pieces of advice.

    1. Knowledge is power and will help you to overcome any challenge.
    2. Keep your sense of humor, and don't take yourself too seriously.
    3. We all feel better knowing we have a game plan, so let's get to work!

Wishing you all the best,

Colleen Carter Ster, A.LM.
C.E.O./Founder
Reflections Publishing LLC

Section One

The Resilience Game Plan Pre-Assessment

• *The Resilience Game Plan* Pre-Assessment •

- **STEP #1:** Take this Pre-Assessment before moving forward with *The Resilience Game Plan*.
- **STEP #2:** Rank your Subjective Well-Being (from 1-10) and then ***For every "Yes" response, write an "X" on the right-hand line.**

Subjective Well-Being: (Rank from 1-10)
1. How satisfied are you with your life? (1 Extremely Unsatisfied - to - 10 Extremely Satisfied) _____
2. What are your feelings about people or situations in your life? (1 Extreme Anxiety - to - 10 Extremely Peaceful) _____
3. Do you feel your life has meaning and purpose? (1 Extremely Disagree - to - 10 Extremely Agree) _____

WHAT'S YOUR GAME PLAN? + WARM-UP

Academic Pressures:
1. Do you feel you belong and are connected at your school?
   ☐ Yes - I belong to teams/clubs   ☐ No - I feel like an outsider   *** (If "Yes," write "X" here:)** _____
2. Do you find your schoolwork engaging and interesting?
   ☐ Yes - I am learning for the "love of learning"   ☐ No - I am a "robo-learner"/only learn for tests   _____
3. Do you find your schoolwork meaningful and relevant to real life?
   ☐ Yes - I am learning life-long skills   ☐ No - I am a "robo-learner"/only learn for tests   _____
4. Do you feel respected and valued at school?
   ☐ Yes   ☐ No   _____
5. Do you have a close connection to at least one teacher at school?
   ☐ Yes - list name: _____   ☐ No   _____

Habit Formation: New Habits and Breaking Old Habits:
1. Do you have habits you want to break? If Yes, list: _____ _____
2. Do you have new habits you want to form? If Yes, list: _____ _____

What's Your Legacy? Knowing Your Core Values:
1. How do you want to be remembered after you graduate? List: _____

Who Are Your Personal "Cheerleaders," Coaches, and/or Mentors:
1. Do you have a mentor/cheerleader in your life?
   ☐ Yes - list name: _____   ☐ No   _____

WHAT'S YOUR GAME PLAN? + LIFE CHOICES

Self and Identity: List Your Peer Friend Group: _____
1. Do you associate your identity with your peer group? If "Yes," list your friend group on the line above and put "X" here: _____

Social Media:
1. Do you feel good about yourself after spending time on Social Media (e.g., Instagram, Snapchat, and TikTok)?
   ☐ Yes - I feel good about myself.   ☐ No - I feel worse about myself   _____

Time Management - Life Balance:
1. Do you think you have a good life balance?
   ☐ Yes   ☐ Average   ☐ No   _____

WHAT'S YOUR GAME PLAN? + LIFE CRISES

Abuse - Domestic, Physical, and Verbal:

1. Do you have a concern of feeling unsafe at school and home?
   ☐ Yes - List location: _____ ☐ No _____

2. Do you feel anxious at home (i.e., not enough food or do not feel protected)?
   ☐ Yes - List concern: _____ ☐ No _____

Anxiety:

1. Do you consider yourself an anxious person? If yes, list things that make you feel anxious:
   ☐ Yes - List: _____ ☐ No _____

Depression:

1. Do you feel depressed or down? If yes, list why you may feel this way or what makes you depressed:
   ☐ Yes - List: _____ ☐ No _____

Substance Abuse - Alcohol and Drugs:

1. Do either you, a friend, or a family member abuse alcohol and drugs?
   ☐ Yes - List: _____ ☐ No _____

Self-Harm:

1. Have you ever wanted to hurt yourself?
   ☐ Yes - List how you would hurt yourself: _____ ☐ No _____

WHAT'S YOUR GAME PLAN? + RELATIONSHIPS

Bullying/Cyberbullying:

1. Have you ever been bullied or been the recipient of cyberbullying?
   ☐ Yes - List situation: _____ ☐ No _____

Family or Guardian:

1. How would you rate your relationship with your family or guardian?
   ☐ Good ☐ Average ☐ Bad - List situation: _____

Friendship:

1. Are you in a peer-pressuring and/or non-supportive friend group?
   ☐ Yes - List your friends: _____ ☐ No _____

Peer Pressure:

1. Have you ever been put in a peer pressure situation?
   ☐ Yes - List situation: _____ ☐ No _____

List Your Stress Level Today (1 = not very stressed and 10 = very stressed) **(1-10)** _____

© 2023 Reflections Publishing LLC. All rights reserved.
This book is sold with the understanding that the publisher and the author are not engaged in rendering medical, legal, or other professional advice or services.
If professional assistance is required, the services of a competent professional should be sought.

Section Two

Reflections Publishing Communication Assessment

Reflections Publishing Communication Assessment

Below, you will find questions to read and answer. The purpose of this assessment is to help you understand how your communication skills play a role and affect the way you communicate with others. For example, this questionnaire will show you why you might be struggling to communicate with a particular someone. If you pay attention to how an individual communicates with you, then you will likely find that this is their "Preferred Method of Communication"—meaning this is the best way to connect with them. Friends, family, fellow students, co-workers, neighbors, and group members can miscommunicate for years until someone in the relationship is willing to notice the disconnect and address the problem. Communication skills are valuable interpersonal tools for you to learn at a young age so you can use these skills during your academic years, when entering into personal relationships, and eventually navigating professional work environments.

You can find more detailed information about each of the "Preferred Methods of Communication" on **pages 27-29**.

WHAT IS YOUR PREFERRED METHOD OF COMMUNICATION?

Choose One:
- ☐ Compliments and Praise
- ☐ Feeling Respected
- ☐ Friendliness and Caring
- ☐ Helping Hand
- ☐ Hugs
- ☐ Spending Time Together
- ☐ Token of Friendship/Gift-Giving
- ☐ Unconditional Love
- ☐ Other: _____

WHAT IS YOUR SECOND PREFERRED METHOD OF COMMUNICATION?

Choose One:
- ☐ Compliments and Praise
- ☐ Feeling Respected
- ☐ Friendliness and Caring
- ☐ Helping Hand
- ☐ Hugs
- ☐ Spending Time Together
- ☐ Token of Friendship/Gift-Giving
- ☐ Unconditional Love
- ☐ Other: _____

WHAT IS YOUR THIRD PREFERRED METHOD OF COMMUNICATION?

Choose One:
- ☐ Compliments and Praise
- ☐ Feeling Respected
- ☐ Friendliness and Caring
- ☐ Helping Hand
- ☐ Hugs
- ☐ Spending Time Together
- ☐ Token of Friendship/Gift-Giving
- ☐ Unconditional Love
- ☐ Other: _____

Additional Things to Think About:

- "Preferred Method of Electronic Communication?"
  ☐ Talking on Cell Phone ☐ Texting on Cell Phone ☐ Email ☐ Instagram ☐ SnapChat ☐ TikTok ☐ Other: _____
- Is your "Preferred Method of Communication" the same for your family and friends? _____
- Was there an event in your life that changed how you communicate with friends, family, coworkers, and schoolmates?
- Do you find it more difficult to communicate with people you are really close to or love? _____
- Do you have at least one person in your life that you can talk to when you are going through a tough time? _____

Ways to Improve Your Communication:

- Listen more than you talk, so you know what to discuss; try to separate issues, so things are not as overwhelming; be in sync with the person you are talking to and maintain an open mind; and keep emotions in check.

© 2024 Reflections Publishing LLC. All rights reserved.

Section Three

How *The Resilience Game Plan* Will Benefit You

How *The Resilience Game Plan* Will Benefit You

I did not "get the memo" that life was supposed to be perfect. We all have something we are working to overcome as we progress through different chapters in our lives. While it might appear everyone around you has a perfect life—that simply is not true. We all deal with something. If you take *The Resilience Game Plan: The Teen Playbook for Developing Cognitive, Communication, and Mindfulness Life Skills (The RGP)* seriously and learn the tips and tools in the workbook—you will find *The RGP* knowledge extremely helpful and beneficial to you throughout your lifetime.

Developing a Growth Mindset

First of all, *The RGP* will help you learn how to have a growth mindset—which is the best way to tackle different situations you encounter throughout life. The advantage of learning this skill set now is that when you develop a growth mindset, you will learn at a young age that through your hard work and determination, you can achieve a stronger academic performance and gain more confidence in your abilities. Evidence-based research conducted by Carol Dweck indicates that the earlier you can create a foundation of a growth mindset along with positive thinking, the sooner you are setting yourself up for a life of success and healthy emotional and social well-being.

When you prioritize your well-being during adolescence, you pour the foundation for your entire body from a cellular level. These cells determine your academic achievement, mental health, and physical well-being. Cellular development can also affect how you will socially adjust into society.

A growth mindset and optimistic thinking are considered habitual explanatory styles. Acquiring habitual explanatory styles during your preteen and teenage years will impact your well-being for the rest of your life. While a parent or guardian likely influences these explanatory styles, they are also influenced by regular interactions with other significant adults in your life (e.g., godparent, advisory or home room teacher, or coach).

Researchers coined the concept of developmental resilience as they discovered that resilient children all seem to possess the following factors:

1. Personal traits (e.g., compassionate to others, confidence in achieving goals, and intelligence)

2. Responsive and supportive caregiver

Unbeknownst to me at the time, I was raised with a growth mindset by my parents, who were educators. They taught me I could do anything I set my mind to do and that failing was okay because I was learning. As teaching professionals, they knew the only way to learn new information was by struggling or experiencing failures along the way. Nobody is born an expert. I grew up watching them return to school to attain multiple master's degrees or work on their Ph.D. They taught me to enjoy the learning process—learning for the love of learning, not focusing on grades.

Research indicates that if you never fail at something when you are young, you are more likely to not know how to cope when you later struggle with something as an adolescent, young adult, and even during your adult years. None of us are perfect, and battling with something and learning how to overcome that struggle is a skill you will use for the rest of your life.

You need to know **you can grow and develop into whoever you want. You can do anything you want; your genetics and/or environment does not hinder you. While these variables can affect us, they do not have to define us**. In fact, researchers are discovering that our brains have the ability to allow us to be life-long learners—with our brains continuing to develop throughout our lifetime. It is through your hard work, determination, attitude, experiences, and specific training that give you your brain power.

The intelligence experts would have the following advice for you:

1. Gilbert Gottlieb, a well-known neuroscientist, believes that your genes require input from your environment. Your genetics are not the only thing that determines your intelligence.
2. Robert Sternber, who is known as an intelligence guru, would tell you that individuals considered experts are typically not people with a fixed mindset, but people engaged in the topic for a desired and specific purpose to learn.
3. Alfred Binet would tell you that **the smartest children in the world in elementary school, do not always end up the smartest adults.**

If you are wondering why the smartest children do not end up as the smartest adults, someone likely raised them with a fixed mindset. As children, somebody probably praised them for their intelligence rather than their effort in learning the subject. Many **children raised with a fixed mindset fear failure**; therefore, when something becomes hard for them, or they receive a bad grade for the first time, they become paralyzed in their learning process.

Why do you need to develop a growth mindset? Two simple answers:

1. **Life is hard and can be challenging.**
2. **Life is a marathon, not a sprint.**

When life gets hard, you need a game plan, and that is where having a growth mindset and utilizing the cognitive, communication, and mindfulness strategies listed in *The RGP* come into play.

Having raised three daughters, I saw firsthand the changes teenagers go through during the formative developmental years. Coupled with the stress of social media, schoolwork, and maneuvering friends and family relationships, I wanted to put them in a giant bubble—bubble wrapping and protecting their developing brains. Why, you ask? The reason for my concern is that the years between early adolescence and young adulthood are a sensitive window of time when social and environmental stress can potentially create a significant negative impact on an adolescent's brain development. and the fact that we have been affected by the pandemic (i.e., keeping us all isolated in our homes with little to no contact with our family and friends), we all can benefit from utilizing *The RGP* and learning the cognitive, communication, and mindfulness strategies listed in this playbook.

Even before the pandemic in March of 2020, I was concerned about the stress that adolescents were experiencing during their middle and high school years. As an adult, I want to apologize for any undue pressures placed on you and want you to use *The RGP* to ultimately learn how to take care of yourself, manage your thoughts and feelings, and give you the tools to make your own decisions.

In the following pages, I am giving you a safe space to download your feelings and some tips and tools to help you navigate this post-pandemic world—so you can live your best life. This first section will walk you through different scenarios in life and provide you with ideas to help you navigate difficult emotions and life situations.

Just remember, your parent(s) or guardian(s) are not going off to your college with you or any other post-high school graduation plans you might have; hence, the importance of learning a growth mindset now. This mindset is a skill you will use for the rest of your life. Also, remember that your parent or guardian had their chance to be your age. Now is your time to make your own decisions; just remember that your decisions and choices may affect you for years to come. This is your life, not their lives or your friend's life. Their anxieties are not your anxieties. Their fears are not your fears. Their past does not have to influence your future. Learn how to make your own decisions because, at the end of the day, you are the person who will live with the consequences of your decisions.

• **Now Apply it with the 3 C's** •

1. Critical Thinking:

- Start with the first paragraph and number each paragraph in the outside margins. Numbering the paragraphs allows you to reference sections to discuss as a group.
- In this section, circle the word **growth mindset** in blue.
- Now explain the benefit of developing a growth mindset versus having a fixed mindset.

_____

_____

2. Collaborate:

- Working with a partner or small group, list some self-talk growth mindset phrases. For example,
  - "I am not afraid to fail. If I miss some problems while I am learning a new concept, that is okay."
  - "Through my hard work, effort, and determination, I can ___."

_____

_____

3. Communicate:

- As a class discussion, share your growth mindset self-talk phrases:

_____

_____

Section Four

How to Become a Resilient Global Changemaker

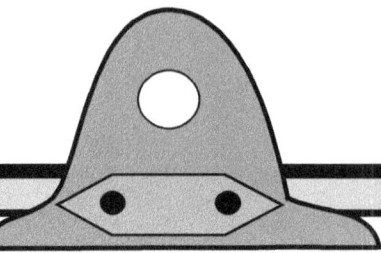

• Resilient Global Changemaker Game Plan •

The qualities below are discussed and integrated throughout *The Resilience Game Plan*. After completing this playbook, you will have increased your well-being and can check the boxes below for your newly gained skills:

☐ **Bridge Builder** who knows how to engage with community members and form intercultural relationships within communities on a local, regional, and global level.

☐ **Collaborative Visionary** who can gather, analyze, and synthesize information with a partner or in a group, then present data results, research, and innovative solutions.

☐ **Common Sense Mastermind** who is level-headed and smart, making good choices and behaving sensibly.

☐ **Community Service Leader** who exhibits prosocial behavior, is conscientious, reliable, relevant, and actively makes a positive impact to optimize human flourishing around the world.

☐ **Compassionate Trailblazer** who is caring, empathetic, happy, kind, and full of gratitude.

☐ **Confident Changemaker** who is balanced, engaging, charismatic, principled, and has high self-esteem and self-worth.

☐ **Critical Thinker** who explores different perspectives with "blue-sky thinking" and is analytical, inquisitive, open-minded, and an active participant in their learning process.

☐ **Global Citizen Contributor** who sees the big picture with an international perspective and is filled with dependability, forward-thinking, honesty, integrity, and social trust.

☐ **Growth Mindset Gamechanger** who has grit and resilience to overcome life difficulties.

☐ **Interpersonal Communicator** who is skilled in improving personal and professional relationships and is a constructive, effective, and respectful problem-solver.

☐ **Knowledgeable Analyst** who, in an unbiased manner, acknowledges any learning gaps, has an analytical nature of knowledge, and applies the Theory of Knowledge (TOK) concepts (e.g., Cultural, Empathy, Evidence, Explanation, Interpretation, Interconnectedness, Justification, Objectivity, Perspective, Responsibility, Truth, Values, and Visionary).

☐ **Lifelong Learner** who is curious and enjoys discovering real-life applications for materials learned across many curriculum subjects (e.g., languages).

☐ **Nature-Conscious Advocate** who implements a daily practice of sustainability and has a healing bidirectional relationship between humanity and our planet.

☐ **Risk-Taking Innovator** who is self-motivated, self-regulated, and forward-thinking.

☐ **Well-Being Connector** who is happy, healthy, and thriving due to their efforts and sense of belonging and social connection at school and within their community.

© 2024 Reflections Publishing LLC. All rights reserved.

Section Five

How to Use *The Resilience Game Plan*

- Six Strategies for Success - 18
- Creating Your "Personalized Game Plan" - 18-19
- How to Use *The Resilience Game Plan* - 20-42

•Six Strategies for Success•

Life happens, and when we hit bumps in the road, we all feel better knowing we have a game plan to navigate our lives through any difficult life scenario. When tough situations occur, you likely get upset or feel disappointed. You get to feel those emotions; however, the end goal is to always keep moving forward with a growth mindset and not get stuck in any situation.

In *The Resilience Game Plan (The RGP),* when a difficult life situation hits, you are going to train your brain to:

1. **Acknowledge the life situation—processing any emotions.**
2. **Allow yourself to feel your emotions—describing your feelings of anxiety or distress.**
3. **Keep moving forward—applying the below steps to overcome your situation.**

• •

• Creating Your "Personalized Game Plan" •

#1 In *The RGP*, you will incorporate these three concepts above into tackling any daily life situation and use the strategies below to create your "Personalized Game Plan."

#2 In *The RGP's* **"What's Your Game Plan" Sections Six-Nine**, you will find many different life topics. In order to successfully incorporate these concepts into your life, you need to learn these strategies and turn them into automatic habits. This game plan will train your brain to identify a situation and quickly process and move through any difficult life situation.

#3 Here is the game plan to become a **Resilient Global Changemaker** in any situation:

⇨ Read the two 4114U (**411**-Information **4**-for **U**-You) pages which will teach you about each life subject.
⇨ Complete the four activity pages to help you learn and process each specific life topic using the below strategies:
  • Strategy #1: Understanding Brain Power - See where and how this situation affects your brain
  • Strategy #2: Learning Cognitive Skills - Identify your thoughts, rate your feelings, and the steps to overcome your obstacle
  • Strategy #3: Learning Communication Skills - Gain interpersonal techniques to improve your relationships
  • Strategy #4: Learning Mindfulness Skills - Learn emotional self-regulation tools to help process your feelings
  • Strategy #5: Developing New Habits - Implement the "Well-Being Habit Tracker's" daily healthy habits
  • Strategy #6: Setting Goals and Reducing Anxiety - Set daily goals using the "Anxiety-Buster To-Do List"

• Six Pages to Create Your "Personalized Game Plan" •
Life happens—here's how you are going to work through it and move forward!

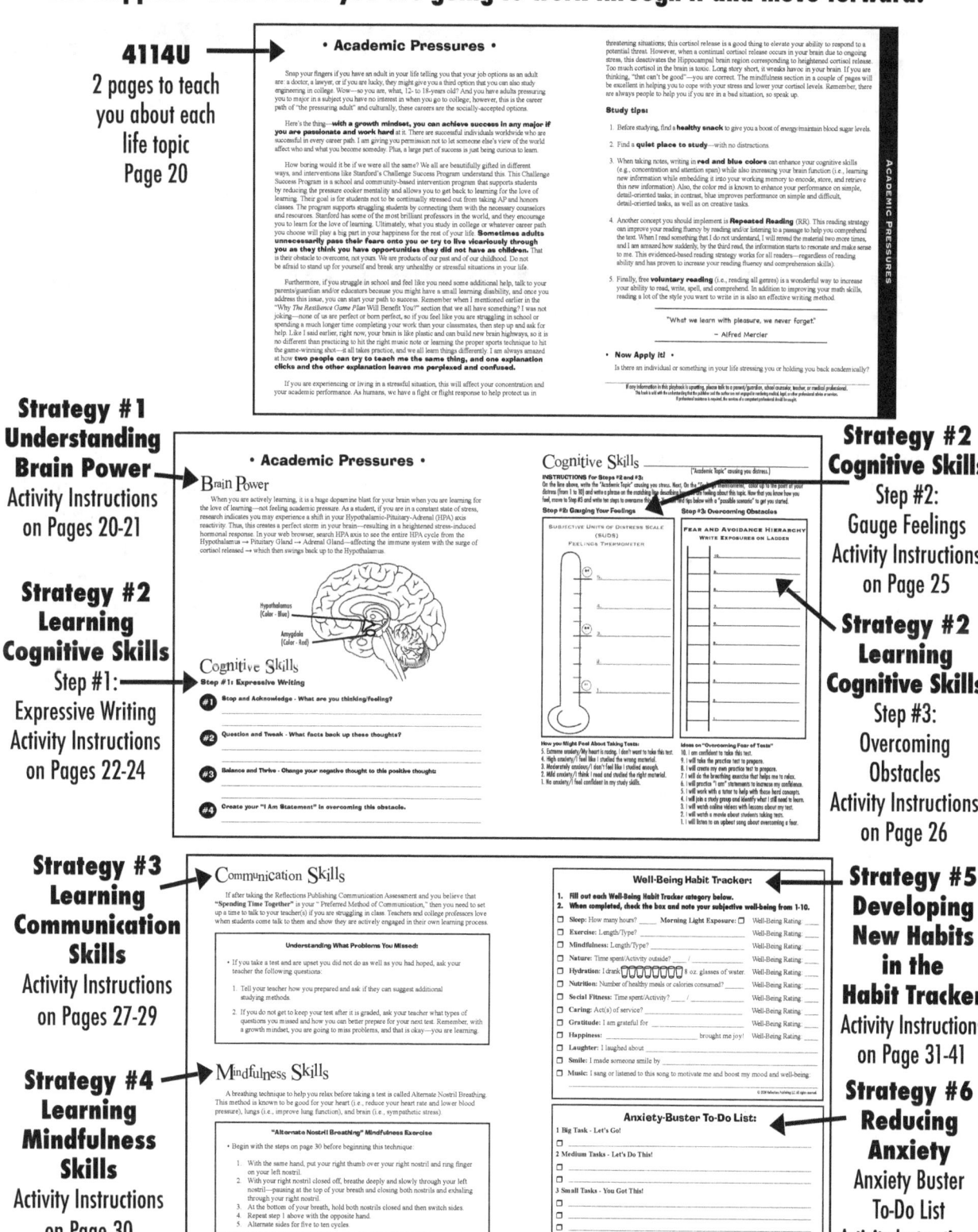

4114U
2 pages to teach you about each life topic
Page 20

Strategy #1
Understanding Brain Power
Activity Instructions on Pages 20-21

Strategy #2
Learning Cognitive Skills
Step #1:
Expressive Writing
Activity Instructions on Pages 22-24

Strategy #3
Learning Communication Skills
Activity Instructions on Pages 27-29

Strategy #4
Learning Mindfulness Skills
Activity Instructions on Page 30

Strategy #2
Cognitive Skills
Step #2:
Gauge Feelings
Activity Instructions on Page 25

Strategy #2
Learning Cognitive Skills
Step #3:
Overcoming Obstacles
Activity Instructions on Page 26

Strategy #5
Developing New Habits in the Habit Tracker
Activity Instructions on Page 31-41

Strategy #6
Reducing Anxiety
Anxiety Buster To-Do List
Activity Instructions on Page 42

HOW TO CREATE YOUR PERSONALIZED GAME PLAN

-19-

• How to Use *The Resilience Game Plan* •

4114U LIFE TOPIC PAGES

For each life topic in *The Resilience Game Plan (The RGP)*, you will find **two 4114U (411-**Information **4-**for **U-**You**) pages** to teach you about each subject. You can then use this newly-learned knowledge to then move onto **four more pages of Brain Power, Cognitive, Communication, and Mindfulness Life Skills**. By the time you work through these six pages for each life topic, you will have created your "Personalized Game Plan."

PLAYBOOK STRATEGY #1: UNDERSTANDING BRAIN POWER

Early adolescence through young adulthood is a sensitive period where social and environmental stressors can potentially alter a developing brain. Harvard scientists David Hubel and Torsten Wiesel named this brain process *plasticity*, which occurs when your brain molds like plastic based on your life experiences.

In the book *Livewired,* neurologist David Eagleman takes the term brain *plasticity* even one step further calling it neuroplasticity. He considers the human brain an "electric living fabric"—continually remolding itself with every life experience. He thinks the brain is a living organism, constantly rewiring itself based on every life situation you experience. Your positive experiences and exposure to external stimuli create beneficial pathways in your brain, and bad experiences create negative changes in your brain. Eagleman coined the phrase *livewire* in place of *plasticity* because the brain is constantly changing and the word *plasticity*, possibly meaning, occurring once and molded for good.

Key Takeaways

1. Experiences early in life are significant in shaping brain development.
2. Adolescence is the window of time to address any possible negative brain changes.
3. All environmental, social, and socio-economical experiences affect brain maturation.

As we move from each life topic in *The RGP*, you will use colored pencils to lightly color every "Key Takeaway" box in yellow (i.e., the color to get noticed). Also, you will color the part of the brain affected by the challenging life scenario. **(See page 154 for the Brain Power Color Chart.)** As you follow instructions in *The RGP* to color parts of the brain, the goal is for you to understand the importance of where and why this particular life topic can negatively affect your brain. Plus, when you apply color to something, this is a good study strategy to implement because it helps you remember things.

Lobes of the Brain
- **FRONTAL LOBE:** voluntary movement, expressive language, planning, impulse control, and managing higher-level executive functions
- **OCCIPITAL LOBE:** vision (visual perception, identifying color, form, and motion)
- **PARIETAL LOBE:** movement and sensation (touch, taste, and temperature)
- **TEMPORAL LOBE:** language (processing auditory information and encoding of memory), emotion, and sexuality

• Human Brain Anatomy •

During your teenage years, your brain is only 80 percent developed—wiring together from the bottom up and from the back to the front. This explains why teens struggle with decision-making and making good choices, as the **Frontal Lobe** area is the last to develop. The synapses strengthen as brain cells in neural pathways and synapses are actively repeated—thus, "**what fires together, wires together**."

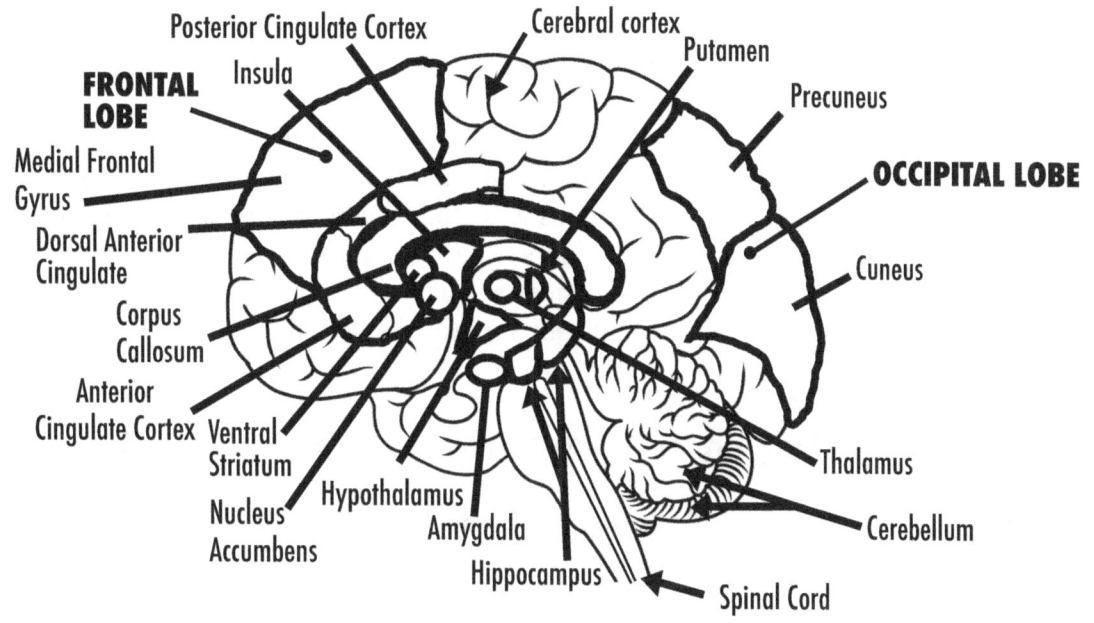

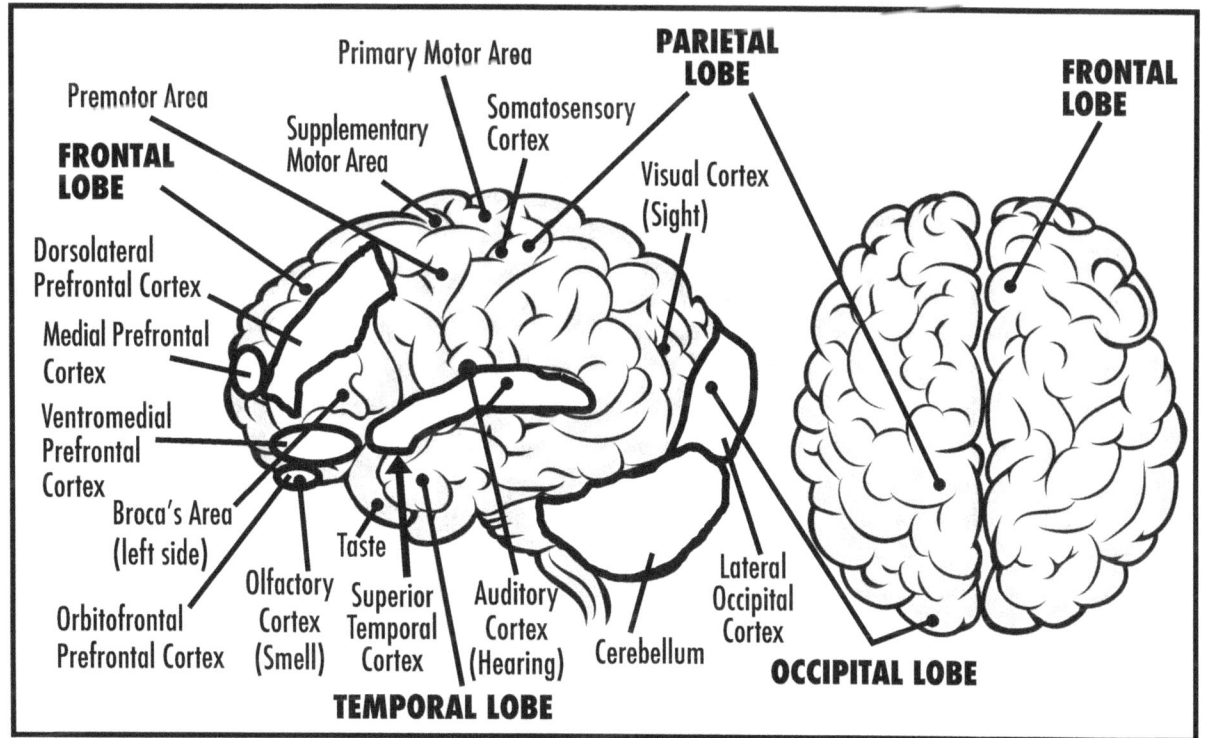

PLAYBOOK STRATEGY #2: LEARNING COGNITIVE SKILLS

Did you know that the average person has around 70,000 thoughts per day? Of those thoughts, 80 percent are negative, and 95 are repetitive. Unless we make a point to retrain our brains, negative thoughts will consume our lives. Cognitive Behavior Specialists have even created a term called Automatic Negative Thoughts (ANT), and nobody likes ants—critters or bad thoughts.

The good news is that we can all build new "brain pathways" and stop negative, obsessive, repeated, and ruminating thoughts. Learning cognitive and communication skills, along with mindfulness techniques, assist in creating these new brain pathways and give you the tips and tools to have in your back pocket when you need them most. *The RGP* includes concepts such as determining your values, setting your goals, understanding your emotions, identifying anxiety in your body and the cause, matching your thoughts to feelings, recording your thoughts, feelings, actions, and behaviors, and practicing mindfulness behaviors until they are habits. Also, the benefit of learning these cognitive skills techniques is that when you feel depressed or anxious, *The RGP* strategies will teach you to automatically replace negative thoughts with more productive, positive, and beneficial cognitions.

The Cognitive Skills Training is Divided into the Following Three Steps:

Step #1: Expressive Writing Activity (to Overcome _____)

Instructions:

This section is a safe space to process your feelings, thoughts, and any stress you might be experiencing. You are guided through this expressive writing exercise with four prompts:

#1 **Stop and Acknowledge - What are you thinking/feeling?**
This prompt encourages you to stop, catch, and acknowledge any anxious, fearful, negative, or stressful thoughts ruminating (i.e., repeatedly over and over) in your brain.

#2 **Question and Tweak - What facts back up these thoughts?**
Next, you want to question any negative or stressful thoughts and whether you have any evidence or facts to support why you are feeling a certain way.

#3 **Balance and Thrive - I will change this negative thought in my head to this positive thought:**
Then, put a stop sign up in your brain to halt the ruminating negative and stressful thinking and redirect and pave a new highway in your brain with a positive thought process.

#4 **Create your "I Am Statement" in overcoming this obstacle:**
Next, creating a powerful "I Am Statement" is an excellent way to practice a growth mindset through repetitive verbal affirmation with positive statements. Phrases such as "I am worthy" and "I am a hard worker" can build self-esteem and boost motivation.

Additionally, creating an "I Am Statement" is a self-affirmation that can provide a barrier to harmful or threatening experiences, lower your feelings of stress, and improve your physical and mental well-being. Through "I Am Statements," these affirmations can elevate a student's academic performance. When you look through the lens of personally adopting a growth mindset, you are expanding your mind—academically, behaviorally, and emotionally.

"I Am Statements" are included in *The RGP* because these self-affirmations have potentially long-lasting effects as they can replace negative, ruminating thoughts by creating an adaptive, positive feedback loop in your self-related processing and reward pathways in your brain.

Mechanism	Associated Brain Function Components
• Self-processing	Medial Prefrontal Cortex + Posterior Cingulate Cortex
• Valuation systems	Ventral Striatum + Ventromedial Prefrontal Cortex

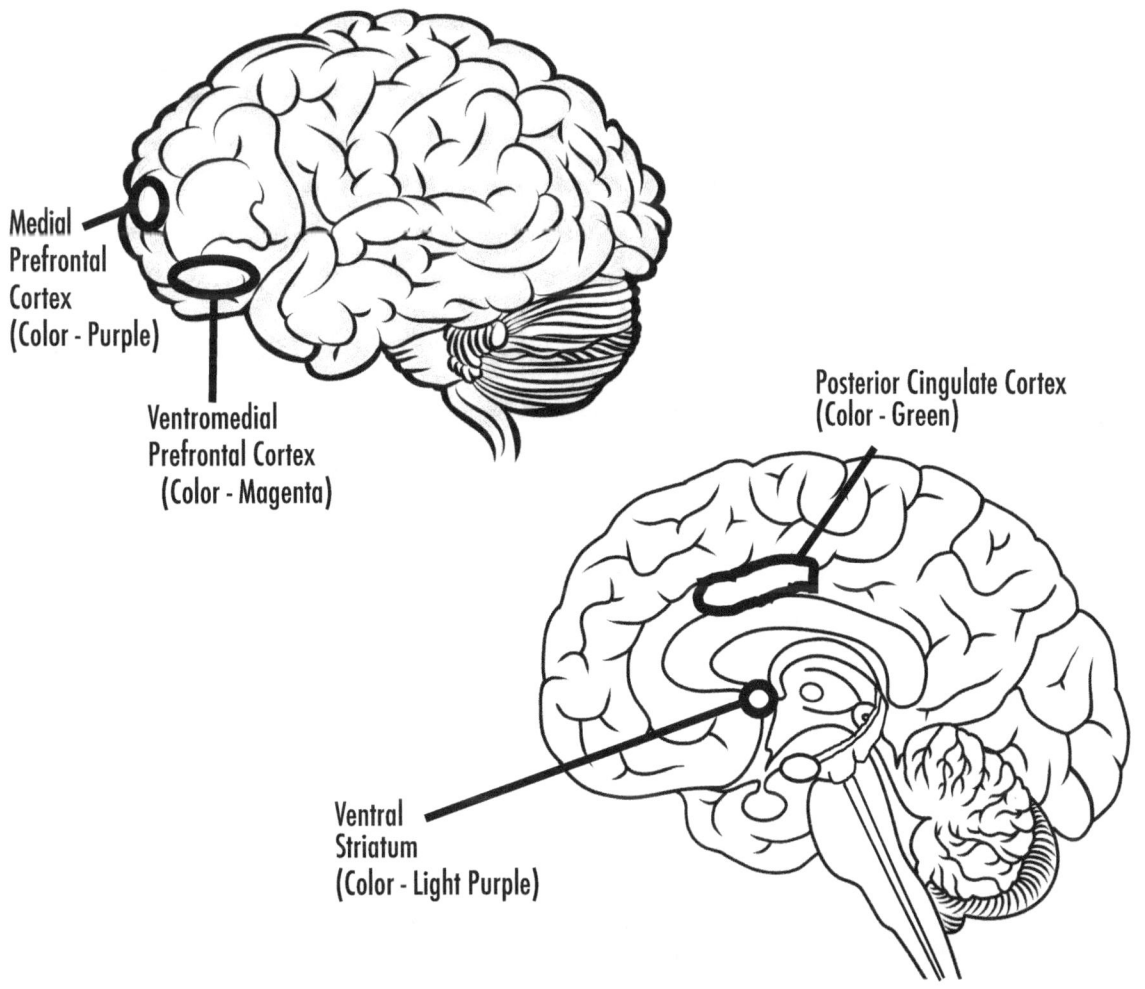

• Example of Step #1 - Expressive Writing to Overcome a Fear of Dogs

For training purposes, you will learn the three "**Cognitive Skills**" steps in *The RGP* playbook, using the life topic of **Overcoming a Fear** and example of how to **Overcome a Fear of Dogs**. This exercise gives you permission to process your feelings and allows you to acknowledge the life situation you are working to overcome.

Instructions:

This section is a safe space for you to process your feelings, thoughts, and any stress you might be experiencing. On the blank line, you will list the fear you are wanting to overcome. In this instance, the example is **overcoming a fear of dogs**.

Next, you are guided through the following expressive writing exercise with four writing prompts:

Cognitive Skills

Step #1: Expressive Writing Activity to Overcome a Fear of Dogs

#1 **Stop and Acknowledge - What are you thinking/feeling?**
When I see a dog, I am afraid the dog is going to bite me. I feel like I am going pass out from the anxiety it causes me. I freak out whenever I see a dog, even when I know I will not come into contact with the dog.

#2 **Question and Tweak - What facts back up these thoughts?**
Why do I feel this way? I have never been bitten by a dog, so why do I assume a dog is going to bite me?
My mom is afraid of dogs, so maybe that is why I am scared? I have no reason to be fearful of dogs.

#3 **Balance and Thrive - Change your negative thought to this positive thought:**
I want to change my scared and fearful thoughts about dogs to this positive thought:
When I see a dog, it makes me smile and I feel happy; I am no longer afraid of dogs.

#4 **Create your "I Am Statement" in overcoming this obstacle.**
I am a courageous person that wants to try new things and become more adventurous.

After you work through the four writing prompts and have a better idea of how you are feeling, you will move on to **Step #2 - Gauging Your Feelings**.

Cognitive Skills

I want to overcome my fear of dogs.
―――――――――――――――――――――――――――――
(Write the "Fear" causing you distress that you want to overcome.)

Example of Step #2 - Gauging Your Feelings

For training purposes, we will continue with the example of **Overcoming a Fear of Dogs**. In this particular activity you will gauge your feelings on the provided Subjective Units of Distress Scale (SUDS) "Feelings Thermometer." This is an excellent way to step back, acknowledge, and rate your level of anxiety/distress. To assist you in learning this new concept, you will find suggestions and ideas to help guide you to create your own list for each life topic in *The RGP* playbook. The goal is to learn how to assess your feelings and always keep moving forward to overcome your obstacles.

Instructions:

When you see the SUDS "Feelings Thermometer" illustration in each life topic section in *The RGP* playbook, you will:

- Use this gauge (on your right) to determine your SUDS rating. You will start at the bottom of this thermometer and list your feelings of anxiety/distress from 1 to 5. The bottom of this scale is marked in "units" with a coordinating line for you to **itemize your feelings from:**
  1. your least anxious and distressing thoughts
     up to
  2. your most anxious and distressing thoughts.

- Now, color your way up to the emotion you are feeling (between 1 to 5.)

- Once you determine your level of anxiety/distress, you move straight to **Step #3** where you will create the necessary steps in your ladder to overcome your obstacle.

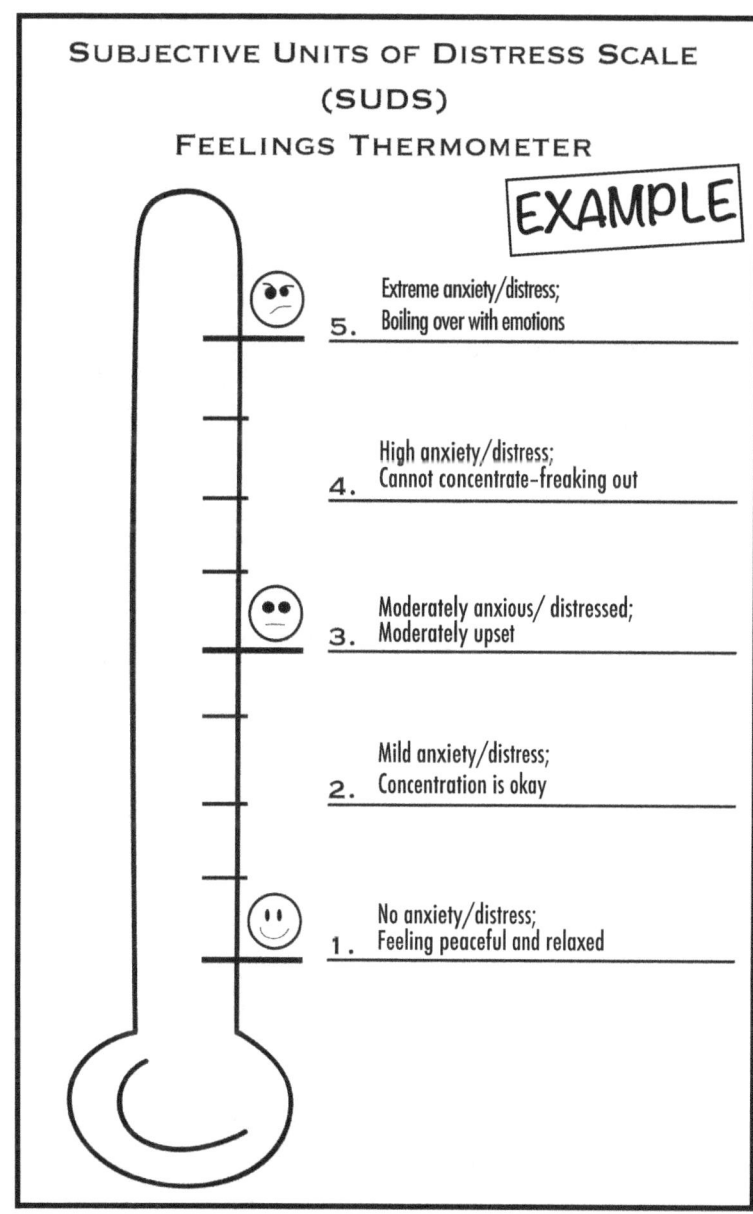

-25-

Cognitive Skills

I want to overcome my fear of dogs.
(Write the "Fear" causing you distress that you want to overcome.)

Example of Step #3 - Overcoming Obstacles

You have now completed **Step #2 - Gauging Your Feelings** to identify your anxiety and distress level and SUDS rating.) **Step #3** will keep you moving forward and building your "Fear and Avoidance Hierarchy Ladder." This framework provides an exposure and response prevention (ERP) plan that identifies what will personally help you to work through your specific fears. As you build this framework, you must turn your focus inward as you self-assess what is triggering you and the baby steps you will need to take to overcome the situation.

Instructions:

- Using the **Overcoming a Fear of Dogs** example, start at the bottom of the ladder (with your easiest exposure) and list your first baby step to overcome this obstacle. Step-by-step you will continue to build your ladder until you get to the top (with your most feared exposure.) At this point, you will have **overcome your fear of dogs** and **exposed yourself to 10 different "feared" scenerios**. You will have succeeded in overcoming your obstacle.

- You will quickly master this technique by repeatedly utilizing this strategy with any tough situation that comes your way. Life is not perfect, so the goal is to always be moving forward and use these coping skills to tackle any difficult life situation.

- Like **Step #2, Step #3** will also include suggestions and ideas, listed below the "Fear and Avoidance Hierarchy Ladder" illustraton for each life topic in *The RGP* playbook. A possible scenario is given for each life topic as an "idea starter" to help guide you to create your own list of exposures for the topic you choose.

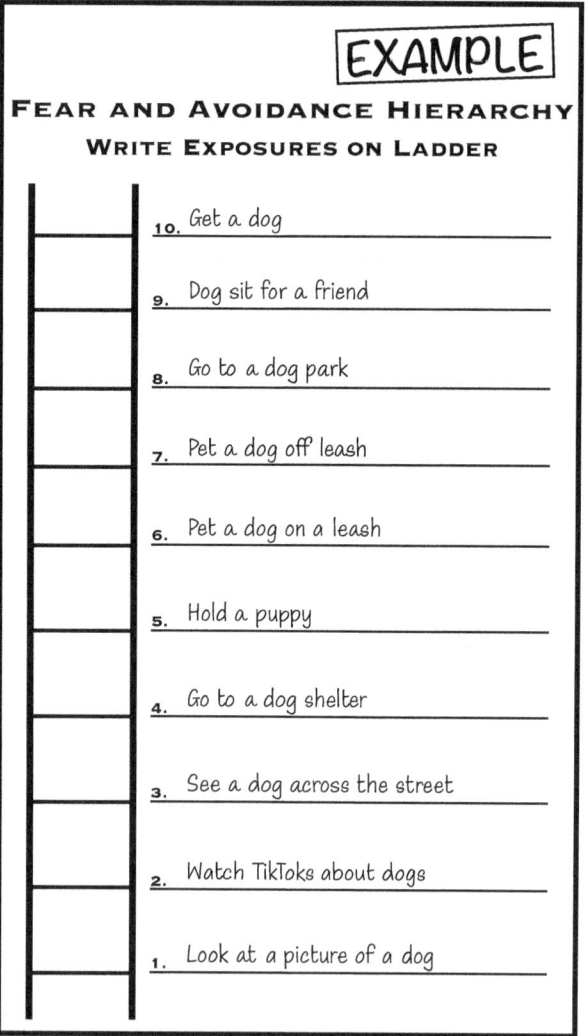

EXAMPLE

FEAR AND AVOIDANCE HIERARCHY
WRITE EXPOSURES ON LADDER

10. Get a dog
9. Dog sit for a friend
8. Go to a dog park
7. Pet a dog off leash
6. Pet a dog on a leash
5. Hold a puppy
4. Go to a dog shelter
3. See a dog across the street
2. Watch TikToks about dogs
1. Look at a picture of a dog

PLAYBOOK STRATEGY #3: LEARNING COMMUNICATION SKILLS

As you progress through *The RGP*, by learning the communication skills for each life topic, you will gain knowledge that can help you achieve your goals. Words are powerful and game-changing. If you learn these communication skills at a young age, then you can significantly improve and impact your interactions with family members, friends, neighbors, and coworkers.

When working with children, tweens, teens, and emerging young adults, I always say **you do not have to be the smartest person in the room.** However, you do **need to have strong communication skills, common sense, a good attitude, be a hard worker (who is on time and present), and most importantly—always be kind and respectful**. The goal is to equip you with adaptive communication skills to make sure you have healthy and meaningful relationships in your life. Having strong communication skills allows you to know how to connect with people and reach your full potential. Communication plays a key role in interpersonal problem-solving skills, and these skills can improve relationships and deter the development of depressive symptoms in individuals.

Furthermore, just like we all learn in various ways, we communicate in different ways too. Back in 2008, working with my three daughters and my Girl Scout troop, we started a questionnaire to help identify ways that children and adults prefer to communicate and how their "Preferred Methods of Communication" can change over the years due to their environment and life events.

To discover your "Preferred Methods of Communication," go to page 10 to take the Reflections Publishing Communication Assessment. This questionnaire asks individuals of all ages to select their *Top Three* "Preferred Methods of Communication," which are listed in detail on the following **pages 27-29**.

• "Preferred Methods of Communication" •

• Compliments and Praise

Everyone enjoys receiving praise, but for some individuals receiving praise is crucial to their personal development. One way to tell if somebody thrives with praise is if they are constantly giving you compliments. This is a tell-tale sign that this is the best way to communicate with this individual.

• Feeling Respected

When used as a noun, respect can mean when a person shows respect to another person or as a verb when you respect someone. Respect is also used in deference to an elder or to be polite; however, respect can run much deeper on a fundamental human level. True respect should lead us to oppose discrimination against other individuals (i.e., age, gender, sexuality, race or religion). Respect can stand for not silencing or insulting another human being—even if we fundamentally disagree with them.

Respect for some people is just for you to take them seriously—even at young ages. Bottom line—when someone treats you in a way you would never consider treating them, it can be hard to process and feel respected.

• Friendliness and Caring

As television personality, Mr. Rogers always said, "If you don't have anything nice to say, don't say anything at all." We all struggle with processing behaviors that are different from the way we personally operate; however, for people who consider caring/compassion, friendliness, and kindness at the top of their list, a bully or relational aggression is devastating to them. Plus, it takes much more energy to be mean than to be kind, and mean people are typically just insecure. Individuals who know their self-worth and identity do not generally put down or bully others.

• Helping Hand

The best way to identify a person who prefers this "Method of Communication" is somebody who is always helping others. If you enjoy helping other people, the research supports that you will likely experience increased well-being. For males, this includes experiencing positive social relations, the feeling of purpose/meaning in life, and self-acceptance. For females, this also includes pro-social interactions, a sense of purpose/meaning in life, and better overall health.

By cultivating a civic responsibility at a young age, you lay a framework for yourself of caring, compassion and sensitivity towards others. By learning compassionate skills at a young age, you are preparing yourself to be a future problem solver in our multifaceted, diverse, and complicated world. If you are volunteering, please do it for the right reasons and not just to list on your college applications.

• Hugs

The power of physical touch or a hug can fill a person's love tank. This same theory applies to people who desire a hug or physical touch as their primary way to show affection to others.

• Spending Time Together

One way to identify the importance of quality time for a person is if they always ask you if you are free to get together or the plan to get together next time. Analyzing research from the American Time Use Survey, Price (2008) discovered that the quality of time between a parent and child decreases as a child gets older; hence, these findings significantly correlate the birth order to a child's outcome. Furthermore, in a family with two children, research shows that the first-born child receives 40 percent more time than the second-born child.

At the end of the day, when someone tells you that spending time with you is crucial to them, then make sure you are fully present and listening when you are with them.

- **Token of Friendship/Gift-Giving**

    Can you think of a person who often gives you gifts? If so, this signals that gift-giving is an important form of communication to this person. You could spend 24 hours a day/7 days a week with this person, but if you are not giving them even small tokens to show your affection, their love tank will not be filled.

    Note: Since close relationships are linked to an individual's sense of self, you (as the gift giver) are motivated to purchase a gift that you know your friend wants to receive; however, you may experience internal conflict when buying a gift that differs from your own personal identity and self-concept.

    Knowing and understanding the internal battle a purchaser experiences can explain how this can elevate a person's inner need to validate oneself with material items. This is also why a person whose preferred method of communication is gifting will not fill their energy tank unless they are buying or receiving gifts.

- **Unconditional Love**

    Some may question if unconditional love is actually a form of communication, but functional neuroimaging scans prove this to be true. When comparing romantic love to maternal love in the brain, researchers discovered that analyzing overlapping regions in the brain's reward system proved unconditional love as a form of communication. Their findings showed a significant activation location in the experimental group when compared to the control group. Additionally, the Beauregard et al. (2009) findings illustrate certain brain regions that highlight "unconditional love," which is mediated by a distinct neural network relative to that mediating other emotions. This network contains cerebral structures known to be involved in romantic love or maternal love. Some of these structures represent key components of the brain's reward system.

- **Summary**

    Identifying and recognizing a family member, friend, or coworker's preferred "Method of Communication" is the key to having successful relationships. Knowing your communication strengths will also help you to identify your communication weaknesses. This assessment has shown that we communicate better with people we do not know well. For those who experience this, the communication challenge is to learn how to best communicate with our close family and friends. When we feel hurt by family members, separating the anger and putting ourselves in a place to speak calmly is hard. Instead, we often push buttons to get even because we know that person so well we know exactly what will sting or strike a chord.

PLAYBOOK STRATEGY #4: LEARNING MINDFULNESS SKILLS

Mindfulness techniques are considered a state of consciousness where you will focus on a moment-to-moment awareness of your internal and external state (e.g., emotions, physical sensations, and thoughts) in a non-judgmental way. These three components, *intention*, *attention*, and *attitude*, are also addressed in this section. For each life topic, you will find a specific mindfulness meditation technique to help you work through challenging life scenarios. The goal of learning mindfulness skills is to learn emotion regulation tools that you can quickly access to assist you when processing any overwhelming emotions. Hölzel et al. (2011) believe that mindfulness has the ability to alleviate mental health and stress-related symptoms. The below four mechanisms are linked with neuroplastic changes in the brain. Neuroimaging studies show how these associated brain functioning components and mechanisms work synergistically—while also enhancing self-regulation.

Mechanism	Associated Brain Function Components
1. Attention regulation	Anterior Cingulate Cortex
2. Body awareness	Insula; Temporo-Parietal Junction
3a. Emotion regulation: reappraisal	Dorsolateral Prefrontal Cortex
3b. Emotion regulation: exposure, extinction, and reconsolidation	Ventromedial Prefrontal Cortex; Hippocampus; Amygdala
4. Change in perspective on the self	Medial Prefrontal Cortex; Posterior Cingulate Cortex; Insula; Temporo-Parietal Junction

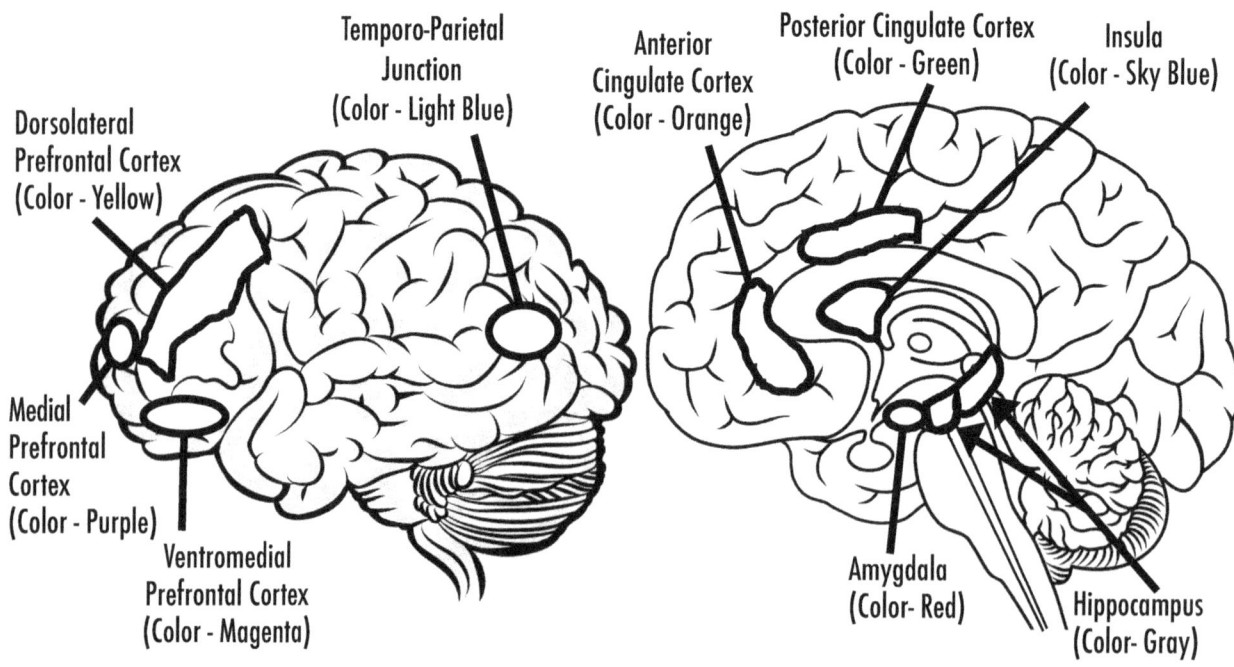

PLAYBOOK STRATEGY #5: DEVELOPING NEW HABITS

You might find you are familiar with some concepts in *The RGP*; however, incorporating these new habit-forming skills in your daily life may still feel uncomfortable to you. This leads us to wonder:

- What exactly is a habit?
- How do you form a new habit?
- How do you break old habits?
- How long does it take to form a new habit?

Definition of Habit

In Julie Dirksen's book *Design How People Learn*, she defines a habit as "an acquired behavior pattern regularly followed until it becomes *almost involuntary*."

• How to Form a New Habit •

In *The RGP*, you are encouraged to keep an open mind and form some new habits; if you stay in the headspace of developing a growth mindset, these habits will benefit you academically, behaviorally, mentally, and physically.

Dirksen divides the creation of new habit formation into six categories: *an acquired behavior pattern, triggers, motivation, feedback, practice or repetition, and environment*.

#1 The **acquired behavior pattern** addresses the fact that we need to first learn the behavior before we can expect or want to make a new habit.

#2 According to B. J. Fogg, **triggers** are part of his behavior model:

Behavior = Motivation + Ability + Trigger

Fogg maintains the theory that for a new habit to activate in your brain, this *almost involuntary* behavior must have a trigger that activates the new action or habit.

#3 Dirksen continues that for a habit to occur, the learner needs **motivation** and must feel some control in the learning process.

#4 The next component Dirksen lists is **feedback** which she acknowledges is an important part of creating a new habit. Dirksen also states that, unfortunately, very few new habits in the learning process have the luxury of immediate feedback.

Practice and repetition are crucial in the learning process when developing a new habit—to the degree the habit becomes *almost involuntarily*. Dirksen expands on this concept stating that when learning a new habit, this process is different for every person and the following four components come into play:

  i. Complexity and difficulty of a desired new habit
  ii. The mechanism that scaffolds and supports this new habit
  iii. The learner's motivation
  iv. The learner's feedback cycle

 Environment is the last category that Dirksen lists when forming a new habit. Learners are more likely to successfully implement a new habit in their life if they are in a supportive environment. For example, in *The RGP*, I encourage you to get some form of exercise every day. A good way to achieve this goal is to have a workout partner or join a sports team —anything that requires accountability and for you to show up.

Utilizing these six ways to form new habits, you will find a section called **"Well-Being Habit Tracker"** in *The RGP*. From **Exercise** to **Music,** each category is discussed in detail, explaining why they are included in *The RGP* and why you should care about tracking this information. The goal is for you to start noticing patterns as you begin incorporating these concepts into your daily life.

All of these concepts are backed up by years of research with the ultimate goal of teaching you how to take care of yourself. My husband and I raised our children knowing we were not going off to college with them, so these are all concepts that our own children have learned and now incorporate into their daily lives.

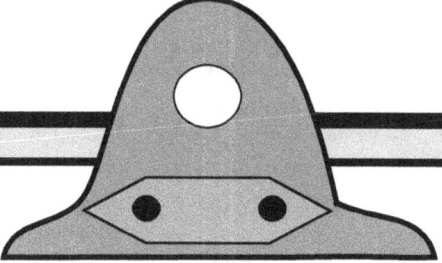

• Well-Being Game Plan •

The RGP "What's Your Game Plan" section will teach you many new life skills. You are encouraged to turn these skills into automatic habits. In addition, in the **Well-Being Habit Tracker** below, you will find many daily habits to incorporate into your life to help you achieve increased well-being.

From the moment you wake up, note the hours of **sleep** you received, and if possible, get outside for some **morning light exposure** to help set your circadian rhythm. You can then conduct the **remaining Well-Being Habit Tracker categories** throughout the day at your convenience while noting your subjective well-being.*

Well-Being Habit Tracker: [EXAMPLE]

1. Fill out each Well-Being Habit Tracker category below.
2. When completed, check the box and note your subjective well-being from 1-10.

- ☐ **Sleep:** How many hours? _____ **Morning Light Exposure:** ☐   Well-Being Rating: ____
- ☐ **Exercise:** Length/Type? _____   Well-Being Rating: ____
- ☐ **Mindfulness:** Length/Type? _____   Well-Being Rating: ____
- ☐ **Nature:** Time spent/Activity outside? ____ / _____   Well-Being Rating: ____
- ☐ **Hydration:** I drank ⬜⬜⬜⬜⬜⬜⬜ 8 oz. glasses of water.   Well-Being Rating: ____
- ☐ **Nutrition:** Number of healthy meals or calories consumed? _____   Well-Being Rating: ____
- ☐ **Social Fitness:** Time spent/Activity? ____ / _____   Well-Being Rating: ____
- ☐ **Caring:** Act(s) of service? _____   Well-Being Rating: ____
- ☐ **Gratitude:** I am grateful for _____   Well-Being Rating: ____
- ☐ **Happiness:** _____ brought me joy!   Well-Being Rating: ____
- ☐ **Laughter:** I laughed about _____
- ☐ **Smile:** I made someone smile by _____
- ☐ **Music:** I sang or listened to this song to motivate me and boost my mood and well-being: _____

© 2024 Reflections Publishing LLC. All rights reserved.

* Subjective well-being is how you feel, your life satisfaction, and if you believe your life has meaning and purpose.
** Bright morning light is known to help you wake up and start your day.

HOW TO USE THE RESILIENCE GAME PLAN

WELL-BEING HABIT TRACKER

Well-Being Habit Tracker Categories

- ### Sleep

Sleep is one of the most important things we do all day, and getting a good night's sleep is critical to your health. According to neuroscientist and author Dr. Frances E. Jensen, **sleep is as important as the air you breathe and the food you eat, and it helps you manage your stress levels.** Also, research indicates that when you get a good night's sleep, everything you learned that day gets stored in your working memory for you to access during your test. So I am giving you permission to go to sleep and not pull an all-nighter; **make sure you get at least 8 hours of sleep**.

Bright Morning Light. When you first wake up, expose yourself to bright morning light (e.g., sunlight or bright white light) to help you wake up and start your day. Many years ago, people lived outdoor lifestyles where sleep, moods, and circadian rhythmic cycles aligned with natural light cycles. For increased well-being, identify activities in nature during daylight hours to help your mood and sleep.

• Exercise

Physical activity (PA). Through evidence-based research, PA is strongly linked to well-being; PA is known to improve physical health which improves your neurocognitive health. PA as "any bodily movement produced by skeletal muscles that requires energy expenditure" and any activity that raises the heart rate above resting levels. Additionally, continued research in this area supports not only a positive relationship between PA and cognitive functions, but also academic achievement. When you get PA, your neurocognitive brain function is enhanced, specifically your executive functions (EF), which is a set of top-down mental processes that allows for controlled and goal-directed behavior.

The research findings show significant benefits and a decrease of anxiety and depression symptoms when a consistent and ongoing training program is conducted (i.e., exercising over 30 minutes a day versus only working out for a couple of days). Moreover, after intense aerobic exercise (i.e., between 30 to 70 percent of maximal heart rate), a reduction in an individual's anxiety and depression is achieved. Even participating in an anaerobic activity, such as stretching, has a significant, positive impact on a person's mood.

Getting outside every day and moving your body in a natural environment can provide psychological restoration and strong long-term health outcomes. Throughout *The RGP*, you will find encouragement to get outside to exercise and get grounded. I am giving you permission to go outside and play.

Sweating/perspiring is how our body regulates its temperature and plays a role in preventing diseases. When you exercise, more sweat is needed to cool your body, and your muscles heat up. When you exercise for longer periods, work out more intensely, or work out in a hot environment (e.g., hot weather or hot yoga class), your sweat loss may cause a water/electrolyte imbalance in your body. Sweat consists of sodium, potassium, calcium, and magnesium, which are electrolytes; if you work out for long periods, you must replenish your body by drinking electrolytes (e.g., electrolyte hydration mix or sports drink). You want to continue to drink water throughout the day. If you have trouble drinking water, you can flavor your water with fruit infusions. You can also replenish your body with foods such as fruits (e.g., avocados, mangoes, pomegranates, and bananas), vegetables (e.g., green leafy vegetables and sweet potatoes), and legumes (e.g., chickpeas, kidney beans, and lentils), and calcium-rich foods (e.g., chicken, fish, milk, and yogurt).

In Persian medicine, sweating is considered to play an essential role in preventing and treating diseases. Sweating contains numerous health benefits (i.e., it removes waste products, maintains your body's health, and keeps your body temperature balanced).

Key Takeaway

- Exercise 30 minutes every day with a consistent and ongoing training program or other planned activity.

- Make sure to sweat every day and drink plenty of water.

• Mindfulness

Through mindfulness practice, individuals can cultivate a heightened focus on the present moment, leading to the development of positive qualities such as joy and compassion. This practice enhances attention, emotions, and behavioral self-regulation skills and improves overall well-being, making it a valuable addition to one's daily routine.

Christine O'Shaughnessy, who leads mindfulness meditation workshops at Harvard University, considers mindfulness a fitness routine to keep your brain healthy. Mindfulness keeps your mind on track by being aware when your mind wanders. Mindfulness is the power of your breath and connecting that breath to your body as you breathe in and out. O'Shaughnessy offers a mindfulness app called Present-Guided Meditation, which offers several free meditation sessions. Also, Harvard researchers discovered that practicing mindfulness 20 minutes a day will help you to be more focused, creative, productive, and less anxious.

In a CNBC interview, Lakhiani says, "For most people, 15 to 20 minutes will give you just the changes that you need. You can take a one- to three-minute dip into peacefulness and see remarkable results. The biggest benefits are going to happen in the first few minutes."

In a neuroscience-based mindfulness intervention program called Training for Awareness, Resilience, and Action (TARA), two different studies with 14- to 18-year-olds who participated in a 12-week group TARA training of mindfulness, yoga, and other therapy techniques showed significant improvements. In the smaller study, the depressed adolescents experienced decreased depressive and anxiety symptoms, along with improved sleep. In the other larger TARA study, the healthy control group reported increased emotional well-being, less anxiety, improved sleep quality, and positive changes within the inner white matter structural brain connectivity and outer gray matter volume.

Key Takeaways

- Research states that **20 minutes a day of meditation is optimal**; even 10 minutes a day delivers healthy brain benefits—which are seen in the first one to three minutes.

- As you practice mindfulness meditation with each life topic in *The Resilience Game Plan*, begin with the following steps before each recommended exercise:

    1. Find a quiet location to relax and either sit on the floor or in a chair.
    2. Align your spine by sitting up straight in a relaxed manner, with head and shoulders relaxed.
    3. Place your arms on each side, setting your hands face up on top of your legs.
    4. Now, close your eyes and start taking deep breaths to relax—noticing the power of your breath and connecting that breath to your body as you breathe in and breathe out.
    5. Since our minds like to wander, with no judgment, if you catch your mind wandering, return your focus to your breath.

- **Nature**

Human survival experiences (i.e., having food, shelter, protection) are ingrained into our homo sapien minds and still influencing brain functionalities in the present day. This therapy highlights the importance of our ancestor's outdoor lifestyle where sleep, moods, and circadian rhythmic cycles are aligned with natural light cycles.

Environmental psychology research studies provide hope that when individuals are immersed in a natural environment, it can provide psychological restoration. Furthermore, spending at least 120 minutes a week in nature or getting outside is associated with positive correlations for both health and well-being. Also, if you can identify some hobbies and/or outlets in nature during hours with sunlight, and you will find that your mood is improved and you will have a better quality night's sleep.

Key Takeaway

- Spending at least 120 minutes a week in nature or outside is associated with positive correlations for both health and mental well-being.

Grounding. When using *The RGP*, if possible, go outside and take advantage of the natural healing power of the earth. Place your bare feet on the concrete, dirt, grass, gravel, or wet sand. If you can get grounded every day, it will calm your busy mind and reduce stress and tension. It shifts your nervous system from a stressed out state to a much calmer state of mind.

If you think of your body as a continuous semiconducting fabric, when you ground it, this negative charge soaks into every part of your body (i.e., interiors of the cell and its nuclei). When these moving electrons are grounded, they quickly neutralize the positive charges in your body.

Mousa (2022) states it is contact with the earth via several channels that could cause a surge of electrons into your body, producing anti-inflammatory effects and immunity enhancement. Mousa also states that while any time spent "getting grounded" is excellent, the optimal amount of time to achieve your ultimate health is grounding for at least 40 minutes daily.

Key Takeaways

- Get "grounded" for at least 40 minutes a day.
- You have been provided with a good excuse regarding why you need to go to the beach or park.

• Hydration

The goal is to drink a minimum of eight glasses of water daily. Our bodies are made of 60% water, so it makes common sense that if we sweat every day, we need to replenish our bodies with water. Mousa (2022) compounds the concept of "getting grounded" with drinking water to help excrete toxins in your body.

Another interesting fact from research is that a drink red in color can encourage us to drink more. It can also increase our mood and cognitive abilities.

Maintaining hydration is highly linked with a person's excellent physical condition and cognitive performance. With the brain comprised of 70% water (compared to 60% in the human body), staying hydrated is essential, as an adequately hydrated brain is known via brain imaging to improve mood, enhance memory, and decrease anxiety symptoms.

Key Takeaways

- The goal is to drink a minimum of 64 ounces of water daily.
- A drink red in color will increase your mood, cognitive abilities, and your desire to drink more fluid. Add a touch of cherry, cranberry, or pomegranate natural juice to your water.

• Nutrition

In one sentence, the summation of this category is—**you are what you eat.** When adolescents do not eat a proper nutritious diet, then cognition is impaired, working memory is compromised, and social cues and empathy are lacking. This causes a higher-level of anxiety and bad decisions to be made. As your body grows, focus on eating a whole-food diet rich in vitamins and nutrients.

In the *Appendix* on **page 153**, you will find a **Nutrition Game Plan.** You can make copies of that page or start a daily food log on your computer or in a "Notes" section on your cell phone. Keeping track of what time of day you eat, where you eat, how you feel/think when eating, what foods you are eating, and "other" (keeping track of healthy meals or daily calories consumed) helps you to keep track of the foods that make you feel good or bad.

- **Social Fitness**

In addition to maintaining our physical fitness, we must also invest in our social fitness. A Harvard study conducted over eight decades by Waldinger & Schulz (2023) can be summarized into eight words and two sentences:

"Good relationships keep us healthier and happier. Period."

Furthermore, Waldinger & Schulz (2023) discuss several longitudinal studies that also report significant findings on the importance of human connections; these studies report that if people live lonely lives, they also have a shorter life expectancy (Seewer et al., 2022). In fact, Great Britain is addressing this public health concern in their country by appointing a Minister of Loneliness.

Umberson & Mortez (2010) expand on this thought process that the social relationships in your life have short- and long-term impacts on your physical and mental health. They also state that the social skills you develop during childhood have a cumulative effect progressing into adulthood.

Layard (2020) connects many concepts, life skills, and strategies in *The Resilience Game Plan*. In the "Well-Being Habit Tracker," Layard encourages you to practice your "Social Fitness" and prosocial behavior—accomplished by showing empathy, compassion, and "Caring" through acts of service. As Layard supports with his research, for you to experience happiness, you need to practice your "Social Fitness" by spending time with family and friends, getting involved in social activities, and having a sense of belonging in your school and community.

- **Caring**

    As mentioned in the "Preferred Method of Communication - Helping Hand" section, it is important to learn the life skills of being a caring, compassionate, empathetic, respectful, and sensitive person so we can make a positive difference to those in our community and around the world. By taking on this global civic responsibility framework, you become a community service leader who is conscientious, reliable, relevant, and always actively making a positive impact within communities worldwide. You exhibit prosocial behavior (compassion and social trust) and perform acts of service, such as exhibiting the daily practice of sustainability (composting and picking up trash) to collecting hygiene kit items to pass out to the homeless population.

- **Gratitude**

    Gratitude is an emotion and attribute that, when practiced daily, is strongly correlated to your overall health and well-being. Incorporating the daily practice of gratitude helps you open your eyes to all of the positive aspects of your life that you may not stop to appreciate until you write them down in your "Well-Being Habit Tracker." To help you get started, here are some questions to assist you in your daily practice:
    - **Awe and Wonder** - What causes you to stop and pause in awe to appreciate a certain beauty?
    - **Thankfulness** - Identify the aspects and people in your life where you feel thankful.
    - **Verbalize Your Appreciation** - Write down phrases you say to others to express your thanks.
    - **Life is Short** - List the positive experiences in your life, along with future bucket list items.

    When you practice gratitude daily, you are paving the neural pathways in your brain to make it an automatic habit to recognize all of the positive aspects of your life. In a study with teenagers and young adults, MRI imaging captured the practice of gratitude journaling in the ventromedial prefrontal cortex and nucleus accumbens areas, considered "value-sensitive" and reward systems cortical brain regions. Researchers discovered these brain changes lead to more prosocial behaviors and moral emotions known to increase your well-being.

- **Happiness**

    According to the University of Oxford's Wellbeing Research Centre's *World Happiness Report*, several factors influence your happiness and well-being. In this report, Oxford researchers analyzed the results of children, adolescents, and young people asking these subjective well-being questions:
    - **Are you happy or satified with your life?**
    - **What are your feelings and emotions regarding people or situations in your life (positive - joy and happiness or negative - sad and anxious) ?**
    - **Do you feel your life has purpose and meaning?**

    Become skilled and trust yourself to self-assess your well-being. You are reliable and capable of addressing these questions. Your well-being now affects your happiness into adulthood and your desire to continue setting high goals, which can lead to a better job and increased income.

    Also, identifying carefree activities at your age is important. Having hobbies and interests can help you to lead a well-balanced life (e.g., physical and social activity, volunteering, and outdoor activities).

- **Laugh**

Laughter is a known thing to have physiological, psychological, social, spiritual, and quality-of-life benefits. In contrast, as found in other areas of medicine, no adverse effects are known. The therapeutic efficacy of laughter is typically induced by external stimuli (i.e., a display of positive emotion, or self-induced laughter). Since the brain cannot distinguish between internal versus external stimuli, similar benefits are assumed to be achieved with both factors. **Researchers continue to monitor laughter as a healing agent since it possesses many positive and quantifiable effects on an individual's health.** In the "Well-Being Habit Tracker," you are asked to name something that makes you laugh each day, as well as list a way you made someone smile.

- **Smile**

Theory and research indicate that individuals with more frequent positive emotions are better at attaining goals at work and have better mental health, physical health, and longevity (Abel & Krueger, 2010). Even fifty years later, research still supports these facts claimed by Izard (1971), stating that positive and negative emotions significantly correlate with an individual's personality and life outcome—influencing how that person will act, think, react, and interact with others.

- **Music**

Going back to the prehistoric era, music has always played a vital role in expressing emotion (i.e., compassion and fear), as well as serving relaxation and healing purposes. Hippocrates, the founding father of rational medicine, and Plato are known to utilize music to soothe patients.

A learned, cognitive response validates the effectiveness of music; the associated learning process can get rooted in your memory. Research also states that **music increases dopamine and serotonin levels in the brain.** Listening to music is known to reach a cellular and epigenetic level in the human body. So get your groove on in the **"Well-Being Habit Tracker"** and list a song that lifts your spirits and motivates you to overcome any challenging situation.

PLAYBOOK STRATEGY #6: SETTING GOALS AND REDUCING ANXIETY

This sixth strategy of "Reducing Anxiety Through Goal Setting" piggybacks perfectly to the previous five strategies you just learned. When the cognitive, communication, and mindfulness skills learned in *The RGP* turn into automatic habits, along with ways to incorporate healthy daily habits in the "Well-Being Habit Tracker," are then combined with this **Anxiety-Buster To-Do List** activity, then you have created an overall mind and body wellness plan for yourself.

      Learning Cognitive, Commununication, and Mindfulness Life Skills
+ Implementing the Well-Being Habit Tracker Categories
+ Setting Goals to Reduce Anxiety in Anxiety-Buster To-Do List
= Healthy Well-Being of Mind and Body

While this **Anxiety-Buster To-Do List** exercise can be used on a daily basis, for the purposes of *The RGP*, you will see this **Anxiety-Buster To-Do List** chart at the end of every *RGP* life topic as you create your "Personalized Game Plan" for that particular topic. By using this **Anxiety-Buster To-Do List**, you will increase your ability to accomplish your goals and timely complete your tasks by listing out: **1 Big Task, 2 Medium Tasks, and 3 Small Tasks**.

According to Masicampo & Baumeister (2011), when you outline or create a list of your goals, you will experience the following:

- Several psychological benefits (i.e., reduces anxiety and keeps focus on success)
- As research indicates from the Zeigarnik Effect, unfinished goals will not deter you from interrupting thoughts, as unaccomplished goals are just distracting.
- When you create and commit to your game plan, it will open up your mind to other pursuits—allowing you to be more creative too.

Anxiety-Buster To-Do List: EXAMPLE

1 Big Task - Let's Go!
- ☐ _____

2 Medium Tasks - Let's Do This.
- ☐ _____
- ☐ _____

3 Small Tasks - You Got This.
- ☐ _____
- ☐ _____
- ☐ _____

© 2024 Reflections Publishing LLC. All rights reserved.

Section Six

What's Your Game Plan?

Warm-up

LIFE TOPICS:

- Academic Pressures - 44
- Habit Formation: Forming New Habits and Breaking Old Habits - 50
- What is Your Legacy? - Core Values - 56
- Who are Your Mentors/Coaches? - 62

• Academic Pressures •

With a growth mindset, you can achieve success in any class if you are passionate and a hard worker. We all have different skills and talents. If you struggle in school and feel like you need some additional help, talk to your caregiver (parent or guardian) and/or a teacher because you might have a small learning disability. Once you address this issue, you can start your path to success.

Remember when I mentioned earlier in the "How *The Resilience Game Plan* Will Benefit You?" section that we all have something? I was not joking—none of us are perfect or born perfect, so if it takes you longer than your classmates to complete your work, step up and ask for help. Like I said earlier, right now, your brain is like plastic and can build new brain highways, so it is no different than practicing to hit the right music note or learning the proper sports technique to hit the game-winning shot—it all takes practice, and we all learn things differently. I am always amazed at how **two people can try to teach me the same thing, and one explanation clicks and the other explanation leaves me perplexed and confused.**

If you find school is too stressful, this will affect your concentration and your academic performance. As humans, we have a fight or flight response to help protect us in threatening situations; this cortisol release is a good thing to elevate your ability to respond to a potential threat. However, when a continual cortisol release occurs in your brain due to ongoing stress, this deactivates the Hippocampal brain region corresponding to heightened cortisol release. Too much cortisol in the brain is toxic. Long story short, it wreaks havoc in your brain and can significantly impact your academic performance. The mindfulness section in a couple of pages will be excellent in helping you to cope with your stress and lower your cortisol levels. Remember, there are always people to help you if you are in a bad situation, so speak up.

```
"What we learn with pleasure, we never forget."
         - Alfred Mercier
```

Study tips:

1. Before studying, find a **healthy snack** to give you a boost of energy/maintain blood sugar levels.

2. Find a **quiet place to study**—with no distractions.

3. When taking notes, writing in **red and blue colors** can enhance your cognitive skills (e.g., concentration and attention span) while also increasing your brain function (i.e., learning new information while embedding it into your working memory to encode, store, and retrieve this new information). Also, the color red is known to enhance your performance on simple, detail-oriented tasks; in contrast, blue improves performance on simple and difficult, detail-oriented tasks, as well as on creative tasks.

4. Another concept you should implement is **Repeated Reading** (RR). This reading strategy can improve your reading fluency by reading and/or listening to a passage to help you comprehend the text. If you do not understand something the first time you read it, then reread the material two more times. You will be amazed how suddenly, by the third read, the information starts to resonate and make sense. This evidence-based reading strategy works for all readers—regardless of reading ability and has proven to increase your reading fluency and comprehension skills).

5. Finally, free **voluntary reading** (i.e., reading all genres) is a wonderful way to increase your ability to read, write, spell, and comprehend. In addition to improving your math skills, reading a lot of the style you want to write in is also an effective writing method.

• Now Apply it! •

Is there an individual or something in your life stressing you or holding you back academically?

_____

_____

_____

_____

_____

_____

If any information in this playbook is upsetting, please talk to a parent/guardian, school counselor, teacher, or medical professional.
This book is sold with the understanding that the publisher and the author are not engaged in rendering medical, legal, or other professional advice or services.
If professional assistance is required, the services of a competent professional should be sought.

• Academic Pressures •

Brain Power

When you are actively learning, it is a huge dopamine blast for your brain when you are learning for the love of learning—not feeling academic pressure. As a student, if you are in a constant state of stress, research indicates you may experience a shift in your **Hypothalamic-Pituitary-Adrenal (HPA) axis** reactivity. Thus, this creates a perfect storm in your brain—resulting in a heightened stress-induced hormonal response. In your web browser, search HPA axis to see the entire HPA cycle from the **Hypothalamus → Pituitary Gland → Adrenal Gland**—affecting the immune system with the surge of cortisol released → which then swings back up to the **Hypothalamus**.

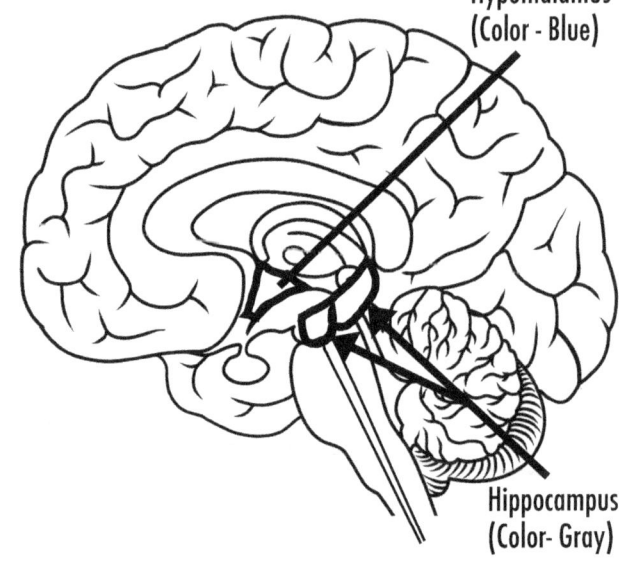

Hypothalamus (Color - Blue)

Hippocampus (Color - Gray)

We all have a fight or flight response to help protect us in threatening situations; this cortisol release is a good thing to elevate their ability to respond to a potential threat. However, when a continual cortisol release occurs in your brain due to ongoing stress, this deactivates the **Hippocampal** brain region corresponding to heightened cortisol release. Too much cortisol in the brain is toxic.

Cognitive Skills

Step #1: Expressive Writing to Overcome

_____
(Write an "Academic Topic" causing you distress.)

#1 Stop and Acknowledge - What are you thinking/feeling?
_____
_____

#2 Question and Tweak - What facts back up these thoughts?
_____
_____

#3 Balance and Thrive - Change your negative thought to this positive thought:
_____
_____

#4 Create your "I Am Statement" in overcoming this obstacle.
_____

Cognitive Skills

_____

("Academic Topic" causing you distress.)

INSTRUCTIONS for Steps #2 and #3:
On the line above, write the "Academic Topic" causing you stress. Next, On the "Feelings Thermometer," color up to the point of your distress (from 1 to 5) and write a phrase on the matching line describing how you are feeling about this topic. Now that you know how you feel, move to Step #3 and write ten steps to overcome this fear. You can find tips below with a "possible scenario" to get you started.

Step #2: Gauging Your Feelings

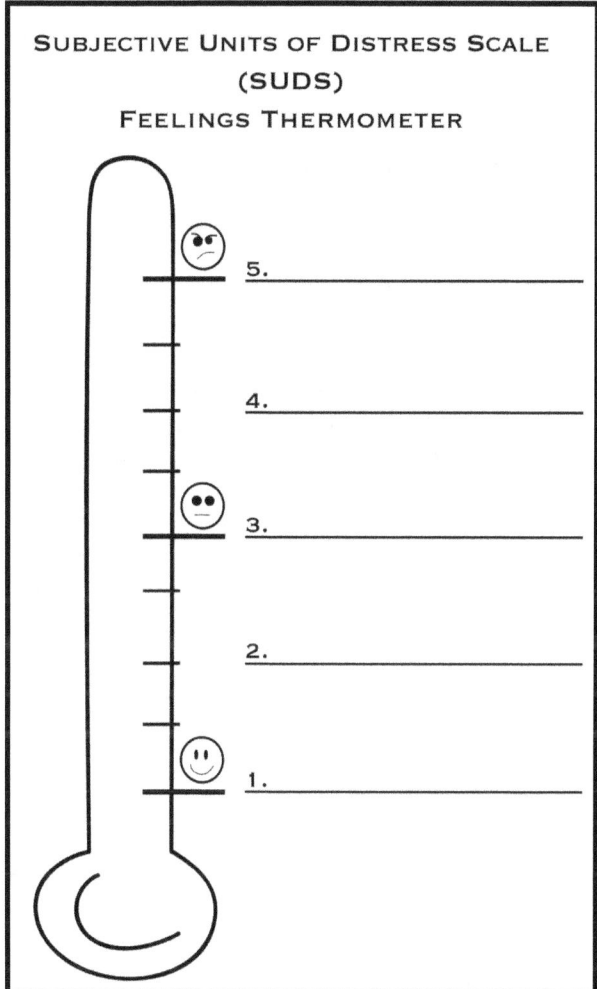

Step #3: Overcoming Obstacles

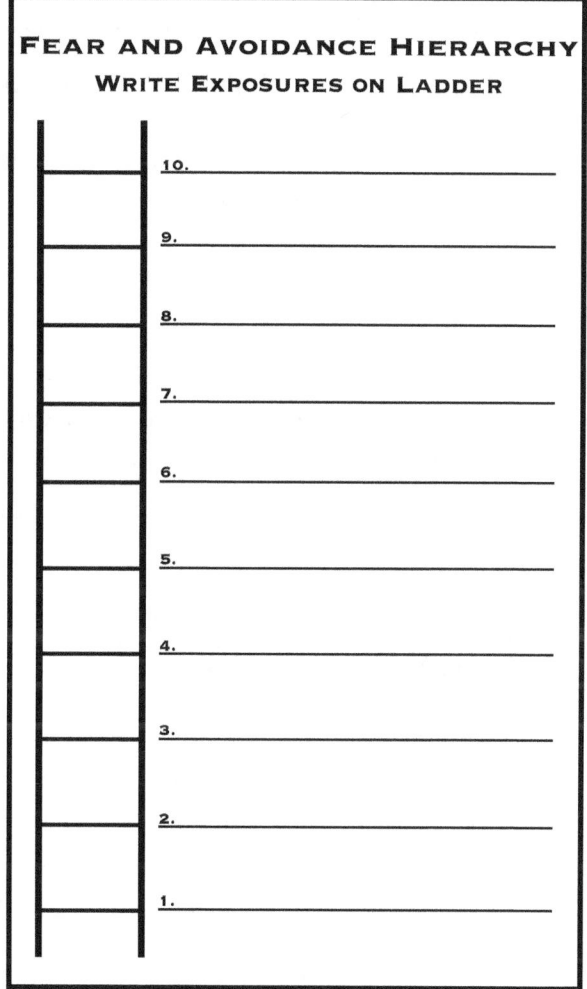

How you Might Feel About Taking Tests:
5. Extreme anxiety/My heart is racing. I don't want to take this test.
4. High anxiety/I feel like I studied the wrong material.
3. Moderately anxious/I don't feel like I studied enough.
2. Mild anxiety/I think I read and studied the right material.
1. No anxiety/I feel confident in my study skills.

Ideas on "Overcoming Fear of Tests"
10. I am confident to take this test.
9. I will take the practice test to prepare.
8. I will create my own practice test to prepare.
7. I will do the breathing exercise that helps me to relax.
6. I will practice "I am" statements to increase my confidence.
5. I will work with a tutor to help with those hard concepts.
4. I will join a study group and identify what I still need to learn.
3. I will watch online videos with lessons about my test.
2. I will watch a movie about students taking tests.
1. I will listen to an upbeat song about overcoming a fear.

Communication Skills

If after taking the Reflections Publishing Communication Assessment and you believe that **"Spending Time Together"** is your "Preferred Method of Communication," then you need to set up a time to talk to your teacher(s) if you are struggling in class. Teachers and college professors love when students come talk to them and show they are actively engaged in their own learning process.

Understanding What Problems You Missed:

- If you take a test and are upset you did not do as well as you had hoped, ask your teacher the following questions:

    1. Tell your teacher how you prepared and ask if they can suggest additional studying methods.
    2. If you do not get to keep your test after it is graded, ask your teacher what types of questions you missed and how you can better prepare for your next test. Remember, with a growth mindset, you are going to miss problems, and that is okay—you are learning.

Mindfulness Skills

A breathing technique to help you relax before taking a test is called Alternate Nostril Breathing. This method is known to be good for your heart (i.e., reduce your heart rate and lower blood pressure), lungs (i.e., improve lung function), and brain (i.e., sympathetic stress).

"Alternate Nostril Breathing" Mindfulness Exercise

- Begin with the steps on page 30 before beginning this technique:

    1. With the same hand, put your right thumb over your right nostril and ring finger on your left nostril.
    2. With your right nostril closed off, breathe deeply and slowly through your left nostril—pausing at the top of your breath and closing both nostrils and exhaling through your right nostril.
    3. At the bottom of your breath, hold both nostrils closed and then switch sides.
    4. Repeat step 1 above with the opposite hand.
    5. Alternate sides for five to ten cycles.

Well-Being Habit Tracker:

1. **Fill out each Well-Being Habit Tracker category below.**
2. **When completed, check the box and note your subjective well-being from 1-10.**

- ☐ **Sleep:** How many hours? _____ **Morning Light Exposure:** ☐   Well-Being Rating: _____
- ☐ **Exercise:** Length/Type? _____   Well-Being Rating: _____
- ☐ **Mindfulness:** Length/Type? _____   Well-Being Rating: _____
- ☐ **Nature:** Time spent/Activity outside? ____ / _____   Well-Being Rating: _____
- ☐ **Hydration:** I drank ☐☐☐☐☐☐☐☐ 8 oz. glasses of water.   Well-Being Rating: _____
- ☐ **Nutrition:** Number of healthy meals or calories consumed? _____   Well-Being Rating: _____
- ☐ **Social Fitness:** Time spent/Activity? ____ / _____   Well-Being Rating: _____
- ☐ **Caring:** Act(s) of service? _____   Well-Being Rating: _____
- ☐ **Gratitude:** I am grateful for _____   Well-Being Rating: _____
- ☐ **Happiness:** _____ brought me joy!   Well-Being Rating: _____
- ☐ **Laughter:** I laughed about _____
- ☐ **Smile:** I made someone smile by _____
- ☐ **Music:** I sang or listened to this song to motivate me and boost my mood and well-being: _____

© 2024 Reflections Publishing LLC. All rights reserved.

Anxiety-Buster To-Do List:

1 Big Task - Let's Go!
- ☐ _____

2 Medium Tasks - Let's Do This!
- ☐ _____
- ☐ _____

3 Small Tasks - You Got This!
- ☐ _____
- ☐ _____
- ☐ _____

© 2024 Reflections Publishing LLC. All rights reserved.

• Habit Formation •

Creating new and breaking old habits is part of having a growth mindset. To recap, below, find the definition of a habit along with the six categories regarding how to form new habits:

Definition of Habit

In the *Design How People Learn book* by Julie Dirksen, she defines a habit as "an acquired behavior pattern regularly followed until it has become *almost involuntary*."

How to Form a New Habit

As discussed in more detail on **pages 31-32**, Dirksen breaks down the creation of habit formation into six categories:
- **Acquired behavior patterns**
- **Triggers**
- **Motivations**
- **Feedback**
- **Practice or repetition**
- **Environment**.

According to Chip and Dan Heath in their book *Switch*, as well as B. J. Fogg's Tiny Habits program, if you are feeling overwhelmed with acquiring a new habit, then name and identify the smallest productive behavior task and make the task feel smaller and more manageable.

How to Break Old Habits

Author James Clear in *Atomic Habits: An Easy & Proven Way to Build New Ones & Break Bad Ones* describes learning new habits as a gradual process. Clear states that if you are struggling to change a habit, then the problem likely is not you, but the "system" that is your normal routine. Clear describes strategies to make new habits include overcoming a lack of motivation and willpower, designing your environment to ensure success, and getting back on track when you fall off course.

Clear states that constantly tweaking and improving your "systems" is the best framework to achieve change. Clear claims that habits are "compound interest" and that **even one percent improvement adds up in the long term**.

Utilizing the example of doing homework with an illustration of a dartboard can help you to work through how to break an old habit. Clear provides **three Layers of Behavioral Change:**

1. **Outcomes** are the first and outer layer in achieving behavioral change. For example, this is a desire to get homework done quicker.

2. **Processing** is the second and middle layer in achieving behavioral change, consisting of steps you will take to change current habits and "systems." Processing considers the steps you might take to become more productive in completing homework.

3. **Identity** is the third and deepest inner layer. This is the ultimate bullseye that addresses how you might need to change your beliefs: address any known or unknown biases; your self-image; or any judgment against yourself or others, etc.

- **Do You Get it?**

1. Below find a **Layers of Behavioral Change** exercise to assist you in forming Identity-Based Habits. This can change "Who you are to become" versus "Outcome-Based Habits." Remember that your behaviors and habits reflect your true identity; thus, the importance of learning habits that align with your identity.

1. **Outcomes:** Color - Blue
   Get homework done quicker

2. **Processing:** Color - Green
   Steps to take to help you get homework done faster and be more productive:
   1. _____
   2. _____
   3. _____
   4. _____

3. **Identity:** Color - Red
   Ideas on how to change any beliefs, biases, your self-image, and any judgment you have against yourself or others which affect and determine your ability as a student:
   1. _____
   2. _____
   3. _____
   4. _____

2. List two new habits you want to form:
   1. _____
   2. _____

3. List two habits you need to break:
   1. _____
   2. _____

If any information in this playbook is upsetting, please talk to a parent/guardian, school counselor, teacher, or medical professional.
This book is sold with the understanding that the publisher and the author are not engaged in rendering medical, legal, or other professional advice or services.
If professional assistance is required, the services of a competent professional should be sought.

HABIT FORMATION

• Habit Formation •

Brain Power

Habit activation in the brain takes place in your **Medial Prefrontal Cortex** which stores long-term assessments of your environmental experiences. In contrast, your short-term memories are actively embedded into your **Hippocampus**. Impulse control is located in the **Dorsolateral Prefrontal Cortex** and in the **Anterior Cingulate Cortex** (Bonnici et al., 2012).

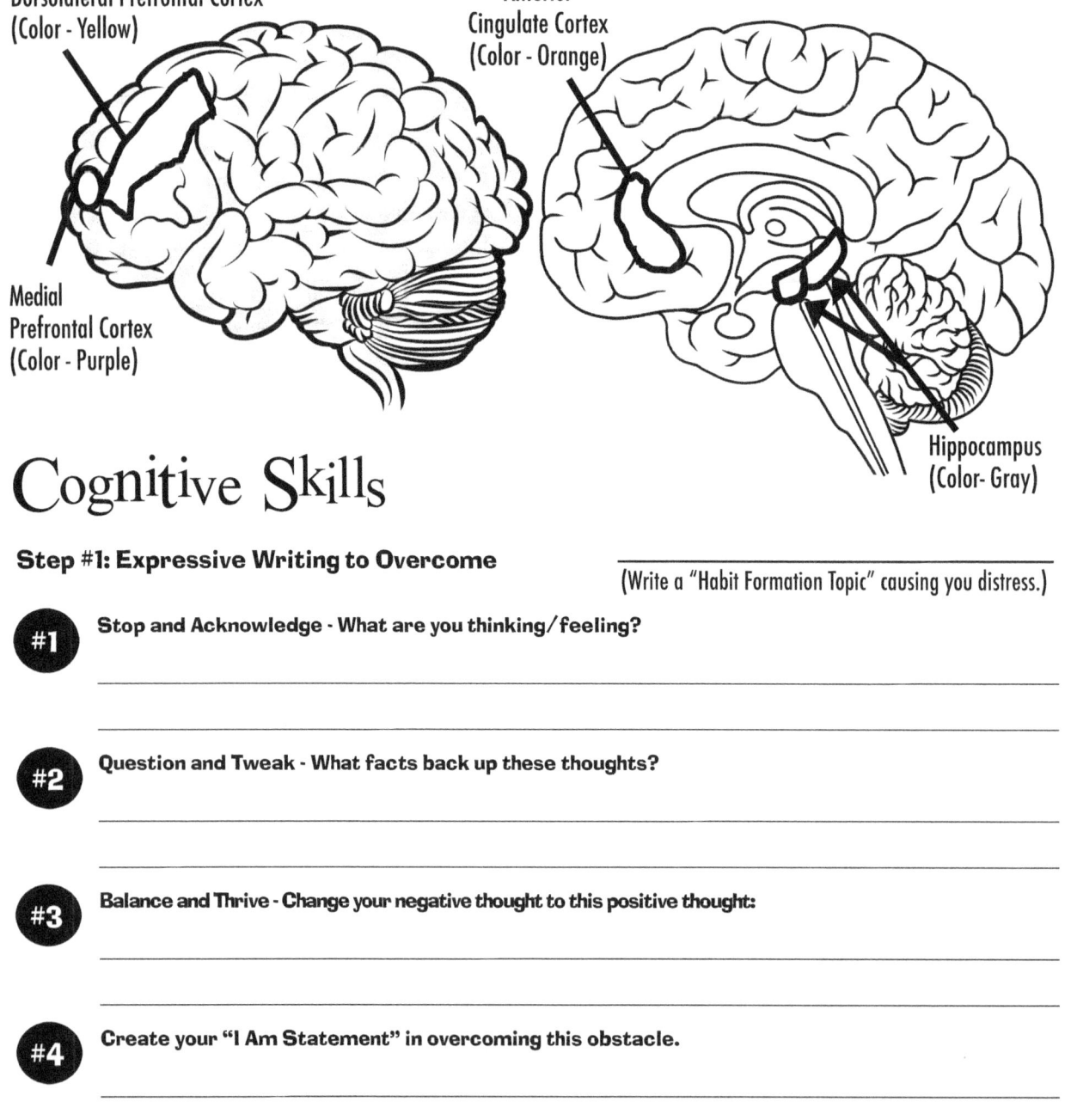

Dorsolateral Prefrontal Cortex (Color - Yellow)

Medial Prefrontal Cortex (Color - Purple)

Anterior Cingulate Cortex (Color - Orange)

Hippocampus (Color - Gray)

Cognitive Skills

Step #1: Expressive Writing to Overcome

_____
(Write a "Habit Formation Topic" causing you distress.)

#1 Stop and Acknowledge - What are you thinking/feeling?
_____
_____

#2 Question and Tweak - What facts back up these thoughts?
_____
_____

#3 Balance and Thrive - Change your negative thought to this positive thought:
_____
_____

#4 Create your "I Am Statement" in overcoming this obstacle.
_____

Cognitive Skills

(Write a "Habit Formation Topic" causing you distress.)

INSTRUCTIONS for Steps #2 and #3:
On the line above, write the "Habit Formation Topic" causing you stress. Next, On the "Feelings Thermometer," color up to the point of your distress (from 1 to 5) and write a phrase on the matching line describing how you are feeling about this topic. Now that you know how you feel, move to Step #3 and write ten steps to overcome this fear. You can find tips below with a "possible scenario" to get you started.

Step #2: Gauging Your Feelings

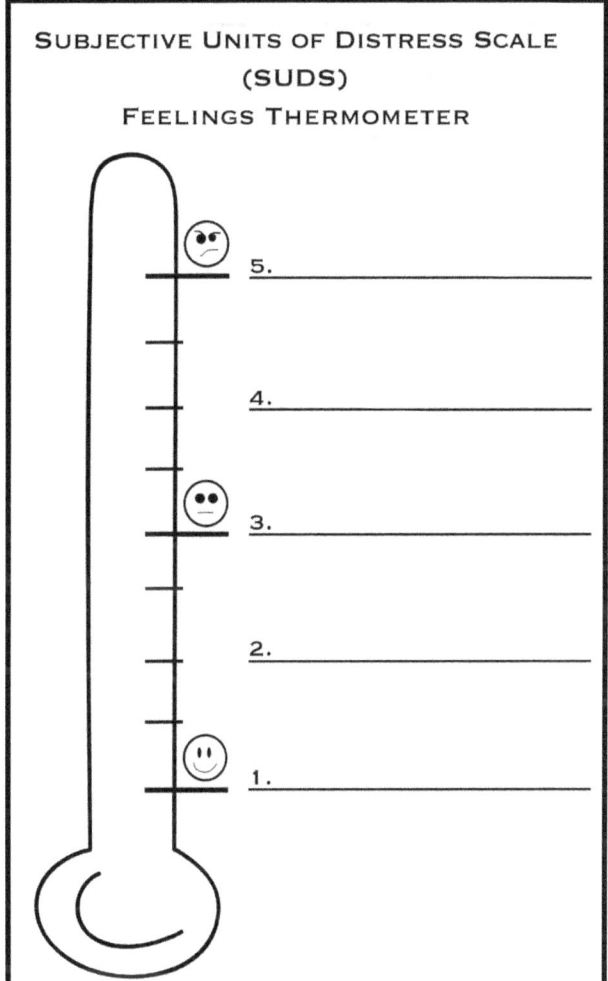

Step #3: Overcoming Obstacles

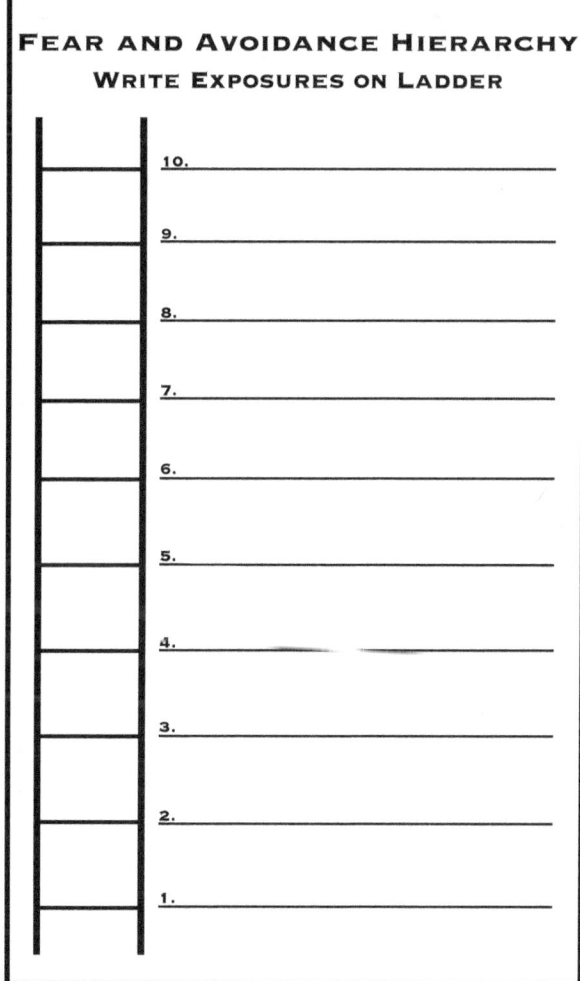

How You May Feel About Breaking a Habit:
5. Extreme anxiety/I feel extreme distress with change.
4. High anxiety/My heart is racing thinking about change.
3. Moderately anxious/I've encountered a roadblock.
2. Mild anxiety/I feel ready for something new.
1. No anxiety/I love learning new things.

Creating a New Habit to Wake Up Early:
10. I now wake up on my own before my alarm goes off.
9. I will leave for school early so I don't have to rush.
8. I will set the tone of my day with calming breathing exercises.
7. I will go outside to see the sun and set my circadian rhythm.
6. I will drink a glass of ice water to wake up my inner body.
5. I will wake up and splash cold water on my face.
4. I will set my alarm to go off at the same time every day.
3. I will watch funny online videos about morning routines.
2. I will watch a movie about a person that is a morning person.
1. I will listen to an upbeat song about starting your day early.

Communication Skills

If you still need to take the Reflections Publishing Communication Assessment, you can do so on **page 10**. If you have formed some bad habits, someone will likely try to talk to you about breaking them and replacing them with new-formed positive habits. Change is hard, but remember that the happiest people are willing to change and evolve.

How to Have a Productive Conversation About Creating New Habits:

- I really want to create the new habit of _____, but _____ is holding me back. I could really use your support to help me overcome this roadblock.
- I recognize I need to break this habit of _____ and I could really use your encouragement because I developed negative emotions around this habit—affecting my confidence.
- This _____ habit is an impulse behavior and I need to break the cycle.

Mindfulness Skills

When addressing habits, the first mindfulness step is to sit in a comfortable position—bringing your awareness to any autopilot action or thoughts your are experiencing (i.e., thinking, doing, or sensing). Pause and breathe through those thoughts—letting those thoughts pass as natural experiences and return your attention as you breathe deeply six times. Next, expand your awareness to your outside surroundings, noticing any lightness or tightness in your body—paying attention to everything around you.

In Maura Thomas' book *Attention Management: How to Create Success and Gain Productivity - Every Day,* she addresses how to use mindfulness to identify cues that evoke your unwanted habits. She also states the fact when we have performed a bad habit for many years, then our body goes into autopilot with that habit. In order to change that unwanted behaviors, she suggests the following technique.

"5 Habitual Cues" Mindfulness Exercise

- Be mindful of these cues that trigger undesired habits:
    1. If a certain **Location** triggers an unwanted habit, then go to another **Location**.
    2. Is there a **Certain Time of Day** that triggers you? If so, be mindful of that trigger.
    3. Be mindful if you notice that your **Emotional State** triggers an unwanted behavior.
    4. Do you find you only conduct the bad habit with **Certain People**?
    5. Avoid a habit if it automatically triggers an **Immediately Preceding Action**.

Well-Being Habit Tracker:

1. **Fill out each Well-Being Habit Tracker category below.**
2. **When completed, check the box and note your subjective well-being from 1-10.**

- ☐ **Sleep:** How many hours? _____ **Morning Light Exposure:** ☐   Well-Being Rating: _____
- ☐ **Exercise:** Length/Type? _____   Well-Being Rating: _____
- ☐ **Mindfulness:** Length/Type? _____   Well-Being Rating: _____
- ☐ **Nature:** Time spent/Activity outside? ____ / _____   Well-Being Rating: _____
- ☐ **Hydration:** I drank 🥛🥛🥛🥛🥛🥛 8 oz. glasses of water.   Well-Being Rating: _____
- ☐ **Nutrition:** Number of healthy meals or calories consumed? _____   Well-Being Rating: _____
- ☐ **Social Fitness:** Time spent/Activity? ____ / _____   Well-Being Rating: _____
- ☐ **Caring:** Act(s) of service? _____   Well-Being Rating: _____
- ☐ **Gratitude:** I am grateful for _____   Well-Being Rating: _____
- ☐ **Happiness:** _____ brought me joy!   Well-Being Rating: _____
- ☐ **Laughter:** I laughed about _____
- ☐ **Smile:** I made someone smile by _____
- ☐ **Music:** I sang or listened to this song to motivate me and boost my mood and well-being: _____

© 2024 Reflections Publishing LLC. All rights reserved.

Anxiety-Buster To-Do List:

1 Big Task - Let's Go!

- ☐ _____

2 Medium Tasks - Let's Do This!

- ☐ _____
- ☐ _____

3 Small Tasks - You Got This!

- ☐ _____
- ☐ _____
- ☐ _____

© 2024 Reflections Publishing LLC. All rights reserved.

• What is Your Legacy? - Core Values •

Determining who you are, what you stand for, and knowing your core values is something only you can decide. Your values, morals, and beliefs steer you in the direction in which you choose to live your life. While you should have trust-worthy mentors along the way to help guide and advise you—only you can truly decide who you want to be someday.

As a tween, the Prefrontal Cortex part of your brain will continue to develop into your twenties—some say the Prefrontal Cortex for males is not fully developed until 29-years-old. This Prefrontal Cortex part of your brain is where your decision-making skills develop. While this part of the brain is still developing into your 20's, just remember that it is a known fact that an individual knows the difference between right and wrong by the age of five-years-old.

In addition to acquiring strong communication skills, a successful person needs to have a good attitude, a strong hard work ethic, be committed to showing up, being on time—always kind and respectful, and most importantly, you need to have common sense. You can be the smartest person in the world, but if you are lacking strong communication skills and do not have common sense, then you will struggle in life.

While your goals may shift throughout your life, your values and morals that you learned and embedded into your personality as a child will guide you as you create your own value system. For you, some of these values may fall into the following categories of:

- Community Service
- Family Values
- Spiritual Values
- Work Ethic

Spending time in reflection will help you to align your morals, priorities, and values. You can use this space to download your thoughts and feelings and dig deep into your core. Follow your gut reactions when you read the guiding questions and write those thoughts down. To help you stay on track, you can write your main thoughts and goals onto a post-it to put in your locker or notebook or make it a screensaver on your cell phone.

"Give every day the chance to become the most beautiful day of your life."
- Mark Twain

1. **What does having common sense mean to you?**

   Wikipedia defines common sense (or simply sense) as sound, practical judgment concerning everyday matters, or a basic ability to perceive, understand, and judge in a manner that is shared by (i.e., "common to") nearly all people.

   _____
   _____
   _____
   _____
   _____

2. **What are you doing now that will create your future legacy?**

   This is your space to write down your hopes and dreams (i.e., college(s) to attend, major you will study in college, career path/future jobs, and future family life):

   _____
   _____
   _____
   _____
   _____

3. **If money were no obstacle, who and what would you be someday?**

   _____
   _____
   _____
   _____
   _____

4. **What steps can you take to make that dream happen?**

   _____
   _____
   _____
   _____
   _____

If any information in this playbook is upsetting, please talk to a parent/guardian, school counselor, teacher, or medical professional.
This book is sold with the understanding that the publisher and the author are not engaged in rendering medical, legal, or other professional advice or services.
If professional assistance is required, the services of a competent professional should be sought.

• What is Your Legacy? - Core Values •

Brain Power

Researchers Falk & Scholz (2018) conducted a meta-analysis of neuroimaging studies that highlighted how the **Ventral Striatum (VS)** and parts of the **Ventromedial Prefrontal Cortex (VMPFC)** play a role in how a person calculates their core values. The **VS** and **VMPFC** analyze a person's decision-making process that ultimately contributes to their final decisions, preferences, and actions. When you select your core values and ultimately determine your personal legacy, you also choose your preferred method of communication and if you will conform to your peers' influence.

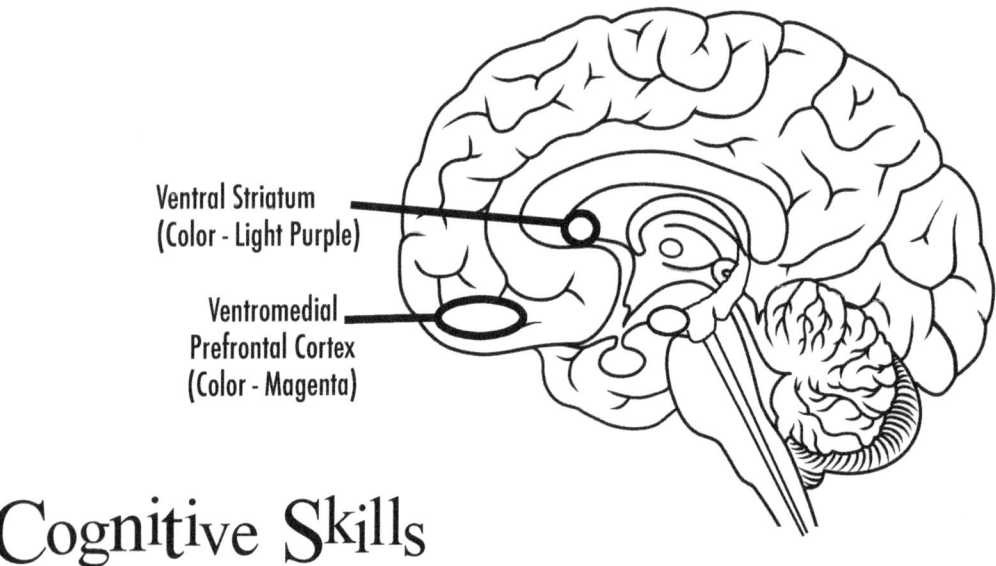

Ventral Striatum (Color - Light Purple)

Ventromedial Prefrontal Cortex (Color - Magenta)

Cognitive Skills

Step #1: Expressive Writing to Overcome

(Write a "Legacy/Core Value Topic" causing you distress.)

#1 Stop and Acknowledge - What are you thinking/feeling?

#2 Question and Tweak - What facts back up these thoughts?

#3 Balance and Thrive - Change your negative thought to this positive thought:

#4 Create your "I Am Statement" in overcoming this obstacle.

Cognitive Skills

_____
(Write a "Legacy/Core Value Topic" causing you distress.)

INSTRUCTIONS for Steps #2 and #3:
On the line above, write the "Legacy/Core Value Topic" causing you stress. Next, On the "Feelings Thermometer," color up to the point of your distress (from 1 to 5) and write a phrase on the matching line describing how you are feeling about this topic. Now that you know how you feel, move to Step #3 and write ten steps to overcome this fear. You can find tips below with a "possible scenario" to get you started.

Step #2: Gauging Your Feelings

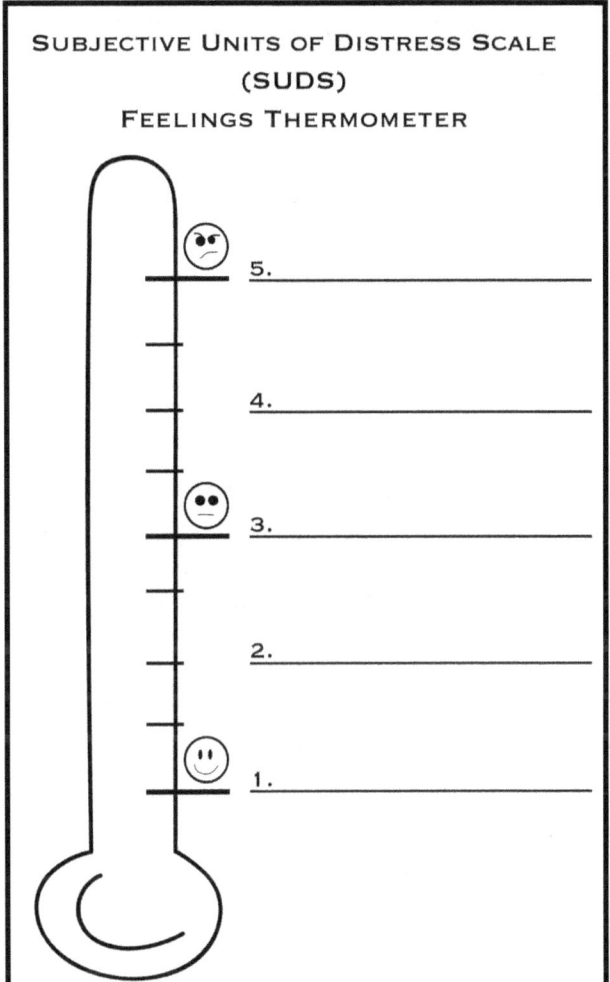

Step #3: Overcoming Obstacles

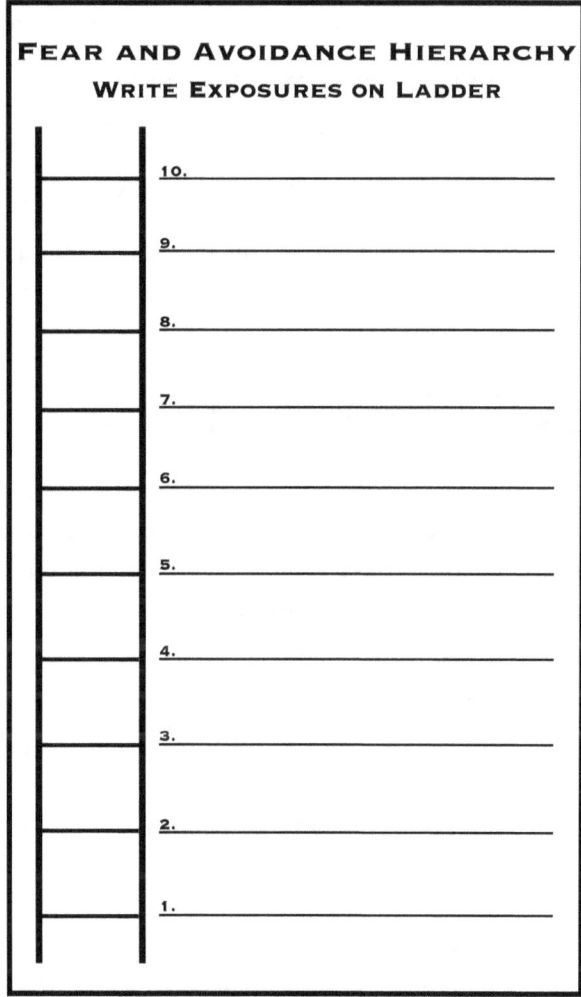

How Do You Feel About Your Core Values?:
5. Extreme anxiety/I feel extreme distress with no values.
4. High anxiety/I lie about my core values.
3. Moderately anxious/I can't stand up for my core values.
2. Mild anxiety/I don't like apologizing for my values.
1. No anxiety/I am extremely confident and know who I am.

Ideas for Fears of Forming My Core Values?:
10. I will be a mentor to others on how to stand up for beliefs.
9. I will join a group that shares my same core values.
8. I will join a group that supports and encourages me.
7. I will do breathing exercises to overcome judgment.
6. I will practice "I am" statements to strengthen beliefs.
5. I will find a friend who thinks like me.
4. I will learn tools to help me be resilient with core values.
3. I will watch funny online videos about making good choices.
2. I will watch a movie about a person deciding who they are.
1. I will listen to an upbeat song about who I am.

Communication Skills

When it comes to your core values, only you can decide what you want your legacy to be someday. When communicating your truth to others, keep your power and acknowledge and appreciate your self-worth. You do not need to apologize for your morals and values—so stand strong to your beliefs.

- Maintain your self-respect—not compromising your values, yet speaking respectfully to others.
- Other people may make different choices in their life—it is not our place to judge them.
- Clearly communicate and stick with your values.
- Always be truthful and do not lie to others—you do not need to feel bad for your beliefs.
- Be confident in your morals and values and be straightforward in your communication.

Mindfulness Skills

This is a mindfulness exercise that will help you to process and help determine your core beliefs. Some of our core beliefs have been programmed into us—consciously and unconsciously. While you may have some positive beliefs, you might also have some negative and self-destructing core beliefs. Take time and explore your thoughts and emotions while doing this mindfulness meditation exercise.

"What are Your Core Beliefs and Values" Mindfulness Exercise

1. Get in a comfortable position and close your eyes. Let your mind wander to thinking about your core values.
2. Take six deep breaths and think of some core values that you believe you have. This will likely be conscious thoughts that have been embedded in us based on our environment (i.e., family, friends, educators, coaches, political views, etc.).
3. Take notice of how your body feels and any sensations you experience such as lightness or tightness in your body.
4. Hold your breath for six seconds and as you exhale, what is the first thought that enters your mind regarding that sensation? Either accept or deny the thought—determining if it aligns with your core values and beliefs.
5. Take another six deep breaths and think of some subconscious cores values that you may or may not know you have (i.e. personal bias).
6. Take notice of how your those sensations make your body feel—acknowledging any lightness or tightness in your body.

Well-Being Habit Tracker:

1. **Fill out each Well-Being Habit Tracker category below.**
2. **When completed, check the box and note your subjective well-being from 1-10.**

- ☐ **Sleep:** How many hours? _____ **Morning Light Exposure:** ☐ Well-Being Rating: _____
- ☐ **Exercise:** Length/Type? _____ Well-Being Rating: _____
- ☐ **Mindfulness:** Length/Type? _____ Well-Being Rating: _____
- ☐ **Nature:** Time spent/Activity outside? ____ / _____ Well-Being Rating: _____
- ☐ **Hydration:** I drank ☐☐☐☐☐☐☐☐ 8 oz. glasses of water. Well-Being Rating: _____
- ☐ **Nutrition:** Number of healthy meals or calories consumed? _____ Well-Being Rating: _____
- ☐ **Social Fitness:** Time spent/Activity? ____ / _____ Well-Being Rating: _____
- ☐ **Caring:** Act(s) of service? _____ Well-Being Rating: _____
- ☐ **Gratitude:** I am grateful for _____ Well-Being Rating: _____
- ☐ **Happiness:** _____ brought me joy! Well-Being Rating: _____
- ☐ **Laughter:** I laughed about _____
- ☐ **Smile:** I made someone smile by _____
- ☐ **Music:** I sang or listened to this song to motivate me and boost my mood and well-being: _____

© 2024 Reflections Publishing LLC. All rights reserved.

Anxiety-Buster To-Do List:

1 Big Task - Let's Go!
- ☐ _____

2 Medium Tasks - Let's Do This!
- ☐ _____
- ☐ _____

3 Small Tasks - You Got This!
- ☐ _____
- ☐ _____
- ☐ _____

© 2024 Reflections Publishing LLC. All rights reserved.

• Who Are Your Mentors/Coaches? •

According to Jack et al. (2013), when individuals have mentors and coaches in their lives then the Positive Emotional Attractor (PEA) is activated in their brains. Neural brain circuits are activated—allowing you to think in a more positive manner and stay motivated. You will visually be able to picture your success and the path you need to take in order to achieve your goals.

Boyatzis (2008) indicates that when individuals receive effective coaching, then the Intentional Change Theory comes into play—creating a behavioral change. This is relevant when your mentor or coach utilizes the Intentional Change Theory to provide you with a common-sense game plan to help you reach your final goals. Boyatzis & Akrivou (2006) believe that when your mentor and/or coach utilizes the Intentional Change Theory, then they are encouraging you to find the following qualities in yourself:

- What is your ideal self?
- What is your calling and purpose and what choices should you make to stay on this track?
- What are your core values, philosophy, and your personal self and identity?
- What are your passions in life?

Conner & Pope (2013) encourage you to make a goal to connect with at least one teacher or school counselor so you can receive any necessary resources to implement any strategies to help reduce any stress. Colarossi and Eccles (2003) also support this notion that finding mentors outside your immediate family circle will help you form a strong sense of self. Phillippo et al. (2017) agree that while you may have a supportive family network, receiving advice and feedback from a mentor will help you form your self-concept and identity formation. Also, Erickson et al. (2009) claim that you will build resiliency if you have trustworthy and nurturing adults in your life who are not in your immediate family circle.

1. **CREATE YOUR OWN DOT • TO • DOT OF A MOUNTAIN—INDICATING THE STEPS YOU NEED TO TAKE TO ACHIEVE YOUR GOALS.**
(I helped to get you started. Think about how a mentor can assist you with addressing any necessary steps and/or setbacks you might experience along the way.

"Without continual growth and progress, such words as improvement, achievement, and success have no meaning."
— Benjamin Franklin

2. Trace or draw a hand below and write the names of five individuals you consider to be a coach, cheerleader, or mentor in your life. Only list people outside your immediate family (i.e., advisory, home room, or music teacher, coach, aunt/uncle).

3. Having trouble coming up with five names? Use this space below to brainstorm areas of your life of someone who could be a possible mentor?

_____

_____

WHO ARE YOUR MENTORS/COACHES?

If any information in this playbook is upsetting, please talk to a parent/guardian, school counselor, teacher, or medical professional.
This book is sold with the understanding that the publisher and the author are not engaged in rendering medical, legal, or other professional advice or services.
If professional assistance is required, the services of a competent professional should be sought.

• Who Are Your Mentors/Coaches? •

Brain Power

As noted on **page 62,** in the research article by Jack et al. (2013), their findings indicate that when individuals have mentors and coaches in their life, the **Positive Emotional Attractor (PEA)** is activated in the brain. Thus, the neural brain circuits activated are indicated below.

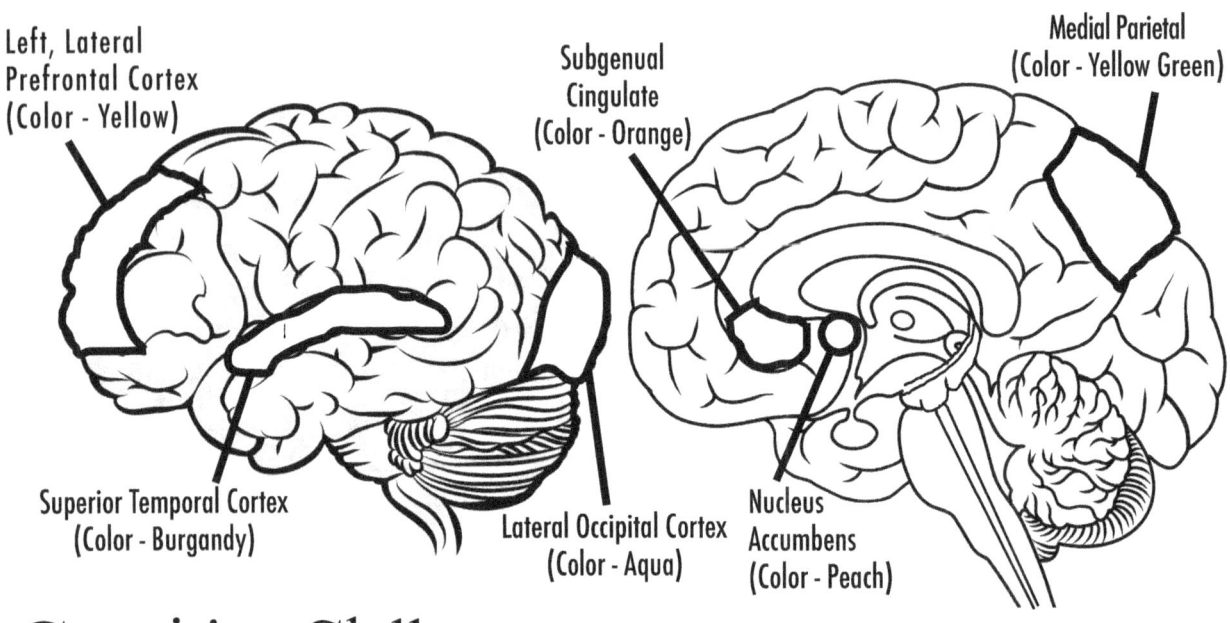

Left, Lateral Prefrontal Cortex (Color - Yellow)

Subgenual Cingulate (Color - Orange)

Medial Parietal (Color - Yellow Green)

Superior Temporal Cortex (Color - Burgandy)

Lateral Occipital Cortex (Color - Aqua)

Nucleus Accumbens (Color - Peach)

Cognitive Skills

Step #1: Expressive Writing to Overcome

(Write a "Mentors/Coaches Topic" causing you distress.)

#1 Stop and Acknowledge - What are you thinking/feeling?
___
___

#2 Question and Tweak - What facts back up these thoughts?
___
___

#3 Balance and Thrive - Change your negative thought to this positive thought:
___
___

#4 Create your "I Am Statement" in overcoming this obstacle.
___

-64-

Cognitive Skills

(Write a "Mentors/Coaches Topic" causing you distress.)

INSTRUCTIONS for Steps #2 and #3:
On the line above, write a "Mentors/Coaches Topic" causing you stress. Next, On the "Feelings Thermometer," color up to the point of your distress (from 1 to 5) and write a phrase on the matching line describing how you are feeling about this topic. Now that you know how you feel, move to Step #3 and write ten steps to overcome this fear. You can find tips below with a "possible scenario" to get you started.

Step #2: Gauging Your Feelings

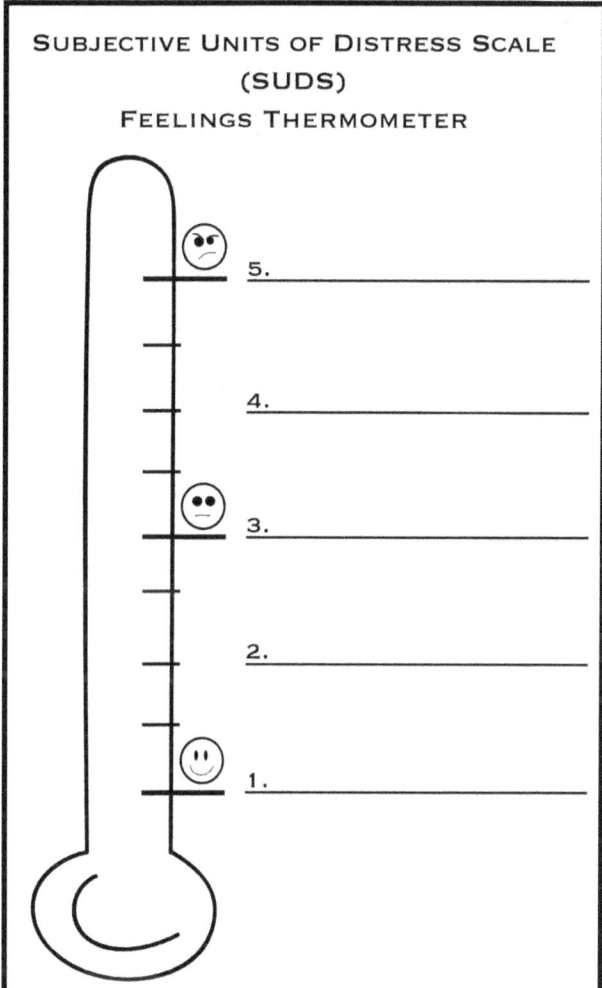

Step #3: Overcoming Obstacles

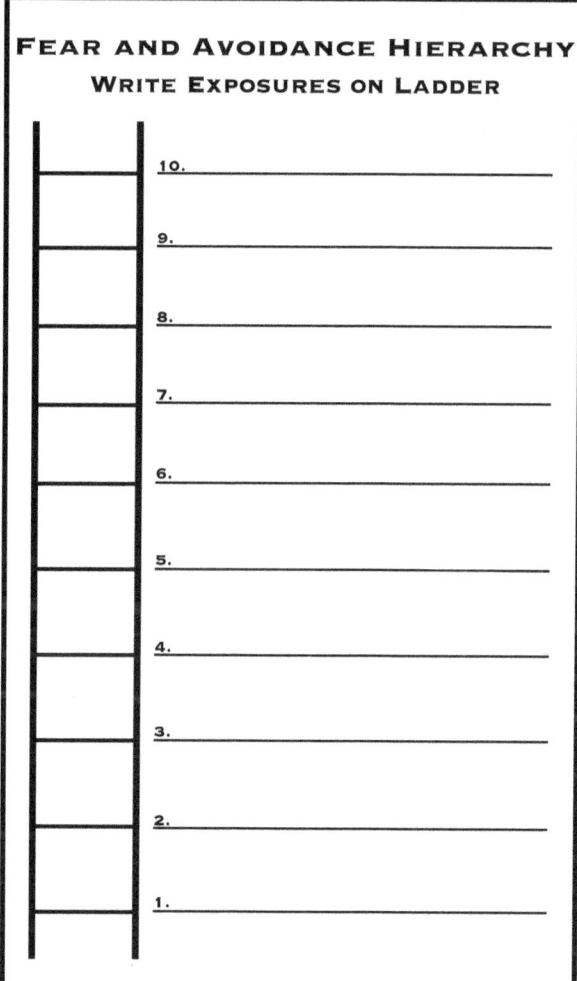

How Do Feel About Your Support System?:
5. Extreme anxiety/I have no mentors in my life.
4. High anxiety/I don't know who to ask to be my mentor.
3. Moderately anxious/I will try to network to find a mentor.
2. Mild anxiety/I will reach out to potential mentors.
1. No anxiety/I have five people I consider mentors to me.

Ideas for Fear of Finding Support System:
10. They said, "Yes!" I'm extremely grateful to find five mentors.
9. Send thank you note after meeting your possible mentor.
8. Approach your possible mentor with confidence to ask them.
7. Prepare and practice for the conversation with possible mentor.
6. Request and schedule a meeting with potential mentor.
5. Create a script in how you will ask someone to be a mentor.
4. Prioritize the list of potential mentors to ask.
3. List a list of potential mentors to ask.
2. Research and reflect on potential mentors to ask.
1. Watch a movie about a coach or mentor in a teen's life.

Communication Skills

If after taking the Reflections Publishing Communication Assessment and you believe that **"Compliments and Praise"** is your " Preferred Method of Communication," then a compliment coming from your mentor or coach will mean a lot to you and also be a big step in forming your identity. As stated in the research article by Phillippo et al. (2017), receiving advice and feedback from a mentor will help you to form your personal self-concept.

If you are struggling how to choose and/or communicate to a potential mentor, here are some tips:

Finding a Mentor

- First, choose an individual who you admire and has the experience, knowledge, and qualities you want to have for yourself some day.
- Build a relationship with your possible mentor and get to know them.
- Be respectful of your mentor's time as you explain to them your goals and aspirations.
- Always express your gratitude toward your mentor with a thank you card or follow-up email.

Mindfulness Skills

Do you get anxiety or feel nervous when you need to talk to someone? If so, just practice this simple mindfulness exercise and it will help to calm your mind and bring focus to the present moment.

"Let's Talk it Out" Communication Mindfulness Exercise

1. Ground yourself in a quiet space, getting in a comfortable position and closing your eyes.
2. Take slow, deep breaths through your nose, allowing your abdomen to rise as you fill your lungs with air. Slowly exhale through your mouth like you are breathing through a straw. Do this six times, letting go of any tension or anxiety that you feel in your body.
3. Let your mind relax, noticing any body sensations (i.e., the weight of your body on the floor).
4. Zero in on areas of your body holding stress—releasing any areas of tension and tightness.
5. Label your emotion of nervousness and think through why you feel this way.
6. Now, place some space between you and your emotion until you feel a sense of calmness.
7. Set your intention on what you want to say, the goal of your conversation, and the message that you want to convey. Kindly remind yourself that you are a capable and strong communicator.
8. Visualize and break your conversation into small, manageable steps.
9. Trust yourself. Release any expectations on the outcome; let the conversation naturally unfold.

Well-Being Habit Tracker:

1. **Fill out each Well-Being Habit Tracker category below.**
2. **When completed, check the box and note your subjective well-being from 1-10.**

- ☐ **Sleep:** How many hours? _____ **Morning Light Exposure:** ☐ Well-Being Rating: _____
- ☐ **Exercise:** Length/Type? _____ Well-Being Rating: _____
- ☐ **Mindfulness:** Length/Type? _____ Well-Being Rating: _____
- ☐ **Nature:** Time spent/Activity outside? ____ / _____ Well-Being Rating: _____
- ☐ **Hydration:** I drank ☐☐☐☐☐☐☐☐ 8 oz. glasses of water. Well-Being Rating: _____
- ☐ **Nutrition:** Number of healthy meals or calories consumed? _____ Well-Being Rating: _____
- ☐ **Social Fitness:** Time spent/Activity? ____ / _____ Well-Being Rating: _____
- ☐ **Caring:** Act(s) of service? _____ Well-Being Rating: _____
- ☐ **Gratitude:** I am grateful for _____ Well-Being Rating: _____
- ☐ **Happiness:** _____ brought me joy! Well-Being Rating: _____
- ☐ **Laughter:** I laughed about _____
- ☐ **Smile:** I made someone smile by _____
- ☐ **Music:** I sang or listened to this song to motivate me and boost my mood and well-being: _____

© 2024 Reflections Publishing LLC. All rights reserved.

Anxiety-Buster To-Do List:

1 Big Task - Let's Go!
- ☐ _____

2 Medium Tasks - Let's Do This!
- ☐ _____
- ☐ _____

3 Small Tasks - You Got This!
- ☐ _____
- ☐ _____
- ☐ _____

© 2024 Reflections Publishing LLC. All rights reserved.

Section Seven

What's Your Game Plan?

Life Choices

LIFE TOPICS:

- Self and Identity - 70
- Social Media - Setting Boundaries - 76
- Time Management - Life Balance - 82

• Self and Identity •

This topic of Self and Identity follows the concept of "What is Your Legacy? - Core Values" nicely. Arkes & Kajdasz (2011) considers the self as:

> **"A stable essence or core
> that predicts their behavior,
> that who they are matter
> for what they do, and
> that what they do
> reflects who they are."**

Arnett (2018) defines identity as a period of time in an adolescent's life when they tend to self-assess **who they are** (their abilities and characteristics), **what they believe** (their belief system and core values), **how they get along** with others (their personal relations), and **where/how do they fit** (into the world around them).

When people try to define themselves, they typically want to describe themselves with stable and consistent traits in mind. Individuals typically use adjectives and action verbs to describe themselves (English & Chen). Utilizing a Self-Evaluation Maintenance (SEM) Model of Social Behavior formulation by Tesser (1988), a positive sense of self-esteem can emerge when "both stability and changeability" are part of the equation. **This SEM Model is comprised of two dynamic processes:**

- **The reflection process**
- **The comparison process**

These two processes interact during self-evaluation in opposite ways, but both have the interactive quality of their predictions.

Additionally, as a teenager, according to Michael A. Hogg, part of your self and identity is associated to the social group at school you associate with because your peer group strongly influences:

- **How you view yourself and who you are as a person**
- **Your attitude and values**
- **Actions you take and how you assimilate into the world around you**

Throughout your life, you will grow and evolve as you mature, but just remember to always think for yourself and not let your social identity with a group affect your behavior, decisions, and forming any unwanted biases and discrimination against others.

Thinking with a growth mindset, read the questions below and ask yourself how you view yourself today and how would you like to change going forward?

1. **Compassion Towards Yourself and Others:**
   _____
   _____
   _____
   _____

2. **Hobbies (i.e., Athleticism, Musically-Talented):**
   _____
   _____
   _____
   _____

3. **Intelligence:**
   _____
   _____
   _____
   _____

4. **Personality:**
   _____
   _____
   _____
   _____

5. **Make Your Own Category** _____ **:**
   _____
   _____
   _____
   _____

SELF AND IDENTITY

If any information in this playbook is upsetting, please talk to a parent/guardian, school counselor, teacher, or medical professional.
This book is sold with the understanding that the publisher and the author are not engaged in rendering medical, legal, or other professional advice or services.
If professional assistance is required, the services of a competent professional should be sought.

• Self and Identity •

Brain Power

In a research report by McAdams & Krawczyk (2014) studying the different components of identity, different neuroimaging tasks showed participants conducting tasks related to social activities and physical appearance—through the use of descriptive phrases. Both tasks consisted of reading and responding to statements with three different perspectives: Self, Friend, and Reflection. Significant differences were found in fMRI activation channels relating to self-knowledge ('I am', 'I look') and perspective-taking ('I believe', 'Friend believes') statements in the **Precuneus**, along with two areas of the **Dorsal Anterior Cingulate**, and the left **Medial** (middle) **Frontal Gyrus**.

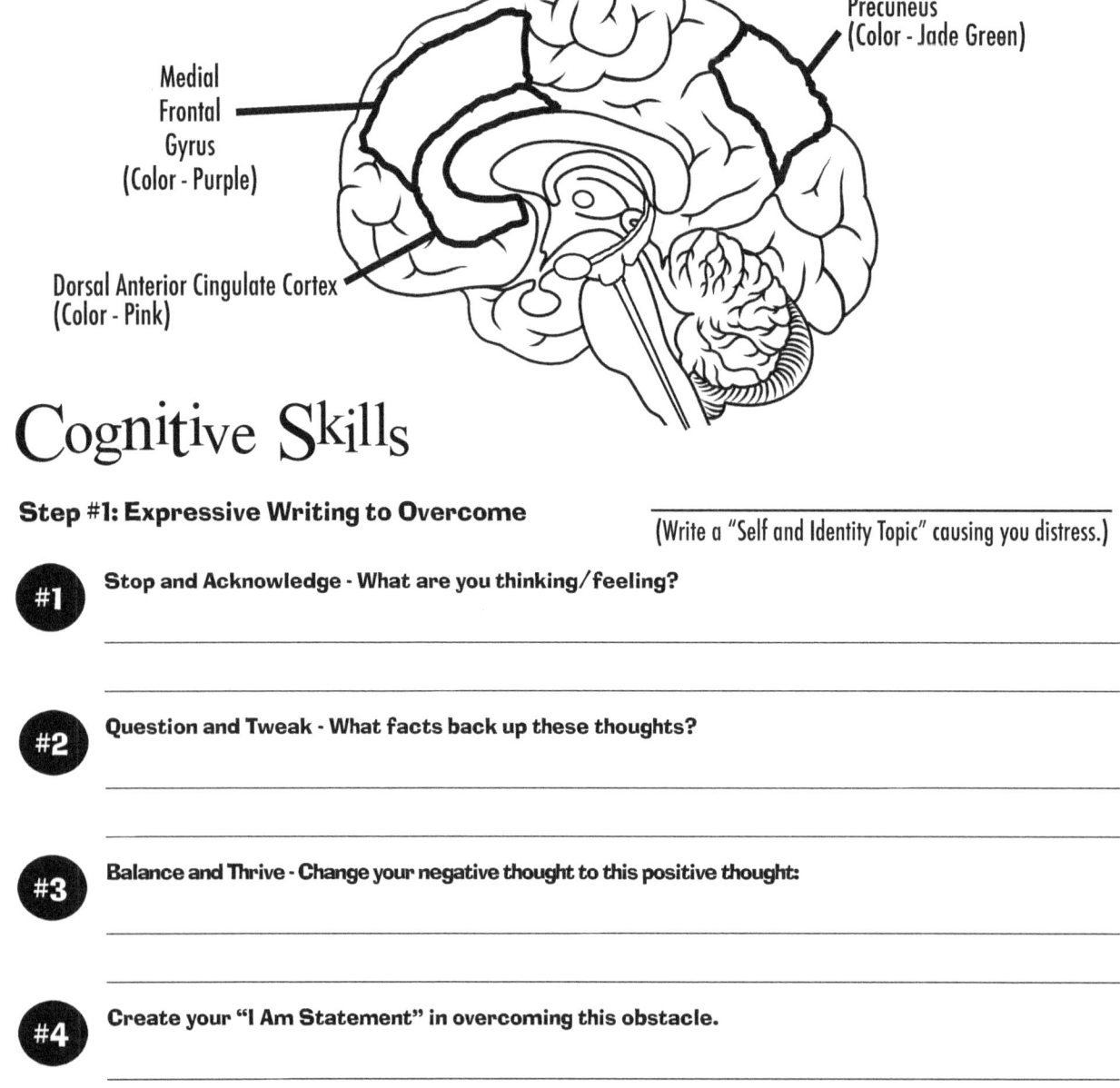

Cognitive Skills

Step #1: Expressive Writing to Overcome

(Write a "Self and Identity Topic" causing you distress.)
_____

#1 Stop and Acknowledge - What are you thinking/feeling?
_____
_____

#2 Question and Tweak - What facts back up these thoughts?
_____
_____

#3 Balance and Thrive - Change your negative thought to this positive thought:
_____
_____

#4 Create your "I Am Statement" in overcoming this obstacle.
_____

Cognitive Skills

_____ (Write a "Self and Identity Topic" causing you distress.)

INSTRUCTIONS for Steps #2 and #3:
On the line above, write a "Self and Identity Topic" causing you stress. Next, On the "Feelings Thermometer," color up to the point of your distress (from 1 to 5) and write a phrase on the matching line describing how you are feeling about this topic. Now that you know how you feel, move to Step #3 and write ten steps to overcome this fear. You can find tips below with a "possible scenario" to get you started.

Step #2: Gauging Your Feelings   Step #3: Overcoming Obstacles

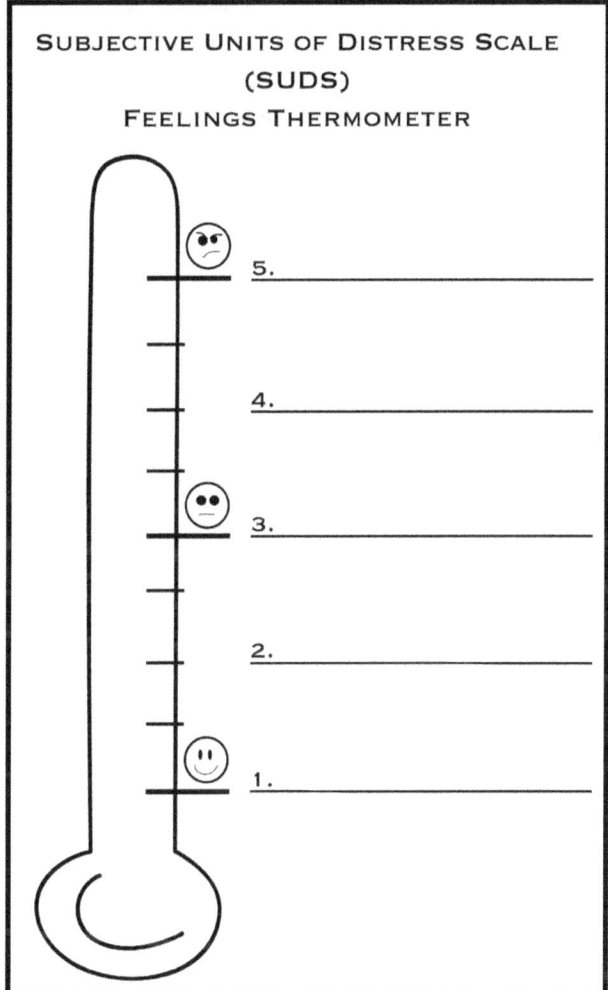

How Do Feel About Your Sense of Self?:
5. Extreme anxiety/Who am I?
4. High anxiety/I feel like have a good sense of self.
3. Moderately anxious/What is my identity?
2. Mild anxiety/I know who I am; my life is on track.
1. No anxiety/I feel confident and know who I am.

Thoughts on Identifying Your Sense of Self:
10. I will teach a class on Self and Identity.
9. I will take a class and gain a better sense of myself.
8. I will discuss with a friend about personal self and identity.
7. I will read books about on the topic Self and Identity.
6. I will practice "I am" statements to increase my confidence.
5. I will meet with a counselor to help with my self and identity.
4. I will journal about movies I've watched on self and identity.
3. I will watch online funny videos about identity crisis.
2. I will watch a movie about soul searching.
1. I will listen to an upbeat song about self-contentment.

Communication Skills

Your middle and high school years are formative years of self-discovery when you start searching for your identity. This process can be difficult for adults and teens as you start separating your identity from your family unit—likely beginning to push back against your parent/guardian with challenging questions and behaviors. Just remember that the adults in your life really want to be there for you and help you process and navigate this exciting time as you search and create your own identity. If **"Feeling Respected"** is one of your "Preferred methods of communication," then this is the time to show it and prove you are worthy of your parents/guardian trusting you as you test the boundaries. Remember, respect goes both ways, and it is something that is earned.

- Now is the time you will begin learning negotiation skills as you have conversations about wanting to change your curfew, start dating, and possibly change how you dress.
- You might take small risks—testing the limits as you process possibly changing your self-image.
- Make sure to keep the communication lines open with your parent/guardian with clear, straightforward, and honest communication. Here are some respectful conversation starters:
    1. **Pick the right moment and start the conversation with gratitude and appreciation:**
       Thank you for trusting me and letting me go out on the weekends with my friends.
    2. **Stay calm and respectful, highlight ways you are responsible, and give a reasonable proposal:**
       Since I always get home on time, I would like to propose a trial period to extend my curfew to 11 p.m. I will always text you where I am and if my plans change. It is hard to go to the movies with my friends with a 10 p.m. curfew and I feel rushed to get home on time.

Mindfulness Skills

How you perceive yourself will typically directs your thoughts and guide your decisions to help you to determine how you choose to shape and mold your personal identity.

"Who Am I" Self and Identity Mindfulness Exercise

1. Get in a comfortable position and close your eyes. Spend five minutes letting your mind wander—asking yourself the following questions:
    - What unique qualities do you have and that you are proud of?
    - What qualities do others tell you that you have?
    - What inspires you and makes you feel alive?
    - Do you believe you are living out your life purpose?
    - Who do you admire and consider a role model. What traits do they have that you like?
2. Take notice of how your body feels and any sensations you experience such as lightness or tightness in your body.

Well-Being Habit Tracker:

1. **Fill out each Well-Being Habit Tracker category below.**
2. **When completed, check the box and note your subjective well-being from 1-10.**

☐ **Sleep:** How many hours? _____ **Morning Light Exposure:** ☐   Well-Being Rating: ____

☐ **Exercise:** Length/Type? _____   Well-Being Rating: ____

☐ **Mindfulness:** Length/Type? _____   Well-Being Rating: ____

☐ **Nature:** Time spent/Activity outside? ____ / _____   Well-Being Rating: ____

☐ **Hydration:** I drank 🥛🥛🥛🥛🥛🥛🥛🥛 8 oz. glasses of water.   Well-Being Rating: ____

☐ **Nutrition:** Number of healthy meals or calories consumed? ____   Well-Being Rating: ____

☐ **Social Fitness:** Time spent/Activity? ____ / _____   Well-Being Rating: ____

☐ **Caring:** Act(s) of service? _____   Well-Being Rating: ____

☐ **Gratitude:** I am grateful for _____   Well-Being Rating: ____

☐ **Happiness:** _____ brought me joy!   Well-Being Rating: ____

☐ **Laughter:** I laughed about _____

☐ **Smile:** I made someone smile by _____

☐ **Music:** I sang or listened to this song to motivate me and boost my mood and well-being:
_____

© 2024 Reflections Publishing LLC. All rights reserved.

Anxiety-Buster To-Do List:

1 Big Task - Let's Go!

☐ _____

2 Medium Tasks - Let's Do This!

☐ _____

☐ _____

3 Small Tasks - You Got This!

☐ _____

☐ _____

☐ _____

© 2024 Reflections Publishing LLC. All rights reserved.

• Social Media - Setting Boundaries •

According to the Child Mind Institute, tweens, teenagers, and young adults use social media the most. The concern about too much screen time for your age group is that while your brain is forming, social media can negatively impact your self-esteem and trigger self-harm ideation. The research conducted by the Child Mind Institute continues that too much screen time is also associated with not getting enough sleep, developing anxiety, and also linked to the onset of mental health symptoms.

The Child Mind Institute also reports that tweens, teenagers, and young adults who are constantly using social media increase their chances of developing depression from between 13 to 66 percent. Twenge et al. (2018) agree with this study, stating that since 2010, screen time and mental health issues have continued trending upward—claiming adolescent depression and self-harm are highly linked. With data collected between 2010-2015, eighth- through twelfth-grade students, Twenge et al. (2018) reported a 33 percent increase in depressive symptoms, while the suicide rate among females also increased.

Social media can also be a huge source of distraction and procrastination, keeping you from your homework and harming your academic performance. Also, remember that social media can portray a distorted sense of reality, making you feel unnecessarily insecure. Since people can use apps to make their pictures perfect, most of what you see on social media is not real. Be aware that social media can make you feel inferior, jealous, and envious of others when you compare yourself to a fake or photoshopped image.

Social media can also interfere with your sleep schedule, as the blue light emitted from your computer and cell phone disrupts melatonin production (the hormone that helps you fall asleep). When you do not get enough sleep on a nightly basis, you will be very tired, which leads to poor concentration at school.

Here are some ways you can use social media in a healthy manner:

1. Set a timer to limit the amount of time you spend on social media.

2. Make sure to follow accounts that only leave you feeling good about yourself.

3. When making comments on a person's post, only write positive things—only writing something that you would also say to someone face-to-face.

Social media can be a helpful and powerful tool—keeping us connected and sharing valuable ideas. Just keep in mind that what you see on social media accounts are often a distorted version of reality and edited to a point of unrealistic expectations. Use the space below to brainstorm in groups and then as a class on ways to improve your social media presence.

1. **List ways that social media is helpful:**
    a. _____
    b. _____
    c. _____

2. **List some ways that social media is harmful to your self-esteem:**
    a. _____
    b. _____
    c. _____

3. **What to keep in mind when scrolling through social media accounts:**
    a. _____
    b. _____
    c. _____

4. **Doodle and Draw:**

If any information in this playbook is upsetting, please talk to a parent/guardian, school counselor, teacher, or medical professional.
This book is sold with the understanding that the publisher and the author are not engaged in rendering medical, legal, or other professional advice or services.
If professional assistance is required, the services of a competent professional should be sought.

SOCIAL MEDIA - SETTING BOUNDARIES

• Social Media - Setting Boundaries •

Brain Power

A research study analyzing social feedback processing in adolescents highlighted increased brain activity in the **Dorsal Medial Prefrontal Cortex**, **Anterior Cingulate Cortex**, and Bilateral **Insula** areas. The report emphasized that neuroimaging captured how females in their late adolescent years change their behavior based on feedback from their peers. The findings indicated a significant association between media-by-peer interactions and a female's future interpretation of an ideal female body.

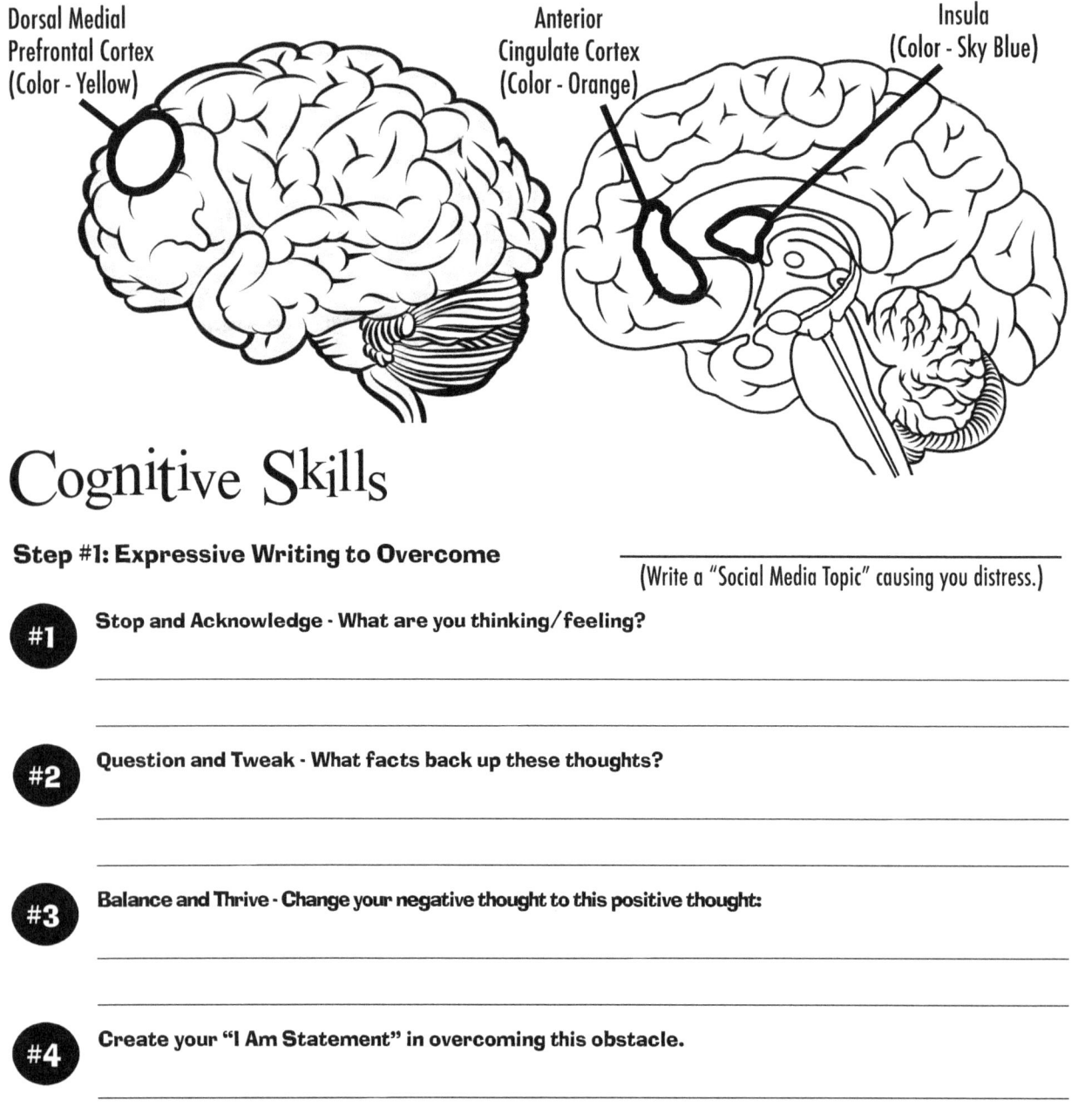

Dorsal Medial Prefrontal Cortex (Color - Yellow)

Anterior Cingulate Cortex (Color - Orange)

Insula (Color - Sky Blue)

Cognitive Skills

Step #1: Expressive Writing to Overcome

(Write a "Social Media Topic" causing you distress.)

#1 Stop and Acknowledge - What are you thinking/feeling?

#2 Question and Tweak - What facts back up these thoughts?

#3 Balance and Thrive - Change your negative thought to this positive thought:

#4 Create your "I Am Statement" in overcoming this obstacle.

Cognitive Skills

(Write a "Social Media Topic" causing you distress.)

INSTRUCTIONS for Steps #2 and #3:
On the line above, write the "Social Media Topic" causing you stress. Next, On the "Feelings Thermometer," color up to the point of your distress (from 1 to 5) and write a phrase on the matching line describing how you are feeling about this topic. Now that you know how you feel, move to Step #3 and write ten steps to overcome this fear. You can find tips below with a "possible scenario" to get you started.

Step #2: Gauging Your Feelings

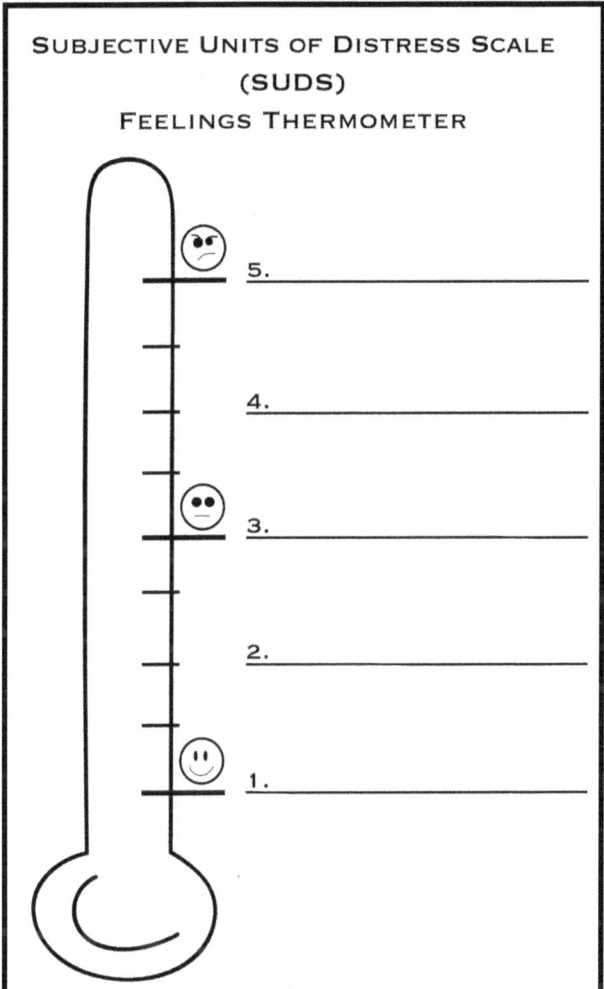

Step #3: Overcoming Obstacles

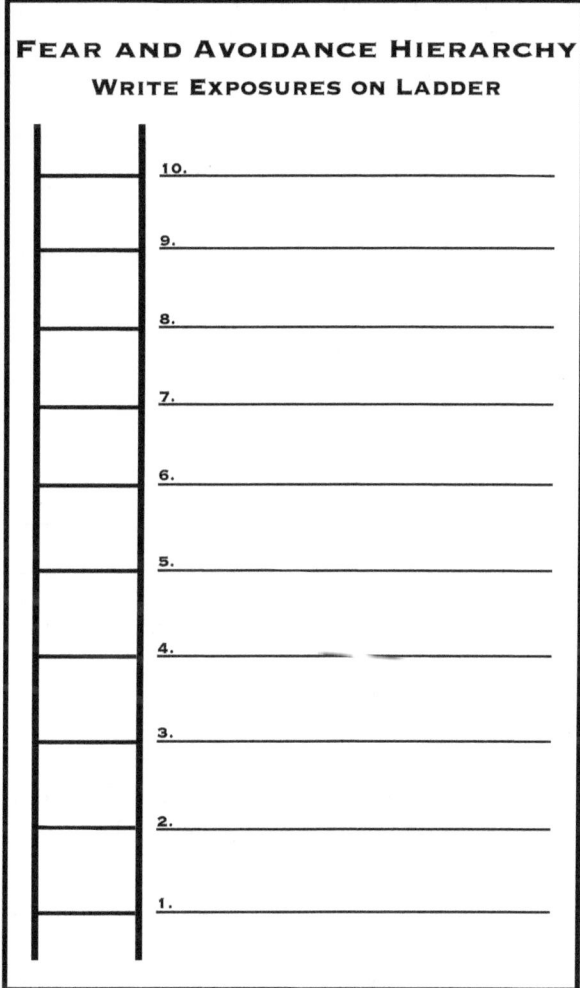

How you May Feel About Social Media:
5. Extreme anxiety/I'm panicking—I have no "likes" on my photo.
4. High anxiety/I feel like everyone is judging me online.
3. Moderately anxious/I feel very self-conscious with my posts.
2. Mild anxiety/I feel I have good social media boundaries.
1. No anxiety/I feel confident in my social media presence.

Ideas on Overcoming Social Media Fears:
10. I am confident in sharing pictures on social media.
9. I longer worry about people judging me.
8. I will not compare myself to others on social media.
7. I will stay away from possible online scams.
6. I will educate myself on cyberbullying.
5. I will stay away from posts that make me feel bad.
4. I will follow positive social media platforms.
3. I will watch online videos about social fears as a teenager.
2. I will watch a movie about middle/high school social fears.
1. I will listen to an upbeat song about overcoming fears.

Communication Skills

I understand how important it is at your age to have a social media presence on sites such as Instagram, TikTok, Snapchat, etc. If you have a social media account, you need to understand that you are creating a digital footprint, and if you think you have deleted something on your account, it actually still exists in "cyberworld." Nothing is ever deleted—even if you "wipe" your phone or computer. Keeping this in mind, the pictures you post, the words you say, and how you present yourself speak volumes about who you are. You will hear adults say how glad they are that social media was not around when they were a kid or they would not have the life or job they have today.

If your "Preferred Method of Communication" is **"Compliments and Praise,"** then just be careful not to let "comments" people make on your post frame your self-worth because online comments are not authentic. Communication is best face-to-face so you can read the person's body language and see their facial expressions. Just remember, if you don't have anything nice to say, don't say it.

Working as a class or in groups, take a few moments to write down a few compliments you can make on a fellow classmate's post:

1. _____.
2. _____.
3. _____.
4. _____.
5. _____.

Mindfulness Skills

Since social media is such a prevalent topic, several mindful meditation tips and tools are recommended below to assist you in keeping your social media stress levels in check.

Social Media Mindfulness Exercise

1. The first thing to remember is that there is nothing wrong with stepping back and taking a break from social media—especially if it makes you feel bad about yourself.
2. Notice how your body feels and any sensations you experience, such as lightness or tightness, when scrolling through social media apps and accounts.
3. Pay attention to how social media affects your mood and overall well-being.
4. You can practice gratitude while scrolling through social media by making positive comments to friends on their posts and practice being happy for others.
5. Take several deep breaths and spend 4-5 minutes reflecting on comments made on your social media posts and how those remarks make you feel. Now, think about possible compliments you could post to someone else on their social media account.

Well-Being Habit Tracker:

1. **Fill out each Well-Being Habit Tracker category below.**
2. **When completed, check the box and note your subjective well-being from 1-10.**

- ☐ **Sleep:** How many hours? _____ **Morning Light Exposure:** ☐   Well-Being Rating: _____
- ☐ **Exercise:** Length/Type? _____   Well-Being Rating: _____
- ☐ **Mindfulness:** Length/Type? _____   Well-Being Rating: _____
- ☐ **Nature:** Time spent/Activity outside? ____ / _____   Well-Being Rating: _____
- ☐ **Hydration:** I drank 🥛🥛🥛🥛🥛🥛 8 oz. glasses of water.   Well-Being Rating: _____
- ☐ **Nutrition:** Number of healthy meals or calories consumed? _____   Well-Being Rating: _____
- ☐ **Social Fitness:** Time spent/Activity? ____ / _____   Well-Being Rating: _____
- ☐ **Caring:** Act(s) of service? _____   Well-Being Rating: _____
- ☐ **Gratitude:** I am grateful for _____   Well-Being Rating: _____
- ☐ **Happiness:** _____ brought me joy!   Well-Being Rating: _____
- ☐ **Laughter:** I laughed about _____
- ☐ **Smile:** I made someone smile by _____
- ☐ **Music:** I sang or listened to this song to motivate me and boost my mood and well-being:
  _____

© 2024 Reflections Publishing LLC. All rights reserved.

Anxiety-Buster To-Do List:

1 Big Task - Let's Go!
- ☐ _____

2 Medium Tasks - Let's Do This!
- ☐ _____
- ☐ _____

3 Small Tasks - You Got This!
- ☐ _____
- ☐ _____
- ☐ _____

© 2024 Reflections Publishing LLC. All rights reserved.

• Time Management - Life Balance •

Life is all about balance and choices regarding how you should spend your time. When you create a schedule and get your work done either early or on time, you will be less stressed. There are several ways for you to have a balance in life, including having strong time management skills. Remember, to learn and gain strong time management skills, it takes a lot of time and practice. Be kind, patient, and committed to reaching your ultimate goals. Celebrate your successes and accomplishments as you progress through your list.

Here are Some Time Management Tips for You to Try:

1. As listed as Playbook Strategy #6: Anxiety Buster To-Do List, **prioritizing tasks into smaller steps relieves anxiety**. Once you put a task on your To-Do List, it frees your brain to spend energy thinking about getting that job done.

2. **Minimize distractions** and find a place where you can focus clearly on the task at hand.

3. To stay on track with your goals, this will include learning to decide what you have time to do now and what you need to save for later. There are only so many hours in the day, so you must learn to say "no" to some things. Our bodies break down and get sick if we try to be Superman or Superwoman. Remember, **you are only human, so keep realistic expectations of yourself**.

4. **Avoid multi-tasking**; focus on one thing at a time and do it well. You chase your tail in a circle like a dog when you try to do too many things at once.

- **List your Game Plan to Achieve a Strong Life Balance and Time Management Skills:**

  _____

  _____

  _____

  _____

  _____

  _____

  _____

  _____

  _____

  _____

- **Doodle or Draw to Help Process Balancing Your Time:**

If any information in this playbook is upsetting, please talk to a parent/guardian, school counselor, teacher, or medical professional.

This book is sold with the understanding that the publisher and the author are not engaged in rendering medical, legal, or other professional advice or services. If professional assistance is required, the services of a competent professional should be sought.

• Time Management - Life Balance •

Brain Power

The **Posterior Cingulate Cortex (PCC)** mediates the students' internally-generated thought processes they experience during emotional and social events. The **PCC** also includes self-directed cognitions and future planning, which is helpful with time management skills.

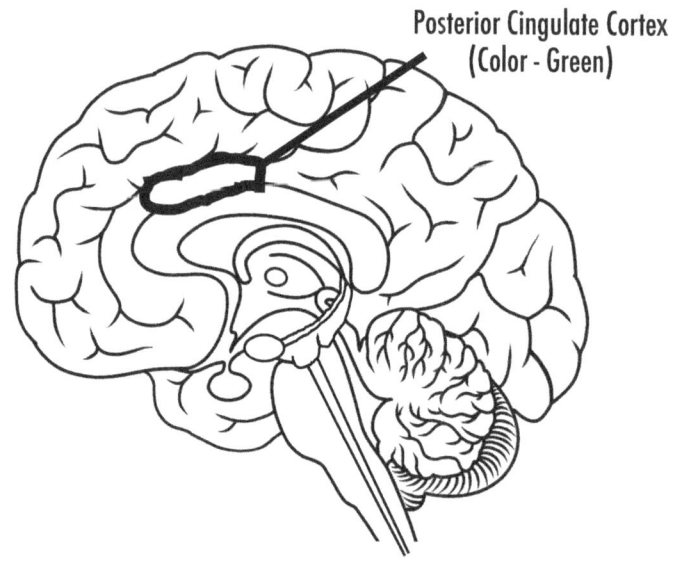

Posterior Cingulate Cortex
(Color - Green)

Cognitive Skills

Step #1: Expressive Writing to Overcome

(Write a "Time Management Topic" causing you distress.)

#1 **Stop and Acknowledge** - What are you thinking/feeling?
_____
_____

#2 **Question and Tweak** - What facts back up these thoughts?
_____
_____

#3 **Balance and Thrive** - Change your negative thought to this positive thought:
_____
_____

#4 Create your "I Am Statement" in overcoming this obstacle.
_____

Cognitive Skills

(Write a "Time Management Topic" causing you distress.)

INSTRUCTIONS for Steps #2 and #3:
On the line above, write the "Time Management Topic" causing you stress. Next, On the "Feelings Thermometer," color up to the point of your distress (from 1 to 5) and write a phrase on the matching line describing how you are feeling about this topic. Now that you know how you feel, move to Step #3 and write ten steps to overcome this fear. You can find tips below with a "possible scenario" to get you started.

Step #2: Gauging Your Feelings   **Step #3: Overcoming Obstacles**

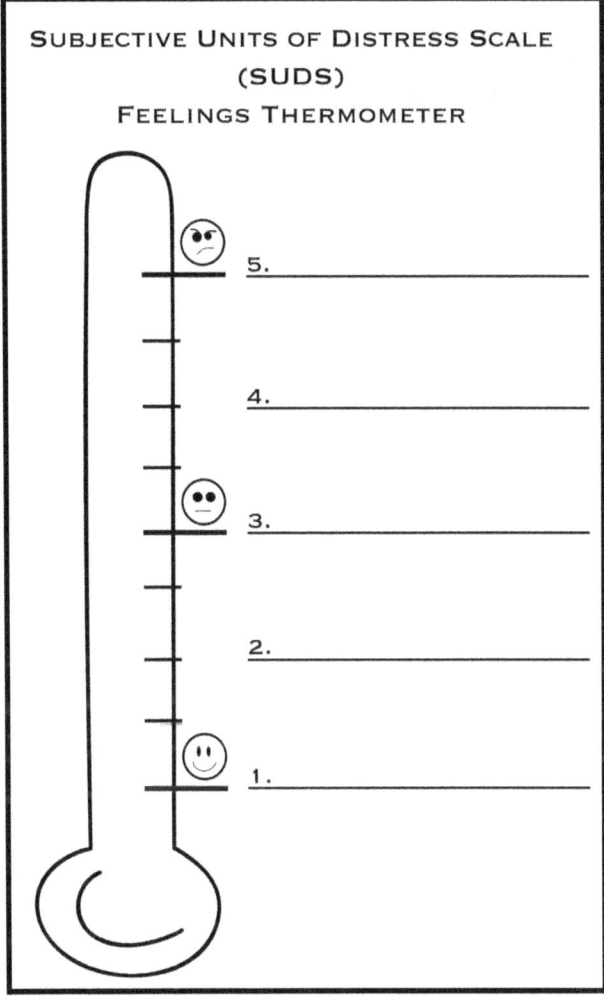

How you May Feel About Time Management:
5. Extreme anxiety/There are not enough hours in the day.
4. High anxiety/I study all the time and I'm still not prepared.
3. Moderately anxious/I don't feel like I studied enough.
2. Mild anxiety/I think I need to reorganize my day.
1. No anxiety/I feel confident in my time management skills.

Overcoming Fears of No Life Balance:
10. I'm confident with achieving my goals in a set amount of time.
9. I will write out my goals to get tasks done on time.
8. I will go outside and journal on ways to balance my life.
7. I will do the breathing exercise to help me focus.
6. I will practice "I am" statements to help balance my life.
5. I will work with a counselor to help with making a schedule.
4. I will join a study group to stay on track with my studies.
3. I will watch online videos about how to balance life.
2. I will watch a movie about balancing everything in life.
1. I will listen to an upbeat song about being overwhelmed.

Communication Skills

Life is full of distractions and difficult decisions on how to best spend your time. Keeping the lines of communication open with your teachers/parent/guardian is important as you process how to balance your life and have good time management skills. If you are having trouble with getting things done on time or feeling overwhelmed, here are some tips on how to ask for help.

If **"Helping Hand"** is your "Preferred Method of Communication," then you, in particular, likely want someone to help you create a game plan to get everything done.

- *I really want to go the band concert on Thursday night, but I am afraid I will not do well on my math test on Friday. What should I do? Can you help me process how to plan this out?*

- *I have an out-of-state soccer tournament this weekend and finals are the following week. I am not guaranteed a sports scholarship, so I need to make sure I am prepared for my tests. I understand there are consequences to my choices and actions. I need help creating a schedule to make sure I am prepared for next week.*

Mindfulness Skills

A mindfulness exercise that is beneficial for time management and to help you find balance in your life is to practice "Single-tasking" versus what most of us do, which is "Multi-tasking." This exercise is good because it helps you focus on one thing at a time—meaning you give this task your full and undivided attention until the job or task is completed. Focusing on just one task will help reduce stress in your life and keep you better engaged and on a schedule to complete the task.

"Single-Tasking" Mindfulness Exercise

1. To begin, choose your one task.
2. Set a timer and commit to working on this task with no disruptions or interruptions.
3. If your mind starts to wander, catch yourself and turn your attention to the task at hand.
4. When the timer goes off, take a break and get some fresh air outside.
5. Take another six deep breaths and think of some subconscious core values you may or may not know you have (i.e., personal bias).
6. Take notice of how those sensations make your body feel—acknowledging any lightness or tightness in your body.

Well-Being Habit Tracker:

1. **Fill out each Well-Being Habit Tracker category below.**
2. **When completed, check the box and note your subjective well-being from 1-10.**

☐ **Sleep:** How many hours? _____ **Morning Light Exposure:** ☐   Well-Being Rating: _____

☐ **Exercise:** Length/Type? _____   Well-Being Rating: _____

☐ **Mindfulness:** Length/Type? _____   Well-Being Rating: _____

☐ **Nature:** Time spent/Activity outside? _____ / _____   Well-Being Rating: _____

☐ **Hydration:** I drank ☐☐☐☐☐☐☐☐ 8 oz. glasses of water.   Well-Being Rating: _____

☐ **Nutrition:** Number of healthy meals or calories consumed? _____   Well-Being Rating: _____

☐ **Social Fitness:** Time spent/Activity? _____ / _____   Well-Being Rating: _____

☐ **Caring:** Act(s) of service? _____   Well-Being Rating: _____

☐ **Gratitude:** I am grateful for _____   Well-Being Rating: _____

☐ **Happiness:** _____ brought me joy!   Well-Being Rating: _____

☐ **Laughter:** I laughed about _____

☐ **Smile:** I made someone smile by _____

☐ **Music:** I sang or listened to this song to motivate me and boost my mood and well-being: _____

© 2024 Reflections Publishing LLC. All rights reserved.

Anxiety-Buster To-Do List:

1 Big Task - Let's Go!

☐ _____

2 Medium Tasks - Let's Do This!

☐ _____

☐ _____

3 Small Tasks - You Got This!

☐ _____

☐ _____

☐ _____

© 2024 Reflections Publishing LLC. All rights reserved.

Section Eight

What's Your Game Plan?

Life Crises

LIFE TOPICS:

- Abuse - Domestic, Physical, and Verbal - 90
- Anxiety - 96
- Depression - 102
- Self-Harm - 108
- Substance Abuse - Alcohol and Drugs - 114

• Abuse - Domestic, Physical, and Verbal •

For starters—It is never okay for you to experience abuse. Whether it is maltreatment, neglect, peer abuse, physical abuse, psychological/mental abuse, or sexual abuse—not even one time is okay. I say this because a dear friend shared with me that if you do not leave the first time a person abuses you, then you likely will never leave. Nontouching ("peeping Tom") and nonverbal (seething glare) are also abuse. The "Communication Skills" section will provide you with some talking points to seek help from a trusted adult.

In 2019, in a Child Maltreatment Report released by the U.S. Department of Health & Human Services, Administration for Children and Families divided almost eight million reported cases of child abuse into the following four categories:

1. **Neglect (74.9%)**
    i. Physical neglect (i.e., lack of basic needs including food, clothing, shelter).
    ii. Emotional neglect (i.e., not providing basic, emotional support and unrealistic expectations of a child's emotional abilities, putting them in danger) (Teicher & Samson, 2016).
2. **Physical abuse (17.5%)**
    i. Any physical action—injuring or putting you in danger (OWH, 2018).
3. **Sexual abuse (9.3%)**
    i. Sexual abuse is defined as any unwelcomed sexual relations where the perpetrator uses force, coercion, and makes threats by an individual they likely know (APA, 2021).
4. **Psychological maltreatment (6.1%)**
    Additionally, according to Zielinski (2009) in an United States childhood maltreatment study with a large sample size of 5,004 participants, this researcher reported the following data:
    • **34.6% of participants experienced child maltreatment**
    a. The breakdown of reported child maltreatment categories in this study were:
        i. Sexual abuse (8%)
        ii. Physical abuse (6.7%)
        iii. Severe neglect (2.9%)
        iv. Various additional maltreatment (13.8%)
    b. With 3.2 % of participants reporting multiple forms of childhood maltreatment

Sensitivity Periods and Risk Factors for Childhood Maltreatment

According to Heim et al. (2013), one reason to take abuse seriously is because if you are exposed to early childhood adversity, they can experience significant neuroplastic changes in the cortex—based on the nature and sensitive developmental timing of the event. The good thing is your brain will attempt to protect itself if you experience an aversive inappropriate event and will not allocate resources to registering the traumatic event—hence, limiting the destructive effect. It is fascinating how your brain will do its best to create adaptive responses to shield you from the abuse or adversity you are experiencing.

You should know that your age plays a significant role when your brain is most vulnerable to the long-term effects of child maltreatment. In a study by Anderson & Teicher (2004) with 596 participants and a mean age of 12.65 years, their brain scans exhibited a reduction in the **Hippocampal** development—highlighting a possible "silent period" between their maltreatment experience and brain alterations. In another research study by Pechtel et al. (2014), they discovered that the adolescent brain, during the time frame of 7- to 14-years-old, is extremely vulnerable to maltreatment and abuse. This was found in fMRI imaging studies as the right **Hippocampal** area had reduced volume.

Sexual abuse cases, reported by Anderson et al. (2008), indicate the **Bilateral Hippocampal** volume showing significant negative altercations when children were exposed to sexual abuse at age 3- to 5-years-old and to a smaller degree in ages 11- to 13-years-old. Furthermore, with sexual abuse, fMRI findings by Heim et al. (2013) show thinning in the **Somatosensory Cortex** layer due to the nature of the abusive touch and negative changes made to the **Visual Cortex** part of the brain region due to facial recognition by the child of their abuser.

Witnessing domestic abuse, per Heim et al. (2013), will show a reduction in gray matter volume in the **Visual Cortex**, as well as in the neural pathways connecting the visual and limbic systems. Smells and odor sensitivity can be epigenetically encoded in the genetic sequence from a feared predator or abuse—affecting the **Olfactory Cortex** (Krusemark et al., 2013; Szyf, 2014).

We cannot pretend abuse does not occur because, according to a community study conducted by Stein et al. (1997), they discovered that 74.2% of females and 81% of males reported exposure to one or more traumatic events in their lifetime.

Early detection for any at-risk child needs to be taken seriously because, for example, if parental verbal abuse starts at the age of three, an fMRI brain scan will likely show elevated gray matter in the **Auditory Cortex** based on studies by Choi et al. (2009) and a study by Tomoda et al. (2011) also showed reduced right **Hippocampal** volume in the abused brain. **The bottom line is that the "act of abuse" a person experiences will leave its mark in a negative way in the brain.**

• •

If you ever experience abuse, draw and/or write out the steps you will take:

If you are experiencing an emergency, please seek immediate assistance from a parent/guardian, school counselor, teacher, or medical professional or call 911.
This book is sold with the understanding that the publisher and the author are not engaged in rendering medical, legal, or other professional advice or services.
If professional assistance is required, the services of a competent professional should be sought.

• Abuse - Domestic, Physical, and Verbal •

Brain Power

Lawson et al. (2017) state that childhood maltreatment can show a reduction in **Hippocampal** volume. Another research study by Heim et al. (2013) reports these changes include cortical thinning in a very specific brain region—mediating the brain's sensory perception and processing areas that are directly correlated to the specific abusive experiences.

- See/Witness abuse → **Visual Cortex**
- Hear abuse → **Auditory Cortex**
- Smells during abuse → **Olfactory Cortex**
- Abusive Touch → **Somatosensory Cortex**

Go to page 21 to color and label the above bolded Cortex regions on this brain image.

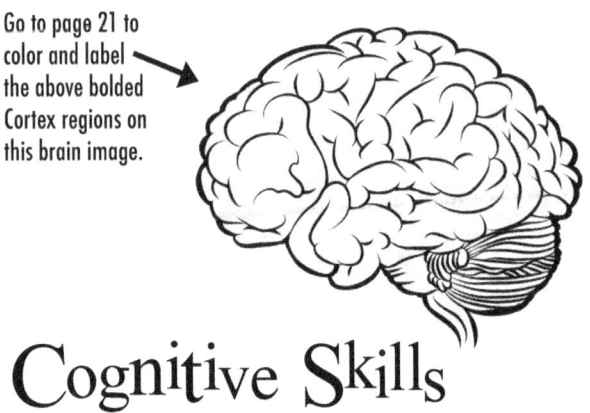

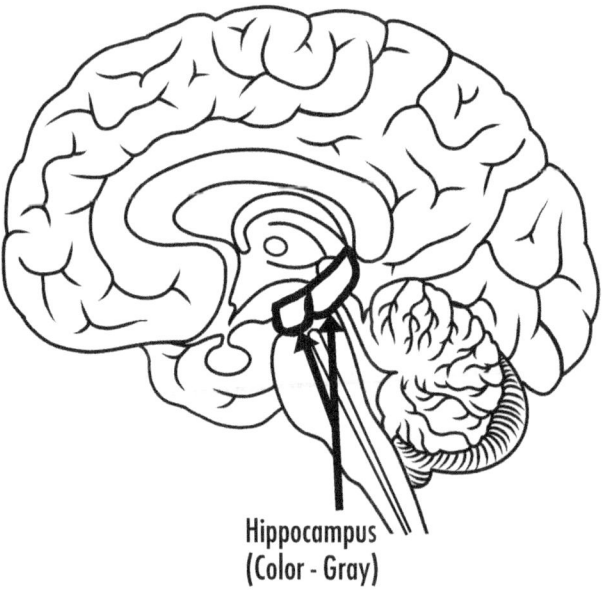

Hippocampus (Color - Gray)

Cognitive Skills

Step #1: Expressive Writing to Overcome

(Write an "Abuse Topic" causing you distress.)

#1 Stop and Acknowledge - What are you thinking/feeling?
_____
_____

#2 Question and Tweak - What facts back up these thoughts?
_____
_____

#3 Balance and Thrive - Change your negative thought to this positive thought:
_____
_____

#4 Create your "I Am Statement" in overcoming this obstacle.
_____

Cognitive Skills

(Write an "Abuse Topic" causing you distress.)

INSTRUCTIONS for Steps #2 and #3:
On the line above, write the "Abuse Topic" causing you stress. Next, On the "Feelings Thermometer," color up to the point of your distress (from 1 to 5) and write a phrase on the matching line describing how you are feeling about this topic. Now that you know how you feel, move to Step #3 and write ten steps to overcome this fear. You can find tips below with a "possible scenario" to get you started.

Step #2: Gauging Your Feelings

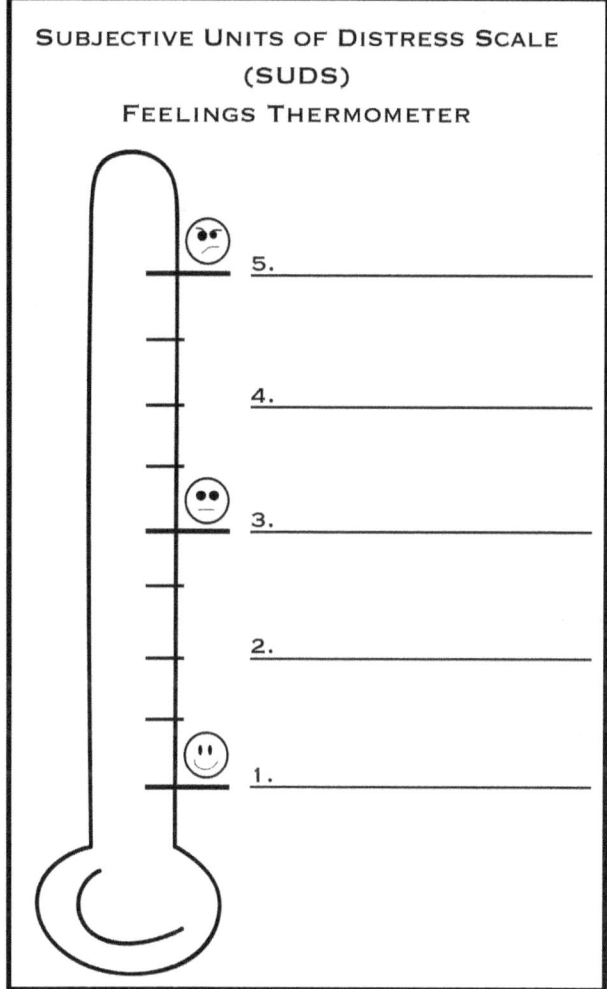

SUBJECTIVE UNITS OF DISTRESS SCALE (SUDS) FEELINGS THERMOMETER

Step #3: Overcoming Obstacles

FEAR AND AVOIDANCE HIERARCHY — WRITE EXPOSURES ON LADDER

How you May Feel About Verbal Abuse:
5. Extreme anxiety/I will burst if someone yells at me.
4. High anxiety/My heart begins racing if someone yells at me.
3. Moderately anxious/I am fearful of someone yelling.
2. Mild anxiety/I know what to say if someone yells at me.
1. No anxiety/I feel confident in my relationships.

Ideas on Overcoming Verbal Abuse:
10. I am confident to stand up for myself against anyone.
9. I will do role-playing to practice standing up for myself.
8. I will journal ideas on what to say if someone yells at me.
7. I will do breathing exercise to help me to relax.
6. I will practice "I am" statements to increase my confidence.
5. I will work with a counselor to help give me tips and tools.
4. I will join a study group and identify what I still need to learn.
3. I will watch online videos about how to stand up for yourself.
2. I will watch a feel good movie about a functional family.
1. I will listen to an upbeat song about healthy relationships.

Communication Skills

As far as abuse is concerned—whether domestic, physical, or verbal, you need to ask for help right away. **Nobody should ever lay a hand on you or abuse you.** There is always a path for you to get out of a bad situation. Many times in abusive relationships, a person will tell you that if you tell on them, they will either hurt someone you love or try to destroy you somehow. Do not let your fear in this situation affect your decision to tell a trusted adult and remove yourself from a bad or potentially dangerous situation. Here are some "I am" statements to help you practice talking to an adult about needing to get out of a bad situation.

Also, if **"Unconditional Love" or "Spending Time Together"** are your "Preferred Methods of Communication," this might be harder for you, but remember that someone who loves you or spends time with you should not be hurting you in any way. That type of attention is not love or quality time.

- I am scared because _____ is doing _____ to me and I need your help.
- I am fearful of what _____ will do to _____ if I report them.
- I am terrified about where I can live if I report _____. I am scared to go home.

Mindfulness Skills

Experiencing abuse can leave a person feeling unsettled as they often feel disassociated with their body. Practicing grounding is one way to shift your focus away from any negative thoughts and emotions and pull yourself to center— becoming present in the moment with all of your surroundings. Below, you will find some grounding techniques that require both your mental and physical attention and energy— allowing your mind a break from all of your swirling, intense thoughts and feelings.

"Getting Grounded" Mindfulness Exercises

1. Sit in a comfortable position and pay attention to the weight of your body on the floor.
2. Do a creative project such as painting or coloring.
3. Go for a walk or hike in nature.
4. Go outside and do yoga on the beach or on the grass barefoot.
5. Call a friend.
6. Organize a "Girl's Night Out" or "Guy's Night Out".
7. Go outside to plant flowers.
8. Sing your favorite song.
9. Cook your favorite meal.

If you are experiencing an emergency, please seek immediate assistance from a parent/guardian, school counselor, teacher, or medical professional or call 911.
This book is sold with the understanding that the publisher and the author are not engaged in rendering medical, legal, or other professional advice or services.
If professional assistance is required, the services of a competent professional should be sought.

Well-Being Habit Tracker:

1. **Fill out each Well-Being Habit Tracker category below.**
2. **When completed, check the box and note your subjective well-being from 1-10.**

- ☐ **Sleep:** How many hours? _____ **Morning Light Exposure:** ☐ Well-Being Rating: _____
- ☐ **Exercise:** Length/Type? _____ Well-Being Rating: _____
- ☐ **Mindfulness:** Length/Type? _____ Well-Being Rating: _____
- ☐ **Nature:** Time spent/Activity outside? ____ / _____ Well-Being Rating: _____
- ☐ **Hydration:** I drank ▯▯▯▯▯▯▯▯ 8 oz. glasses of water. Well-Being Rating: _____
- ☐ **Nutrition:** Number of healthy meals or calories consumed? _____ Well-Being Rating: _____
- ☐ **Social Fitness:** Time spent/Activity? ____ / _____ Well-Being Rating: _____
- ☐ **Caring:** Act(s) of service? _____ Well-Being Rating: _____
- ☐ **Gratitude:** I am grateful for _____ Well-Being Rating: _____
- ☐ **Happiness:** _____ brought me joy! Well-Being Rating: _____
- ☐ **Laughter:** I laughed about _____
- ☐ **Smile:** I made someone smile by _____
- ☐ **Music:** I sang or listened to this song to motivate me and boost my mood and well-being: _____

© 2024 Reflections Publishing LLC. All rights reserved.

Anxiety-Buster To-Do List:

1 Big Task - Let's Go!

☐ _____

2 Medium Tasks - Let's Do This!

☐ _____
☐ _____

3 Small Tasks - You Got This!

☐ _____
☐ _____
☐ _____

© 2024 Reflections Publishing LLC. All rights reserved.

• Anxiety •

Anxiety is like most things in life—some good components and some bad. The good thing about anxiety is that it revs your body up like a car and is beneficial if you are in a dangerous situation because it initiates a fight-or-flight response in your body. This stress response releases cortisol in your brain—allowing your body to jump start quickly and escape the threatening situation.

The bad thing about anxiety is that your body cannot survive in a constant state of stress. I am not saying that your life needs to be perfect and easy every day, but you also cannot stay stressed out either. Puberty is normally the time when anxiety is triggered in adolescents. According to a book by Jensen & Nutt (2015) called *The Teenage Brain*, due to the surge of puberty hormones, teenagers have a much more heightened response to stress than adults. This is why when you get stressed out about midterms or finals, you likely get a headache, an upset stomach, or catch a cold or the flu. Since your brain is actively growing, forming, and wiring itself, literally every day, your brain can either wire itself correctly and effectively or when episodes of extreme stress hit or substance abuse occurs (i.e., drugs and alcohol), the wiring can go wrong—fraying and not connecting properly.

[This is where you say, "That can't be good.]

And I will say, "You're right—this is not good at all."

Now turn to **page 114**, to the section on Substance Abuse: Alcohol and Drugs. Please write the Two Rules you see on that page.

1. _____

2. _____

Quick Tip: If you suffer from anxiety or panic attacks, keep extreme sour or fire hot candy on hand in your backpack. (Ideally, a sugar-free and naturally-colored candy to avoid a spike or drop in your blood sugar or reaction to food coloring.) Research supports that eating extreme sour or fire hot candy can redirect your brain from negative emotions to the sensation in your mouth. For this method to work, be mindful of the candy on your tongue and think to yourself,
 • "What does the candy taste like?"
 • "What does the candy smell like?"
 • "How does the texture of the candy feel on my tongue?"

This technique also aligns with the "Five Senses for Grounding," which includes what you hear, feel, see, taste, and smell. Utilizing these five physical and mental processes shifts your focus from a state of panic or anxiety to a state of mindfulness (Banks & Connell, 2023; Speed & Majid, 2020).

Three more calming techniques are drinking chamomile tea, massaging orange (citrus), lavender, or chamomile essential oils on your skin, and taking a frozen orange from the freezer and noticing the coldness in your hands and the uplifting smell by scratching the orange's skin.

- **Doodle, Draw Your Own Mandala, or Create a Dot•to•Dot:**

    Researchers who study test anxiety among adolescents found that **mandala coloring is linked to an increased state of mindfulness and decreased test anxiety,** so doodle, draw, or make a dot-to-dot to your heart's content (Carsley & Heath, 2019; Cawley & Tejeiro, 2024; Rose & Lomas, 2020).

If you are experiencing an emergency, please seek immediate assistance from a parent/guardian, school counselor, teacher, or medical professional or call 911.
This book is sold with the understanding that the publisher and the author are not engaged in rendering medical, legal, or other professional advice or services.
If professional assistance is required, the services of a competent professional should be sought.

• Anxiety •

Brain Power

Anxiety is a state when the sympathetic nervous system gets stuck. In a research article about adolescents suffering from anxiety, the **Anterior Cingulate Cortex** region of the brain had hypo-activation in anxious adolescents and adults. "The unique U-shaped activation pattern in the **Ventromedial Prefrontal Cortex** in many anxious adolescents may reflect heightened sensitivity to threat and safety conditions."

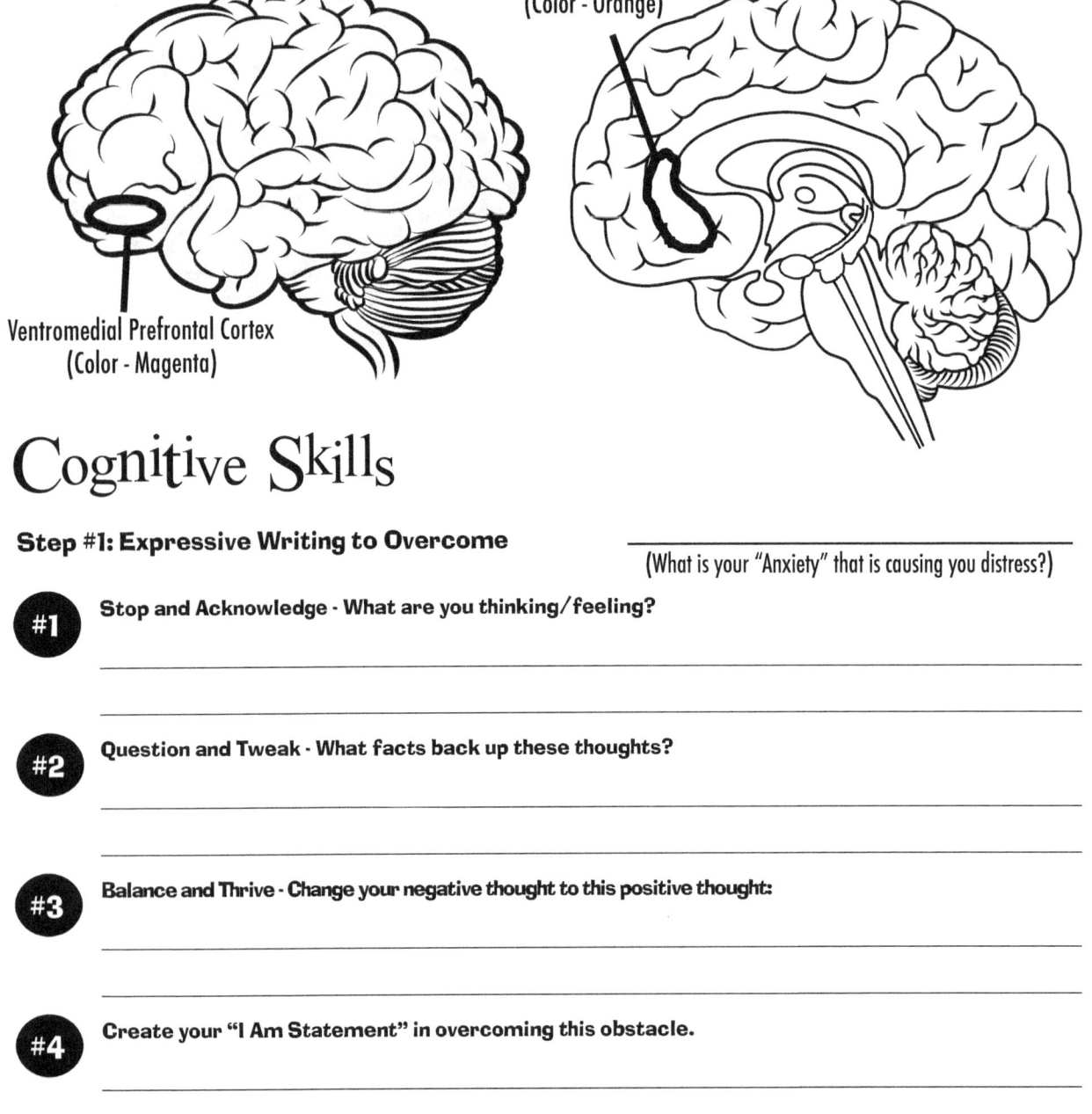

Anterior Cingulate Cortex
(Color - Orange)

Ventromedial Prefrontal Cortex
(Color - Magenta)

Cognitive Skills

Step #1: Expressive Writing to Overcome

_____
(What is your "Anxiety" that is causing you distress?)

#1 **Stop and Acknowledge - What are you thinking/feeling?**
_____
_____

#2 **Question and Tweak - What facts back up these thoughts?**
_____
_____

#3 **Balance and Thrive - Change your negative thought to this positive thought:**
_____
_____

#4 **Create your "I Am Statement" in overcoming this obstacle.**
_____
_____

Cognitive Skills

(What is your "Anxiety" that is causing you distress?)

INSTRUCTIONS for Steps #2 and #3:
On the line above, write what is causing your "Anxiety" and making you stressed. Next, On the "Feelings Thermometer," color up to the point of your distress (from 1 to 5) and write a phrase on the matching line describing how you are feeling about this topic. Now that you know how you feel, move to Step #3 and write ten steps to overcome this fear. You can find tips below with a "possible scenario" to get you started.

Step #2: Gauging Your Feelings

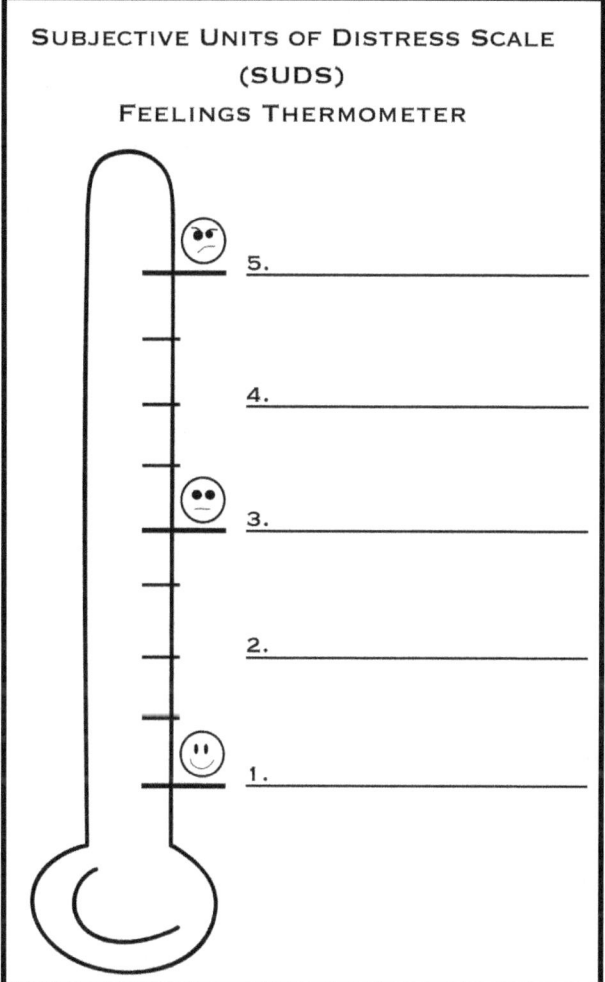

Step #3: Overcoming Obstacles

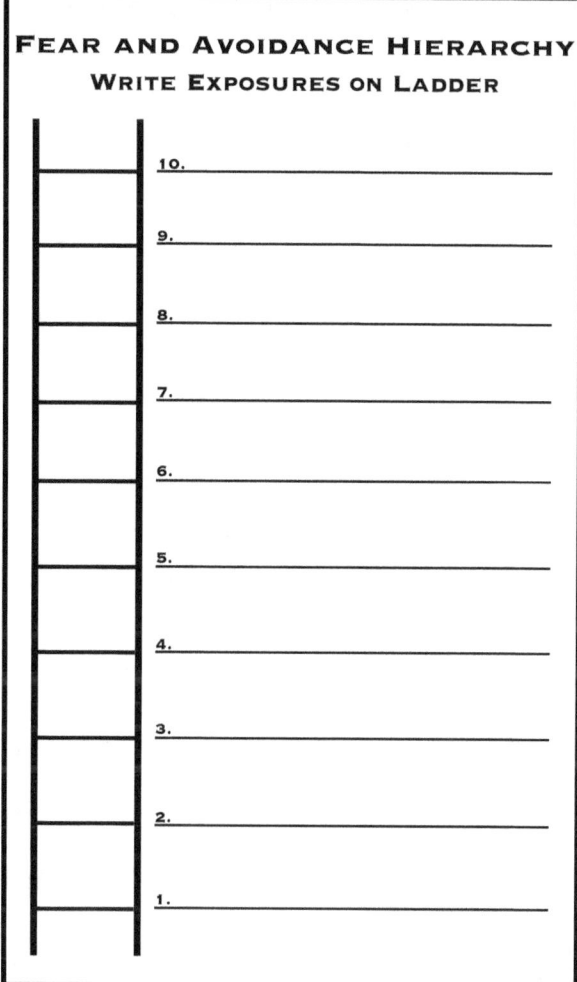

How you May Feel About Social Anxiety:
5. Extreme anxiety/I feel extreme panic in a social situation.
4. High anxiety/I am extremely tense in a social situation.
3. Moderately anxious/I am intensely nervous in a social situation.
2. Mild anxiety/I feel mildly nervous in a social situation.
1. No anxiety/I am completely relaxed in a social situation.

Ideas to Overcome Social Anxiety Fears:
10. I am now confident attending party with no anxiety.
9. I will drive to the party with trusted friends.
8. I will role-play and practice things to say at the party.
7. I will journal ideas on things to say and do at the party.
6. I will go to a counselor to help deal with my social anxiety.
5. I will talk to a trusted friend about my social anxiety.
4. I will take a class on overcoming social anxiety.
3. I will watch online videos on overcoming social anxiety.
2. I will watch a movie about college parties.
1. I will listen to an upbeat song about going to a party.

Communication Skills

If **"Spending Time Together"** is your "Preferred Method of Communication," you, in particular, need to speak up because you likely need someone to spend time with you and help you process your anxious feelings. Learning what you need at a young age to help you process and move through a difficult or anxious situation is key to living a happy life. Here are some tips to get the conversation going with a trusted adult or friend and space to write your own:

- I am nervous about what _____ is doing to me and I need your help.

- I am struggling with _____. Can you help me make this problem more manageable?

- I am feeling anxious about _____ and wondering if you can give me some possible ideas or solutions to help me stop worrying about this situation.

- I am concerned about being able to trust _____ because I do not think their actions toward me are something that I should tolerate. Can you help me get out of this situation?

- _____
  _____.

Mindfulness Skills

Using specific and directed exposure methods can help shut down anxiety. Practice this effective mindfulness exercise for social anxiety called "Noticing and Labeling." With practice, this exercise will help you to remain calm and confident in social situations.

"Noticing and Labeling Feelings" Mindfulness Exercise

1. Get in a comfortable position and close your eyes. Let your mind wander to thinking about what is causing your anxiety.
2. Take six deep breaths—inhaling through your nose and exhaling through your mouth.
3. Bring your attention to the present moment and focus on your breathing.
4. Notice any physical sensation you are feeling—acknowledging any lightness or tightness in your body, such as heart racing or shallow breathing.
5. Acknowledge these sensations without judgment and redirect your thoughts back to center.
6. If your mind wanders, then redirect your thoughts back to your breathing.

Well-Being Habit Tracker:

1. **Fill out each Well-Being Habit Tracker category below.**
2. **When completed, check the box and note your subjective well-being from 1-10.**

- ☐ **Sleep:** How many hours? _____ **Morning Light Exposure:** ☐   Well-Being Rating: _____
- ☐ **Exercise:** Length/Type? _____   Well-Being Rating: _____
- ☐ **Mindfulness:** Length/Type? _____   Well-Being Rating: _____
- ☐ **Nature:** Time spent/Activity outside? ____ / _____   Well-Being Rating: _____
- ☐ **Hydration:** I drank 🥛🥛🥛🥛🥛🥛 8 oz. glasses of water.   Well-Being Rating: _____
- ☐ **Nutrition:** Number of healthy meals or calories consumed? _____   Well-Being Rating: _____
- ☐ **Social Fitness:** Time spent/Activity? ____ / _____   Well-Being Rating: _____
- ☐ **Caring:** Act(s) of service? _____   Well-Being Rating: _____
- ☐ **Gratitude:** I am grateful for _____   Well-Being Rating: _____
- ☐ **Happiness:** _____ brought me joy!   Well-Being Rating: _____
- ☐ **Laughter:** I laughed about _____
- ☐ **Smile:** I made someone smile by _____
- ☐ **Music:** I sang or listened to this song to motivate me and boost my mood and well-being:
  _____

© 2024 Reflections Publishing LLC. All rights reserved.

Anxiety-Buster To-Do List:

1 Big Task - Let's Go!

☐ _____

2 Medium Tasks - Let's Do This!

☐ _____

☐ _____

3 Small Tasks - You Got This!

☐ _____

☐ _____

☐ _____

© 2024 Reflections Publishing LLC. All rights reserved.

• Depression •

Many times, anxiety and depression are co-morbid (i.e., two or more) symptoms. During puberty, this is the time when you might notice feeling anxious and/or depressed for the first time. Your body changes a lot during puberty, so be kind to yourself during this time.

Depression is a state of mind that affects many people at some point. For instance, when a loved one passes away, it is natural to feel depressed for approximately one year after this happens. However, if the depression continues over one year, then it is something you need to address because the sooner you start working to overcome your depressive symptoms, the better. This happens because your brain is "plastic" and "livewired." The sooner you learn tips and tools to navigate your depression, the better your chance of a possible full recovery. Remember, the brain and body will always try to heal, so your fate has not been sealed, and you do not have to remain stuck feeling the way you do..

Below, you will find some interesting research studies. As you read the following four paragraphs, **use a highlighter to mark the intervention results and areas of the brain affected. You can refer back to page 21 to the provided detailed map of the human brain anatomy.**

With the onset of adolescent depression linked to a hormonal mechanism (Patton et al., 1996), adolescence is a critical time when stressors can have a negative affect during this sensitive brain development period (Pechel et al., 2014). Functional MRI (fMRI) imaging studies show improvement in depression symptoms in at-risk youth when intervention treatments are implemented at young ages (Teicher & Samson, 2016; Tymofiyeva et al., 2020).

Approximately 33 percent of diagnosed adults with major depressive disorder know their depression originated during their adolescent years (Goodyer et al., 2011). This is why it is so important to diagnose at-risk adolescents between 11- to 17-years-old when brain maturation is at a significant developmental stage (Chattopadhyay et al., 2017). This has proven to be true in several research studies, including this study of 11- to 17-year-olds by Chattopadhyay et al. (2017) with 116 cross-sectional participants. At-risk designations were able to create potential intervention treatments. Once intervention treatments were initiated, depression symptoms decreased.

In a resting state fMRI study by Straub et al. (2017), 38 participants, ages 13- to 18-years-old, with healthy controls and adolescents with depression, received brain scans before receiving group Cognitive Skills Training sessions. When depressed adolescents are compared before (pre-Cognitive Skills Training) to after (post-Cognitive Skills Training), the brain scans show that functional connectivity significantly increased between the Amygdala and the left Dorsolateral Prefrontal Cortex, Bilateral Dorsal Anterior Cingulate Cortex, and the left Anterior Insula. This proves that doing the Cognitive Skills Training in *The Resilience Game Plan* will significantly improve symptoms in teenagers with depressive symptoms, so let's get to work!

Ways to Cope with Depression:

If you are struggling with depression, seek professional help and talk to a trusted adult such as a parent, teacher, counselor, coach, or healthcare provider. They can offer support, guidance, and resources to help you cope with your symptoms so you can start feeling better. Also, go to the *Appendix* and read the **Depression Game Plan on page 152**.

1. Connect with others, as depression can feel very isolating (i.e., spend time with family and friends; join a sports team or school club; or find a volunteer club in your community.) List your ideas below:
   a. _____
   b. _____

2. Practice Self-Care. List some things that will help you relax and find joy in life.
   a. _____
   b. _____

3. Challenge and replace negative thoughts with positive and self-compassionate ideas.

Doodle or Draw how you are feeling:

If you are experiencing an emergency, please seek immediate assistance from a parent/guardian, school counselor, teacher, or medical professional or call 911.
This book is sold with the understanding that the publisher and the author are not engaged in rendering medical, legal, or other professional advice or services.
If professional assistance is required, the services of a competent professional should be sought.

• Depression •

Brain Power

In a 1,100-participant study of patients diagnosed with depression, fMRI scans were taken, and researchers noted similarities in the brain and categorized their depressive symptoms into four biotypes: the **Insula**, **Orbitofrontal Cortex**, **Ventromedial Prefrontal Cortex**, and multiple subcortical areas (i.e., **Corpus Callosum**, **Hippocampus**, **Amygdala**, **Thalamus**, and **Putamen**).

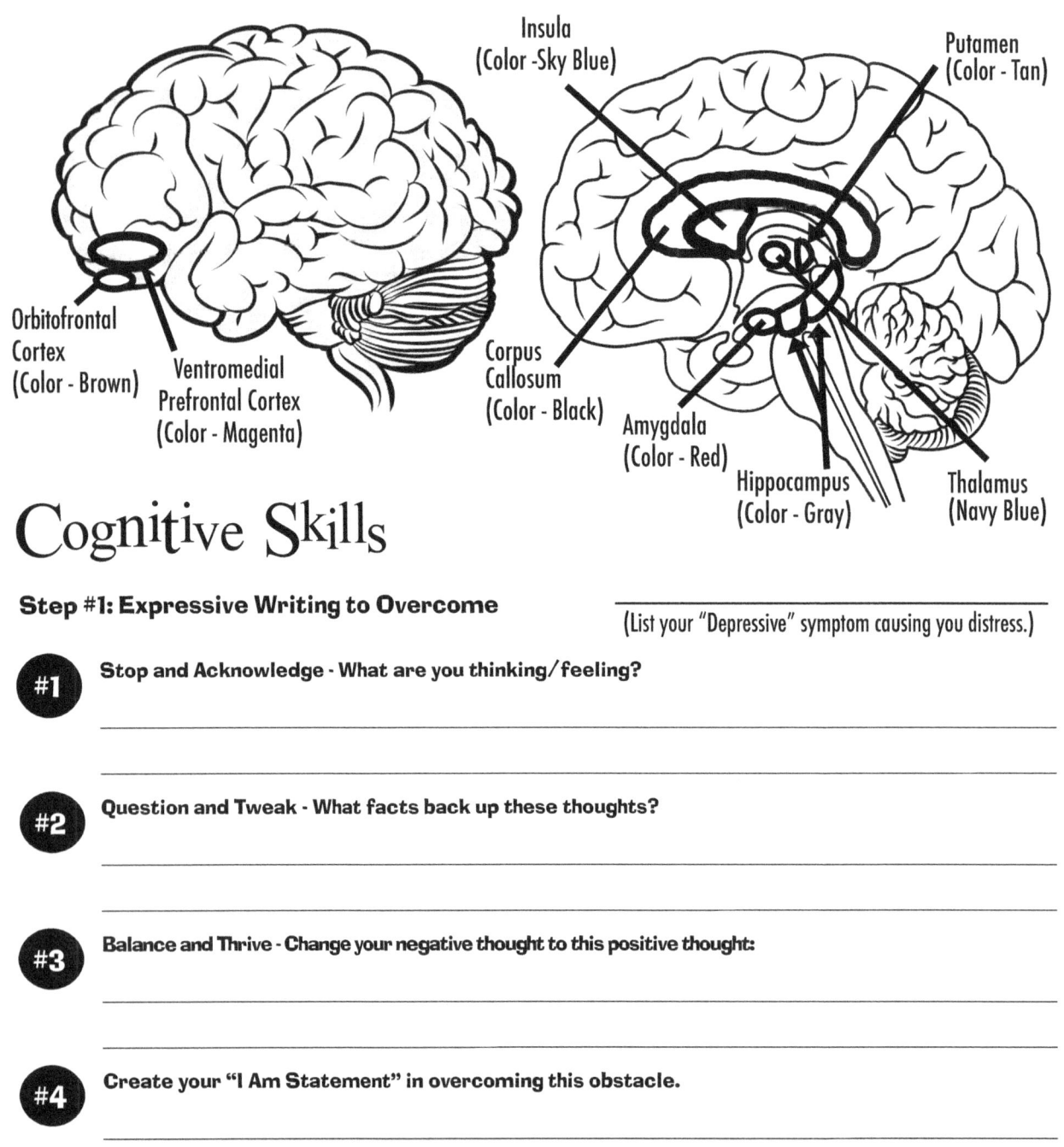

Cognitive Skills

Step #1: Expressive Writing to Overcome

_____
(List your "Depressive" symptom causing you distress.)

#1 Stop and Acknowledge - What are you thinking/feeling?
_____
_____

#2 Question and Tweak - What facts back up these thoughts?
_____
_____

#3 Balance and Thrive - Change your negative thought to this positive thought:
_____
_____

#4 Create your "I Am Statement" in overcoming this obstacle.
_____

Cognitive Skills

(List your "Depressive" symptom causing you distress.)

INSTRUCTIONS for Steps #2 and #3:
On the line above, write a "Depressive" symptom causing you stress. Next, On the "Feelings Thermometer," color up to the point of your distress (from 1 to 5) and write a phrase on the matching line describing how you are feeling about this topic. Now that you know how you feel, move to Step #3 and write ten steps to overcome this fear. You can find tips below with a "possible scenario" to get you started.

Step #2: Gauging Your Feelings

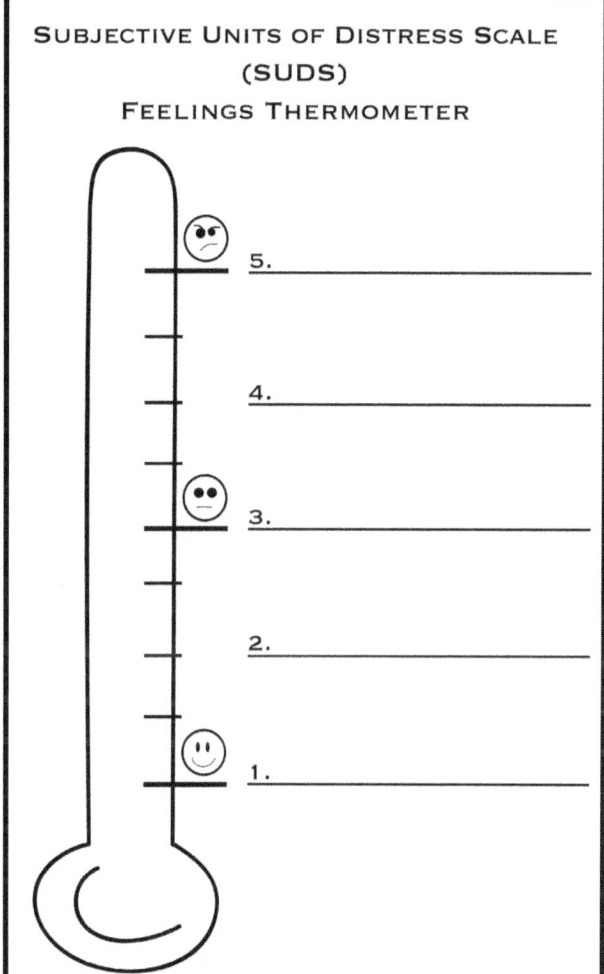

Step #3: Overcoming Obstacles

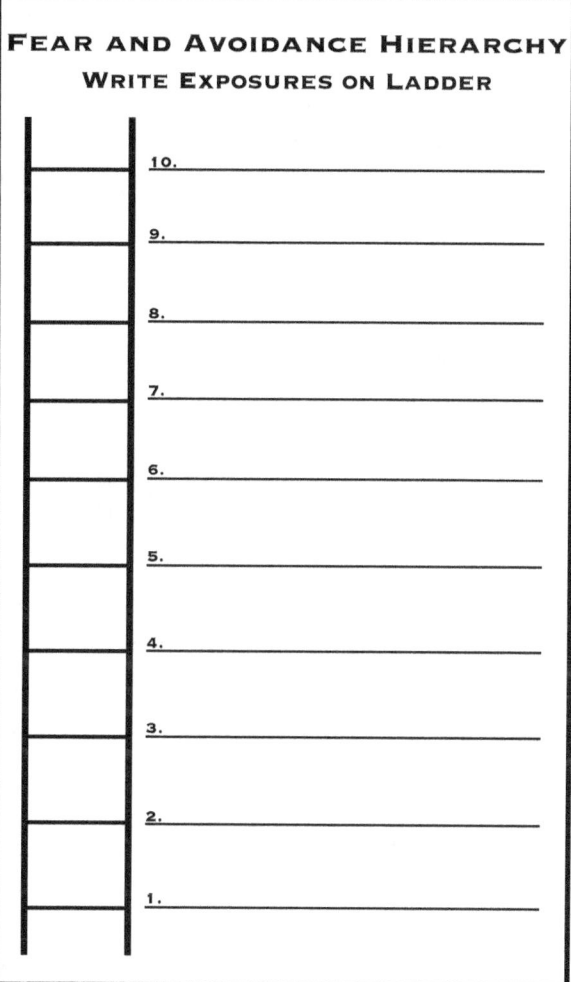

Possible Social Depression Feelings:
5. Extreme anxiety/I'm having a panic attack—can't be social.
4. High anxiety/I feel distressed and want to stay home.
3. Moderately anxious/I don't want to talk to anyone.
2. Mild anxiety/I have a lot of self doubt—feeling down.
1. No anxiety/I am extremely happy all the time.

Ideas on Social Depression Fears:
10. Everyday I'll get outside and keep social connections.
9. I'll get outside, get grounded, and do yoga with a friend.
8. I will work on building a social calendar to get me outside.
7. I will do breathing exercise to bring me peace and calmness.
6. I will practice "I am" statements to increase my confidence.
5. I will build a support system of people who care about me.
4. I'll build self-compassion writing one thing I like about myself.
3. I will watch online videos with tips on overcoming depression.
2. I will watch a movie about a person who is depressed.
1. I will listen to an upbeat song about feeling down.

Communication Skills

With depression, your typical "Preferred Methods of Communication" might not click with you right now because you are not feeling like yourself. Learning some positive self-talk skills to replace those negative, rumination thoughts in your head will help you feel a little better every day.

- Instead of thinking, *I am worthless and can't do anything right.* Change your narrative to the positive thought of *This is the first time I have tried_____. I am just learning and I will do better next time around.*
- Instead of thinking, *I can't believe _____ canceled on me. I knew they didn't like me.* Change your narrative to the positive thought of *I know _____'s mom is sick and needed her to stay home. I should drop off some flowers and let them know I am thinking about them.*
- Instead of thinking, *I know I failed that test. I am so stupid and will never get into college.* Change your narrative to a positive thought: *Everyone in class said this test was hard, so the teacher will likely curve the test. When I see my test, I will ask to talk to my teacher to make sure I understand what I missed.*

If you are experiencing an emergency, please seek immediate assistance from a parent/guardian, school counselor, teacher, or medical professional or call 911.

Mindfulness Skills

According to Boyraz & Lightsey (2012), when you have positive thoughts and practice gratitude, you believe your life has meaning, you approach stressful situations with a positive attitude, and when you are sick, your body will heal faster, and you are in less pain.

"Practicing Gratitude" Mindfulness Exercise

1. Get in a comfortable position and close your eyes. Let your mind wander to thinking about things in your life that you are grateful for and lean into those feelings.
2. Take five deep breaths—breathing slowly in...and out...
3. As you take these breaths, think of something you are grateful for on your inhaled breaths Be conscious and notice how your body feels thinking about these things. What environment you are picturing when you are feeling grateful? Where is your happy place?
4. Again, take five deep breaths—breathing slowly in...and out... Now, this time think of things that make you uncomfortable —questioning things in your life and your happiness.
5. Take notice of how your body feels and any sensations you experience, such as lightness or tightness as your body swirls around these thoughts.
6. Take another five deep breaths —breathing slowly in...and out... reminding yourself of what you are grateful for and where you feel this way. Notice the lightness in your body when you think of yourself in your happy place.

Well-Being Habit Tracker:

1. **Fill out each Well-Being Habit Tracker category below.**
2. **When completed, check the box and note your subjective well-being from 1-10.**

- ☐ **Sleep:** How many hours? _____ **Morning Light Exposure:** ☐   Well-Being Rating: ____
- ☐ **Exercise:** Length/Type? _____   Well-Being Rating: ____
- ☐ **Mindfulness:** Length/Type? _____   Well-Being Rating: ____
- ☐ **Nature:** Time spent/Activity outside? ____ / _____   Well-Being Rating: ____
- ☐ **Hydration:** I drank 🥛🥛🥛🥛🥛🥛 8 oz. glasses of water.   Well-Being Rating: ____
- ☐ **Nutrition:** Number of healthy meals or calories consumed? ____   Well-Being Rating: ____
- ☐ **Social Fitness:** Time spent/Activity? ____ / _____   Well-Being Rating: ____
- ☐ **Caring:** Act(s) of service? _____   Well-Being Rating: ____
- ☐ **Gratitude:** I am grateful for _____   Well-Being Rating: ____
- ☐ **Happiness:** _____ brought me joy!   Well-Being Rating: ____
- ☐ **Laughter:** I laughed about _____
- ☐ **Smile:** I made someone smile by _____
- ☐ **Music:** I sang or listened to this song to motivate me and boost my mood and well-being:
_____

© 2024 Reflections Publishing LLC. All rights reserved.

Anxiety-Buster To-Do List:

1 Big Task - Let's Go!

- ☐ _____

2 Medium Tasks - Let's Do This!

- ☐ _____
- ☐ _____

3 Small Tasks - You Got This!

- ☐ _____
- ☐ _____
- ☐ _____

© 2024 Reflections Publishing LLC. All rights reserved.

• Self-Harm •

At an alarming rate, adolescents with self-injurious thoughts and behaviors (SITBs) are tragically on an upward trend (Nock et al, 2019). Many people consider self-harm and nonsuicidal self-injury (NSSI) a current crisis; however, even going back two thousand years ago, Aristotle described Greek teenagers as "passionate, irascible, and apt to be carried away by their impulses." So why do teenagers act so impulsively and vulnerably to the power of suggestion? It is because, during your formative brain development years, your brain gets "more of a sense of reward than an adult brain." Your brain is in a sensitive state and gets splashed with more dopamine in "sensation-seeking situations" than an adult brain.

A research study by Dartmouth College scientists highlighted in an fMRI experience exactly why and how this happens in your teenage brain. The bottom line is that going back to puberty, the Frontal Cortex in your brain is still wiring itself together, thus making it difficult for you to understand any consequences of your actions and accurately assess risks and rewards. The study described this thought process of costs versus benefits as moving slower in your brain versus an adult's brain. Your brain focuses more on the "reason" you might want to do something versus the consequence of your decision because the areas around your Frontal Lobe are not yet fully connected and wired together. An adult brain's Anterior Cingulate Cortex is fully developed; therefore, this section of the adult brain understands they are about to make a mistake and immediately processes not to go through with the action.

So, you are likely thinking that all of your bad choices are not your fault, and to some degree, that is true, but remember that **you do know** the difference between right and wrong at the age of five. Plus, **when drugs and alcohol are added into the mix, all bets are off because they may cause your brain to be wired incorrectly and therefore your brain may not function properly**.

Research indicates that if you can have a game plan in place when you are struggling with resisting "sensation-seeking situations" and you can redirect your attention and focus to something else, then the moment can pass. Research indicates that **self-harm ideation can pass in fifteen minutes**, so let's get to work and create a game plan to start training your brain to redirect those negative "sensation-seeking temptations" into positive thoughts and actions. These positive thoughts can be anything from remembering how much you were looking forward to the upcoming game against your rival school to knowing how upset your parents, sibling, girlfriend, or boyfriend will feel and miss you, to thinking about your pet at home and them not understanding where you went or why you are not coming home to play with them.

Ideas to help you get through 15 minutes of self-harm ideation:

- _____
_____
_____
_____
_____

- _____
_____
_____
_____
_____

- _____
_____
_____
_____
_____

- _____
_____
_____
_____
_____

- _____
_____
_____
_____
_____

SELF-HARM

Key Takeaway

- **Suicide Hot line: 988**

If you are experiencing an emergency, please seek immediate assistance from a parent/guardian, school counselor, teacher, or medical professional or call 911 or 988.
This book is sold with the understanding that the publisher and the author are not engaged in rendering medical, legal, or other professional advice or services.
If professional assistance is required, the services of a competent professional should be sought.

• Self-Harm •

Brain Power

The **Anterior Cingular Cortex** (which works as a behavior monitor to help identify mistakes) is not fully wired in your adolescent, developing brain; thus, you react impulsively and passionately and cannot process and make good decisions (Jensen & Ellis Nut, 2015). Between adolescence and adulthood, your self-regulation and cognitive control systems mature; thus, your impulsive sensation-seeking and risk-taking behaviors decline as your **Lateral Prefrontal Cortex**, **Parietal Cortex**, and **Anterior Cingular Cortex** are wired together (Steinberg, 2008).

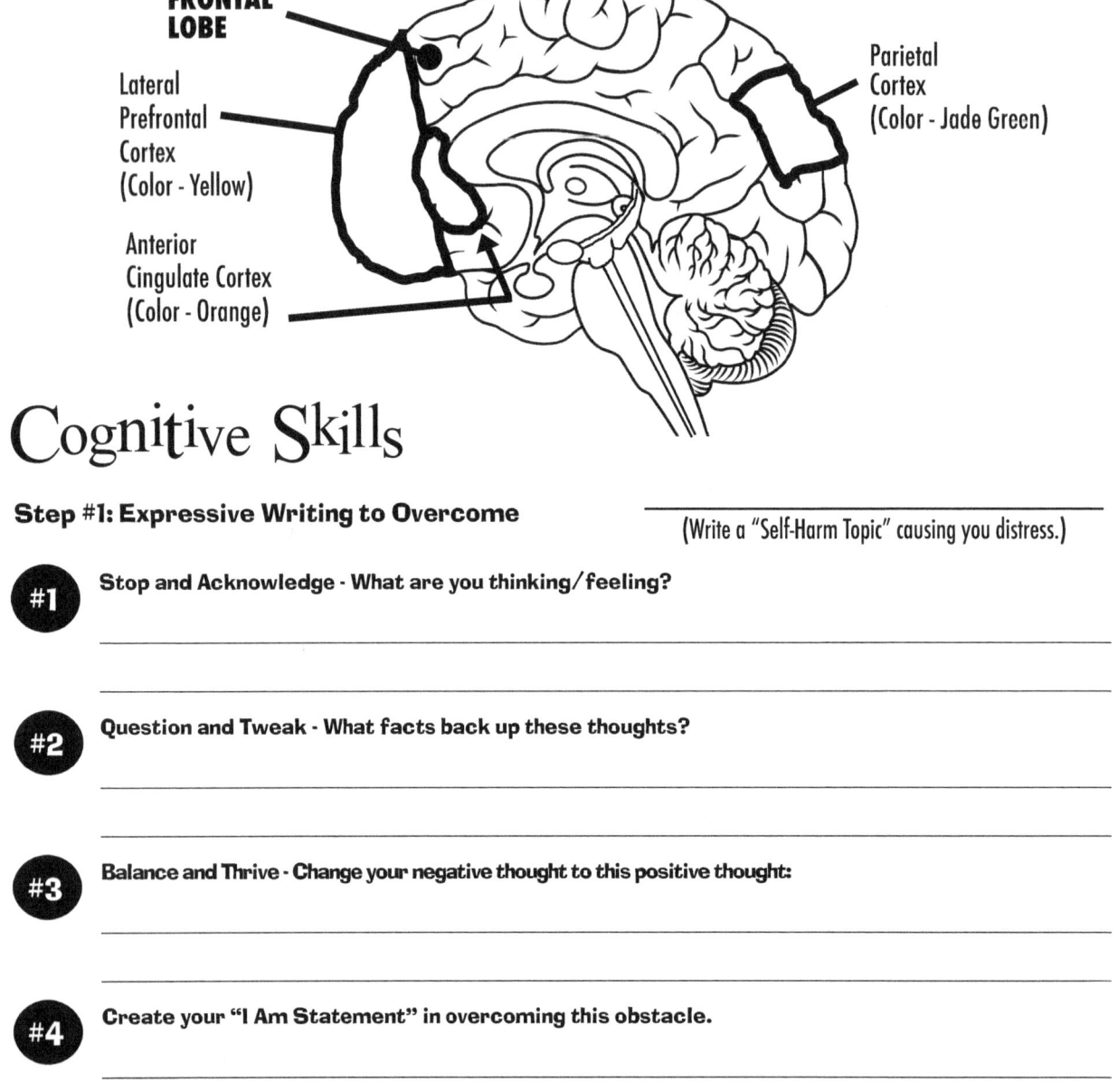

Cognitive Skills

Step #1: Expressive Writing to Overcome

(Write a "Self-Harm Topic" causing you distress.)

#1 **Stop and Acknowledge - What are you thinking/feeling?**

#2 **Question and Tweak - What facts back up these thoughts?**

#3 **Balance and Thrive - Change your negative thought to this positive thought:**

#4 **Create your "I Am Statement" in overcoming this obstacle.**

Cognitive Skills

(Write a "Self-Harm Topic" causing you distress.)

INSTRUCTIONS for Steps #2 and #3:
On the line above, write the "Self-Harm Topic" causing you stress. Next, On the "Feelings Thermometer," color up to the point of your distress (from 1 to 5) and write a phrase on the matching line describing how you are feeling about this topic. Now that you know how you feel, move to Step #3 and write ten steps to overcome this fear. You can find tips below with a "possible scenario" to get you started.

Step #2: Gauging Your Feelings

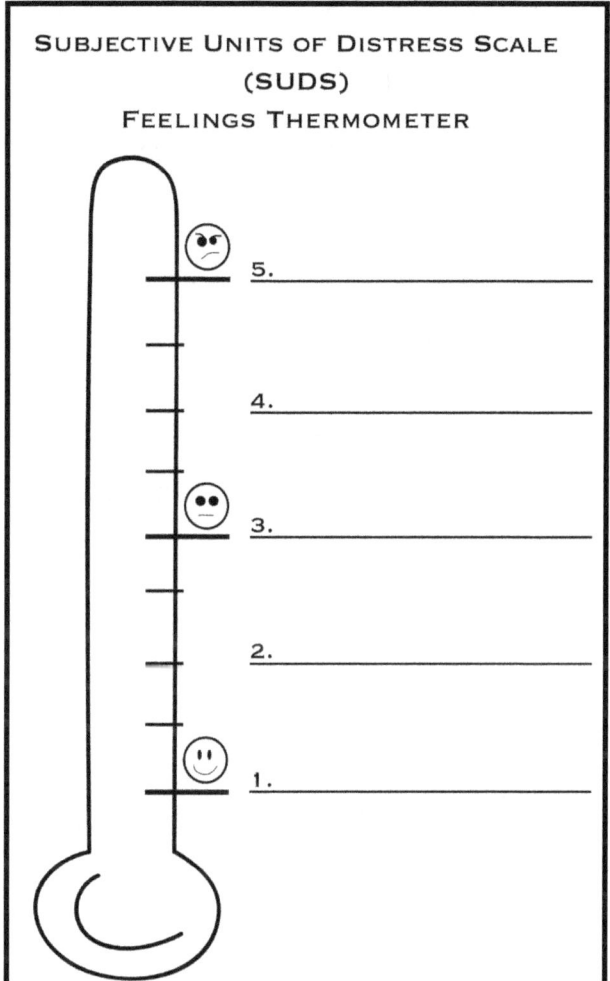

Step #3: Overcoming Obstacles

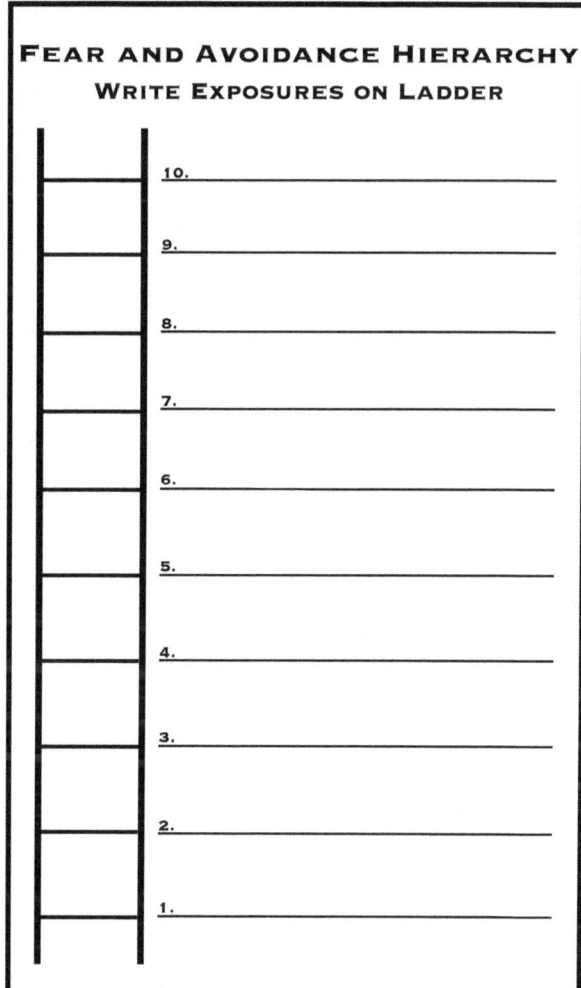

How you May Feel About Self-Harm:
5. Extreme anxiety/I need to seek help immediately.
4. High anxiety/I don't want to continue feeling like this.
3. Moderately anxious/I don't want to be around anyone.
2. Mild anxiety/I feel better pinching myself.
1. No anxiety/I love myself and would never hurt myself.

Ideas on Overcoming Self-Harm Fears:
10. I am confident with no intentions of harming myself.
9. I will help someone else who is struggling with self-harm.
8. I will journal why I ever wanted to commit self-harm.
7. I will do the breathing exercise to help overcome self-harm.
6. I will practice "I am" statements to overcome self-harm.
5. I will join a group self-harm therapy group.
4. I will stay away from friends who self-harm.
3. I will watch a movie about self-harm.
2. I will watch a television show about teen self-harm.
1. I will listen to a song about self-harm.

If you are experiencing an emergency, please seek immediate assistance from a parent/guardian, school counselor, teacher, or medical professional or call 911 or 988.

Communication Skills

If you are in a state of inducing self-harm, then your typical "Method of Communication" likely will not work because you clearly are not yourself. As I mentioned a couple of pages earlier, the added effects of drugs and alcohol can put you in a psychosis state and make you do things to your body that you normally would never consider doing otherwise. Also, many people who inflict self-harm have reported they immediately regret it and realize that what they thought was so horrible really was a solvable problem. Here are some talking points to ask for help:

- I know I joke about suicide all the time, but I really am concerned because I do not feel like myself and I recognize that my thoughts are not safe and I need help.

- I am really stressed, and I haven't slept in weeks. My mind is constantly racing, and I don't see a way out of _____. I can't get through this on my own.

- My girlfriend just broke up with me, and I fear what I will do to myself. Please find someone I can go to for help.

- Kids constantly tease me at school, and I want to go to a different school.

If you are experiencing an emergency, please seek immediate assistance from a parent/guardian, school counselor, teacher, or medical professional or call 911 or 988.

Mindfulness Skills

This mindfulness technique is known to be used by Navy Seals when they are in hypersensitive situations and need to bring their mind back to a relaxed state. When we are ultra stressed or in a hypersensitive state, we may not be aware that we are taking short and irregular breaths, which causes our body to remain in a state of increased and heightened stress and anxiety.

Mindfulness Box Breathing Exercise

1. Get in a comfortable position and close your eyes.
2. Begin taking long, deep breaths and imagine you are tracing a box with your finger in the air with each inhaled and exhaled breath.
3. Inhale your breath for four seconds and draw the right side of a box.
4. Then hold this breath for four seconds—while drawing the bottom of the box.
5. Exhale your breath for four seconds while drawing the left side of you box.
6. Now, hold your breath for four seconds as you draw the top and close the box.
7. Continue this exercise until you feel fully relaxed.

Well-Being Habit Tracker:

1. **Fill out each Well-Being Habit Tracker category below.**
2. **When completed, check the box and note your subjective well-being from 1-10.**

- ☐ **Sleep:** How many hours? _____ **Morning Light Exposure:** ☐   Well-Being Rating: ____
- ☐ **Exercise:** Length/Type? _____   Well-Being Rating: ____
- ☐ **Mindfulness:** Length/Type? _____   Well-Being Rating: ____
- ☐ **Nature:** Time spent/Activity outside? ____ / _____   Well-Being Rating: ____
- ☐ **Hydration:** I drank 🥛🥛🥛🥛🥛🥛 8 oz. glasses of water.   Well-Being Rating: ____
- ☐ **Nutrition:** Number of healthy meals or calories consumed? _____   Well-Being Rating: ____
- ☐ **Social Fitness:** Time spent/Activity? ____ / _____   Well-Being Rating: ____
- ☐ **Caring:** Act(s) of service? _____   Well-Being Rating: ____
- ☐ **Gratitude:** I am grateful for _____   Well-Being Rating: ____
- ☐ **Happiness:** _____ brought me joy!   Well-Being Rating: ____
- ☐ **Laughter:** I laughed about _____
- ☐ **Smile:** I made someone smile by _____
- ☐ **Music:** I sang or listened to this song to motivate me and boost my mood and well-being: _____

© 2024 Reflections Publishing LLC. All rights reserved.

Anxiety-Buster To-Do List:

1 Big Task - Let's Go!
- ☐ _____

2 Medium Tasks - Let's Do This!
- ☐ _____
- ☐ _____

3 Small Tasks - You Got This!
- ☐ _____
- ☐ _____
- ☐ _____

© 2024 Reflections Publishing LLC. All rights reserved.

• Substance Abuse - Alcohol & Drugs •

Instructions: Get a yellow highlighter and mark the sentences that discuss what happens to your developing brain when you consume drugs and alcohol on a daily basis. After reading, discuss as a class.

We generally only have **Two Rules** in our house. Our daughters know the rules, and so do their friends. The **Two Rules** are:

1. **Make Good Choices.**
   - There are always consequences to the decisions and choices you make.
2. **Use Common Sense.**
   - I cannot emphasize this enough. You do not have to be the smartest person in the room, but you need to use common sense. Just think before you act.

I like collaborating and consulting with our daughters when working on projects. I originally had "Substance Abuse" as a couple of bullet points in a section called "Common Sense;" however, one of my daughters advised me not to do that. She explained to me that, as a college student, she knew many people who consumed drugs or alcohol in some form and would be offended if I told them that taking drugs and alcohol during their tween and teen years would damage their brains long term. I explained to her that some recent **research on cannabis is indicating that teenagers with no family history are developing schizophrenia due to daily cannabis use**. It is becoming such a pandemic that my Harvard Psychopharmacology instructor was approved to teach a class on this subject.

I told my daughter that when I had to write a paper for this Psychopharmacology class, my topic was to try and find a medicinal and healthy formulation of cannabis for adolescents to take to alleviate pain. Keeping an open mind, knowing an adolescent who lives in daily chronic pain and living in a state where cannabis is legalized, I was anxious to research and discover if there was a formulation of cannabis that might be a safe option. Also, growing up in Indiana, where both of my grandfathers were farmers, I thought it was worth researching since marijuana was a plant. I had a meeting with my instructor about my paper and explained my frustration of not finding any research to support my hypothesis. You can see for yourself and go to your web browser and type the following keywords:
(adolescent) AND (cannabis) AND (fMRI) AND (schizophrenia).

In continuing this conversation with my daughter, she told me not to say cannabis because kids call it weed. Regardless of whether you call it cannabis, marijuana, or weed, if you consume weed and other drugs daily during your adolescent years while your brain is developing and your brain is "plastic" and "livewired," then the research states your brain may get damaged to the point of no return.

According to the United Nations Office on Drugs and Crime (UNODC), two-thirds of the data reported from participating countries rank cannabis as its primary substance abuse. With weed legalization in some states, adolescents view weed no differently than watching their parents drink alcohol. Weed is getting normalized, with kids saying, "It relaxes me." What is also concerning is that they often do not know **where the weed is coming from or the formulation they are taking**.

Adolescence is a known time when your brain properly wires its fiber tracts—connecting your cognitive, motor, and sensory functions (Paus et al., 1999). This research is part of the reason why there are laws on how old you must be to consume drugs and alcohol. It is not just for adults to be "fun sponges," by saying no. The law is in place to protect your developing brain and for your health and safety. Battistella et al. (2014) reported significant brain atrophy with heavy weed consumption before age 18. Zalesky et al. (2012) found a linear correlation between cannabis toxicity to the brain's white matter and when a person starts cannabis on a regular basis. Harvard Medical School reports that the brain may continue to develop until age 30; hence, the law's current age of 21 may be too young because you should not consume drugs and alcohol while your brain is still developing. Johnson (2022, January 31) agrees based on reports from neuroscience research stating we may need to reconsider the age at which a child becomes an adult.

Researchers are sounding the alarm that we are undergoing a major public health crisis. Curran et al. (2016) report the known crisis that **some individuals are at even more risk of adverse effects of consuming weed—developing symptoms of psychotic illness, cognitive impairment, and long-term addiction**. The Koob and Volkow Model of Addiction explains how the three stages of weed addiction affect three major neurocircuits in the brain.

Meier et al. (2012) reported the following studies: **1.** In New Zealand, individuals who developed a weed addiction during their adolescent years **reported a decline of up to six IQ points. 2.** Another study links cognitive changes to weed consumption with a **decline of eight points**.

Weed contains 100 unique ingredients called cannabinoids, and the two most prominent ingredients are Delta9-tetrahydrocannabinol (Δ9-THC) and cannabidiol (CBD), which tend to have adverse effects on the developing human brain behavior. Research indicates that Δ9-THC impairs learning, produces psychosis-like effects, and increases anxiety. When you purchase drugs in random places because you are underage, you have no idea what you are buying. I can tell you a story of a person who thought they were smoking weed in a vape pen; however, it was laced with a horse tranquilizer. This person almost died, but fortunately, **one of the teenagers on site had some common sense and knew they were protected by The Good Samaritan Law and called 911**. So, I am going to remind you again of Rules #1 and #2 again here:

1. **Make Good Choices.**
2. **Use Common Sense.**

It is normal for pruning to occur in the brain during adolescence (Cohen-Corey, 2002); however, Bossong & Niesink (2010) believed that abnormal pruning likely occurs when the toxic THC enters the brain during the critical time of maturation—affecting the synaptic pruning in the cerebellum (Casu et al., 2005) and Prefrontal Cortex (Bossong & Niesink, 2010).

To recap, research by Meier et al. (2012) indicates in long-term studies that regular weed consumption begins during puberty (the formative brain development years) is linked to severe weed dependence, a gateway to other drugs, lung disease, memory impairment, altering psychosocial development, poorer cognitive performance, and mental health problems (e.g., schizophrenia and bipolar disorder).

If you are experiencing an emergency, please seek immediate assistance from a parent/guardian, school counselor, teacher, or medical professional or call 911.
This book is sold with the understanding that the publisher and the author are not engaged in rendering medical, legal, or other professional advice or services.
If professional assistance is required, the services of a competent professional should be sought.

• Substance Abuse - Alcohol & Drugs •

Brain Power

The term "amotivation syndrome" gets used in individuals because positron emission tomography (PET) shows proof that adolescents who heavily consume weed during their key formative brain development years (i.e., puberty through at least the age of 25-years-old) and used on a regular basis, show a reduction in the **Striatal Dopamine Synthesis**. In a post-mortem study by Rapp et al. (2012), cannabis use is linked to volume loss in the brain—in the **Cingulum**, the **Dorsolateral Prefrontal Cortex**, and the **Cerebellum**.

In a study by Meier et al. (2012) of 1,037 individuals, daily cannabis use was studied beginning with a neuropsychological test when the participants were 13-years-old. Interviews with these same participants took place at the ages of 18-, 21-, 26-, 32-, and 38-years-old. The findings prove a significant life-time, neurotoxic effect on kids that start using weed in their teen years.

Dorsal Striatum "Habit Hub" is tied to amotivation and reduction in Striatal Dopamine Synthesis due to heavy and regular cannabis use (Color - Light Purple)

Cingulum (Color - Orange)

Dorsolateral Prefrontal Cortex (Color - Yellow)

Ventral Striatum "Reward Hub" releases smaller amounts of dopamine due to heavy and regular cannabis use (Color - Light Purple)

Cerebellum (Color - Golden Yellow)

Cognitive Skills

Step #1: Expressive Writing to Overcome

(Write a "Substance Abuse Topic" causing you distress.)

#1 Stop and Acknowledge - What are you thinking/feeling?
_____
_____

#2 Question and Tweak - What facts back up these thoughts?
_____
_____

#3 Balance and Thrive - Change your negative thought to this positive thought:
_____
_____

#4 Create your "I Am Statement" in overcoming this obstacle.
_____

-116-

Cognitive Skills

_____

(Write a "Substance Abuse Topic" causing you distress.)

INSTRUCTIONS for Steps #2 and #3:
On the line above, write the "Substance Abuse Topic" causing you stress. Next, On the "Feelings Thermometer," color up to the point of your distress (from 1 to 5) and write a phrase on the matching line describing how you are feeling about this topic. Now that you know how you feel, move to Step #3 and write ten steps to overcome this fear. You can find tips below with a "possible scenario" to get you started.

Step #2: Gauging Your Feelings

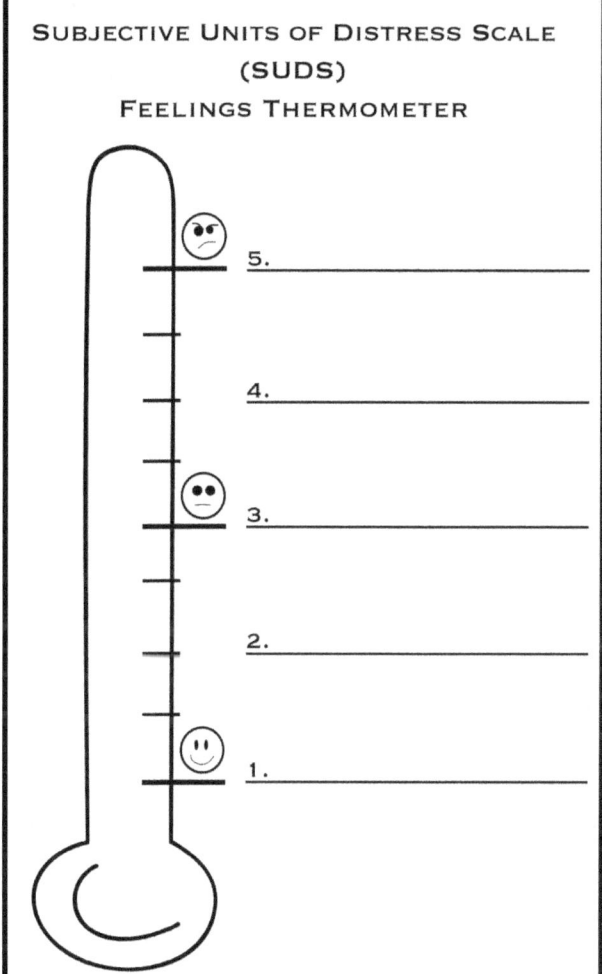

Step #3: Overcoming Obstacles

How you May Feel About Drugs and Alcohol:
5. Extreme anxiety/I can't say, "NO!"
4. High anxiety/My heart is racing with the pressure.
3. Moderately anxious/People won't leave me alone.
2. Mild anxiety/I feel judged that I am not doing drugs.
1. No anxiety/I feel confident in myself; I do not use drugs.

Ideas on Overcoming Drug and Alcohol Use:
10. I am confident I can now say, "NO!"
9. I will practice saying, "NO!" utilizing role playing scripts.
8. I will create a list of "Go-to Phrases" to avoid drugs.
7. I will do breathing exercises to help me relax and refocus.
6. I will practice "I am" statements to increase my confidence.
5. I will hang out with new friends who don't pressure me.
4. I will join group therapy, making new friends who support me.
3. I will watch online videos regarding damage of drug use.
2. I will watch a movie about overcoming drug use.
1. I will listen to an upbeat song about overcoming drug use.

Communication Skills

In today's society, you likely see drug and alcohol use at school, on the weekends, and possibly even at home. If **"Spending Time Together"** is your "Preferred Method of Communication," and if your friends start doing drugs and alcohol, then it might be even more challenging for you to say "No." It is hard when friends you have possibly known since kindergarten start to make choices that do not align with your core values. If I were you, I would start looking for some new friends. We always tell our kids that one easy way out is to blame or use us as an excuse. It works every time. Sometimes, it is not what you say but how quickly you say something in return. Here are some "Go-to Phrases" on things you can say that get you out of the situation without placing judgment on the person trying to coerce you into taking drugs.

- I have an alcohol allergy and get really sick.

- My mom needs me at home to watch my younger sister because our babysitter cancelled.

- I actually have a big tournament tomorrow. I need to be well rested and ready for the game. My coach is also having us text him a picture with a parent/guardian showing we are home.

- Write your own: _____

___

Mindfulness Skills

We can learn a lot about ourselves and our emotions by paying attention and having awarenes regarding how we feel in different environments and situations. Substance abuse is challenging to overcome due to the drugs and alcohol rewiring your brain in a negative manner, but your brain will try to heal itself and mindful meditation can help repair those brain circuits that have gone haywire.

> **"Taking Note of Emotions" Mindfulness Exercise**
>
> 1. Get in a comfortable position and close your eyes. Let your mind wonder—thinking about all of the emotions you are feeling.
> 2. Paying attention to your breathe ask yourself, "how you are feeling?"
> 3. With each thought that comes to mind, take notice of how your body feels and any sensations you experience such as lightness or tightness in your body.
> 4. Pay attention to your breath and ask yourself, "Why I am putting drugs/ alcohol in my body?"
> 5. Again, with each thought that comes to mind, take notice of how your body feels and any sensations you experience such as lightness or tightness in your body. With each negative thought that enters your mind, let it go and redirect that thought to a more productive and positive way to treat your body.
> 6. You can continue this exercise asking yourself additional questions that you want to process.

Well-Being Habit Tracker:

1. **Fill out each Well-Being Habit Tracker category below.**
2. **When completed, check the box and note your subjective well-being from 1-10.**

- ☐ **Sleep:** How many hours? _____ **Morning Light Exposure:** ☐   Well-Being Rating: _____
- ☐ **Exercise:** Length/Type? _____   Well-Being Rating: _____
- ☐ **Mindfulness:** Length/Type? _____   Well-Being Rating: _____
- ☐ **Nature:** Time spent/Activity outside? ____ / _____   Well-Being Rating: _____
- ☐ **Hydration:** I drank ☐☐☐☐☐☐☐☐ 8 oz. glasses of water.   Well-Being Rating: _____
- ☐ **Nutrition:** Number of healthy meals or calories consumed? _____   Well-Being Rating: _____
- ☐ **Social Fitness:** Time spent/Activity? ____ / _____   Well-Being Rating: _____
- ☐ **Caring:** Act(s) of service? _____   Well-Being Rating: _____
- ☐ **Gratitude:** I am grateful for _____   Well-Being Rating: _____
- ☐ **Happiness:** _____ brought me joy!   Well-Being Rating: _____
- ☐ **Laughter:** I laughed about _____
- ☐ **Smile:** I made someone smile by _____
- ☐ **Music:** I sang or listened to this song to motivate me and boost my mood and well-being: _____

© 2024 Reflections Publishing LLC. All rights reserved.

Anxiety-Buster To-Do List:

1 Big Task - Let's Go!

☐ _____

2 Medium Tasks - Let's Do This!

☐ _____

☐ _____

3 Small Tasks - You Got This!

☐ _____

☐ _____

☐ _____

© 2024 Reflections Publishing LLC. All rights reserved.

Section Nine

What's Your Game Plan?

Relationships

LIFE TOPICS:

- Bullying/Cyberbullying - 122
- Caregiver - 128
- Friendships - 134
- Peer Pressure - 140

• Bullying and Cyberbullying •

Bullying is a one-sided act of peer abuse that occurs to an innocent person. While you might think that calling the act of peer abuse is extreme, I believe this terminology is more representative of when one person is mean to another human being—for absolutely no reason.

One of the most challenging concepts for any person to process who receives bullying behavior is that someone would treat you in a way that you would never consider treating someone else. So why are people so mean to each other? Typically, it is because the perpetrator is:

1. Extremely insecure. Individuals who are happy and content do not feel the need to put others down for entertainment.

2. Low in self-confidence. Around third grade, students start to notice and compare themselves to classmates. In some circumstances, this is the age when students start to struggle in school, so to compensate for this insecurity, aggressors start picking on classmates who are good students.

3. Jealous. This is unfortunately an insecurity and habit that some parents pass down to their children and is a learned behavior.

Expert Alison Trachtman Hill, in the Face 2 Face book, encourages people not to call a fellow student a bully but to label the behavior instead of the person. She states **"kids are not good or bad—they make good or bad decisions."** Additionally, she divides the social aspect of peer abuse into the following three roles:

- **The Aggressor:**   This person executes the bad peer abuse behavior.

- **The Target:**   This person receives the peer abuse.

- **The Witness:**   This person is called a "Witness" and not a "Bystander" because if you are a **witness to someone getting picked on then you have a responsibility to report it** to an adult or authority figure.

```
   "Babies are not born with hate or jealousy in their hearts.
   These are learned behaviors. You can choose to be a compassionate
   person who gives unconditional love to all people—regardless of
     ethnicity, gender, race, religion, and socio-economic backgrounds."
                      - Colleen Carter Ster
```

Peer Abuse Defense Shield

Build a shield of defense armor to combat an aggressor's attack:

"Tips and Tools" to Shield Peer Abuse

- Stand tall with your head held high.

- Talk in a strong, confident, and firm voice.

- Look the aggressor in the eye when you talk.

- Let the aggressor's comments bounce off your shield. Do not let their words enter your head or heart.

- Try not to react to the aggressor. A reaction may be exactly what the aggressor is looking to provoke. Breathe deeply and remove yourself from the situation as quickly as possible.

- Stay with a group of friends and aggressors will be less likely to target you.

With cyberbullying, this tactic can feel even worse because the person is not brave enough to be mean to the other person's face. They are hiding behind a computer screen or a cell phone. If you are a victim of cyberbullying, there are steps you can take to shut down the abuse. The first step is to document and log the abuse so you can validate your case. The second step is to then report this abuse to a parent/guardian and/or school official.

If you are experiencing an emergency, please seek immediate assistance from a parent/guardian, school counselor, teacher, or medical professional or call 911.
This book is sold with the understanding that the publisher and the author are not engaged in rendering medical, legal, or other professional advice or services.
If professional assistance is required, the services of a competent professional should be sought.

• Bullying and Cyberbullying •

Brain Power

According to Adams, Sanko, & Bukowski (2011), just the presence of a best friend can serve as a protective buffer against the negative effect of a bad experience on an individual's global self-worth, as well as altercations created in the **Hypothalamic-Pituitary-Adrenal (HPA) axis**—due to less cortisol released.

Use a web search engine to find the location of the **HPA axis** in your brain and then in the space below, draw your own version of a brain labeling the **HPA axis** in your illustration.

Cognitive Skills

Step #1: Expressive Writing to Overcome

(Write a "Bullying/Cyberbullying Topic" causing you distress.)

#1 Stop and Acknowledge - What are you thinking/feeling?
_____
_____

#2 Question and Tweak - What facts back up these thoughts?
_____
_____

#3 Balance and Thrive - Change your negative thought to this positive thought:
_____
_____

#4 Create your "I Am Statement" in overcoming this obstacle.
_____
_____

Cognitive Skills

_____

(Write a "Bullying/Cyberbullying Topic" causing you distress.)

INSTRUCTIONS for Steps #2 and #3:
On the line above, write the "Bullying/Cyberbullying Topic" causing you stress. Next, On the "Feelings Thermometer," color up to the point of your distress (from 1 to 5) and write a phrase on the matching line describing how you are feeling about this topic. Now that you know how you feel, move to Step #3 and write ten steps to overcome this fear. You can find tips below with a "possible scenario" to get you started.

Step #2: Gauging Your Feelings

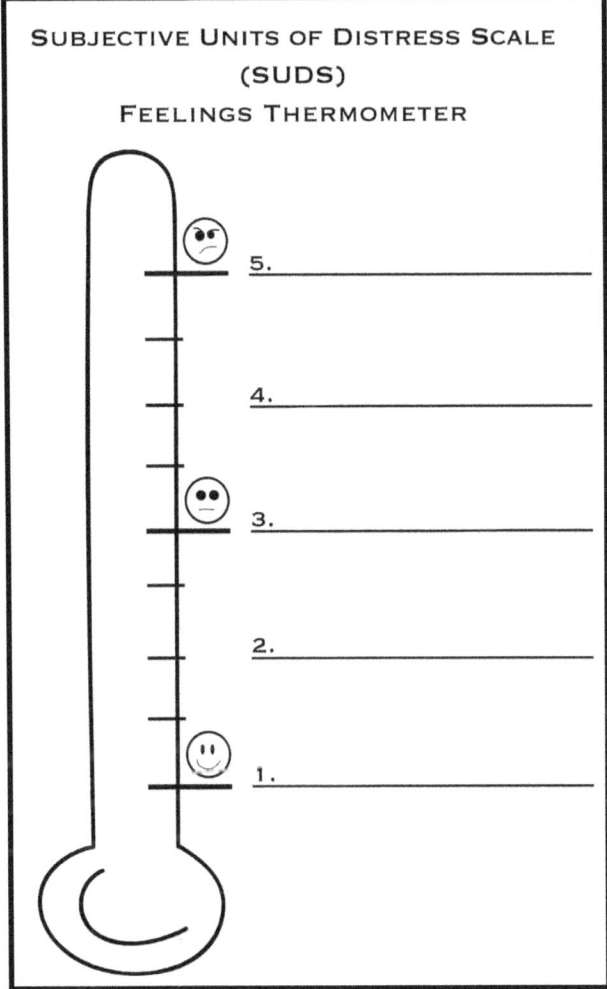

Step #3: Overcoming Obstacles

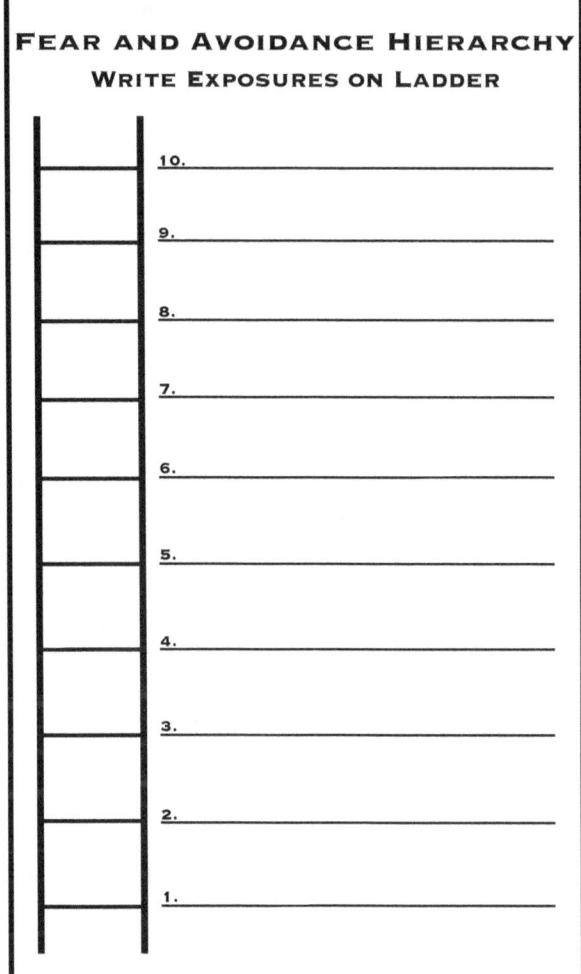

How you May Feel About Getting Bullied:
5. Extreme anxiety/I am severely suffering from peer abuse.
4. High anxiety/I don't see the bullying ever stopping.
3. Moderately anxious/I feel humiliated from bullying.
2. Mild anxiety/This bully is affecting my well-being.
1. No anxiety/I have never experienced a bullying situation.

Ideas on Overcoming Bullying Fears:
10. I am confident to study up to bullies and support others too.
9. I will rehearse with role-playing scripts to respond to bullying.
8. I will create coping strategies so I am prepared for bullying.
7. I will practice breathing exercises to not let bully affect me.
6. I will build self-esteem with practicing "I am" statements.
5. I will run an anti-bullying club at my school.
4. I will join a bullying support group and seek help from teachers.
3. I will watch online videos and TikToks on bullying.
2. I will watch a movie about a student getting bullied.
1. I will listen to an upbeat song about overcoming bullying.

Communication Skills

Witnessing or experiencing peer abuse can be very upsetting; however, you can prepare yourself so you have the tips and tools you need in your back pocket to pull out and utilize when you need them. In order to shut down peer abuse as a "Witness" or "Target," you just need some "Go-To Phrases." Sometimes it does not matter what you say—you just need to have a quick and witty response prepared and ready to go. When creating your "Go-To Phrase," you need to create short, concise, and focused phrases that are direct and to the point with no emotion attached. Stay focused—being kind and direct. Say what you mean; however, be brief—less is more.

Power "Go-To Phrases" and Strategies For the Target: (kid-proven)

1. "Thank you for the compliment." Watch them look confused and walk away.
2. "I'm tired of trying to make sense of your gibberish." Do not give them your power.
3. "Wow, I never heard that one before." Now walk away. They are not worth your time or energy.
4. Practice writing your own: _____

Power "Go-To Phrases" and Strategies for the Witness: (kid-proven)

1. "You are just saying that because you are so insecure. It's not cool to be so hateful."
2. Put post-it notes around school—with the message: No Bullying Allowed. Be Respectful.
3. Practice writing your own: _____

Mindfulness Skills

Mindfulness Awareness Exercise

1. **Awareness:** Stay grounded and keep perspective. Acknowledge and appreciate everything around you and see the big picture.
2. **Meditate:** Connect with your holistic system; peel back the layers and dig deep.
3. **Read:** Continue learning and practicing a growth mindset.
4. **Rest:** Work can only be done in peace; remember to take deep breaths and meditate.
5. **Reflect:** Journal the process of your journey. Observe and accept changes.
6. **Simplify:** Let go and unplug. See your thoughts clearly and do not live in the past.
7. **Gratitude:** Practice being thankful and listen more than you speak.

Well-Being Habit Tracker:

1. Fill out each Well-Being Habit Tracker category below.
2. When completed, check the box and note your subjective well-being from 1-10.

- ☐ **Sleep:** How many hours? _____ **Morning Light Exposure:** ☐   Well-Being Rating: _____
- ☐ **Exercise:** Length/Type? _____   Well-Being Rating: _____
- ☐ **Mindfulness:** Length/Type? _____   Well-Being Rating: _____
- ☐ **Nature:** Time spent/Activity outside? ____ / _____   Well-Being Rating: _____
- ☐ **Hydration:** I drank 🥛🥛🥛🥛🥛🥛 8 oz. glasses of water.   Well-Being Rating: _____
- ☐ **Nutrition:** Number of healthy meals or calories consumed? _____   Well-Being Rating: _____
- ☐ **Social Fitness:** Time spent/Activity? ____ / _____   Well-Being Rating: _____
- ☐ **Caring:** Act(s) of service? _____   Well-Being Rating: _____
- ☐ **Gratitude:** I am grateful for _____   Well-Being Rating: _____
- ☐ **Happiness:** _____ brought me joy!   Well-Being Rating: _____
- ☐ **Laughter:** I laughed about _____
- ☐ **Smile:** I made someone smile by _____
- ☐ **Music:** I sang or listened to this song to motivate me and boost my mood and well-being:
_____

© 2024 Reflections Publishing LLC. All rights reserved.

Anxiety-Buster To-Do List:

1 Big Task - Let's Go!
- ☐ _____

2 Medium Tasks - Let's Do This!
- ☐ _____
- ☐ _____

3 Small Tasks - You Got This!
- ☐ _____
- ☐ _____
- ☐ _____

© 2024 Reflections Publishing LLC. All rights reserved.

• Caregiver •

Family dynamics are quite interesting because as the phrases go—"we all are products of our childhood" and "the apple doesn't fall far from the tree;" these phrases are so true. Thus, as you grow up, what you consider to be a normal family is how you see your family communicate and operate throughout your childhood. Communication-wise, if people in your family yell and argue, then you likely will grow up thinking that yelling and arguing is normal behavior. This is also why individuals who are abused as children continue the cycle of abuse onto their own children.

• Communication from the Caregiver (Parent/Guardian) Perspective

From a parent/guardian perspective, humans have a limited energy supply. Just like an electric car getting plugged into an electrical outlet, it gains the energy it needs to operate. The human body does the same thing except we go to sleep to restore and gain energy for the next day. Just like some electric cars, it has a gas option, and humans can supplement caffeine or exercise to give them a boost; however, if we push too hard, our bodies can break down like a car. When we communicate with people effectively, we use less energy and have more of a reserve to spend that energy elsewhere. If our relations within the family network are positive, then the energy supply is slowly used and can even get restored and regenerated when together. When children know they are loved unconditionally, it creates a workable framework of communication that allows parents to walk alongside them as they grow up and the family network to function in a healthy manner.

• Communication from the Child's Perspective

When children feel they can talk to people without feeling judged, disrespected, or guilty, then they will open up to you. When communicating with people, consider how self-complex a person is and the timing of your communication with them. "Pick your moments" and recognize that when you care about somebody, you do not intentionally push their buttons.

• Creating Family Connections

Why is it so hard to praise the ones we care about the most? Communication becomes fuzzy when we are too busy, too tired, or possibly not wanting to listen to the opinions of friends, family, classmates, or coworkers. An individual cannot address the love tank without first filling their own energy tank. When we communicate with each other in the method that fills our energy and love tanks, then we can function to our full potential—as an individual, parent, spouse, child, classmate, coworker, etc.

"When I was a boy of fourteen, my father was so ignorant I could hardly stand to have the old man around. But when I got to be twenty-one, I was astonished by how much he'd learned in seven years."

- Mark Twain

- **Caregiver (Parent/Guardian) Relations**

The following are some anonymous comments about how well these students reported communicating with their caregivers:

- "I'm terrified of making my parents mad or disappointed. There are things I would prefer to tell people my age than my parents. I don't want to deal with their reactions and make the situation even more emotional."

- "Sometimes I feel like I am not close enough to my parents to talk to them about serious situations. I do not feel they will understand and they will judge me."

- "It depends on the subject."

- "My dad is more shy and I feel like the generational and cultural gap between us (he immigrated to the United States and I am first-generation American born) and it prevents us from having open communication."

- "My feelings will be dismissed or my mom will weaponize what I've told her and she will use it against me."

- "Sometimes I can talk to my parents. My dad is a moody fella, so I have to feel out the vibe first."

- "My dad has a lot of anger issues."

- "My mother tends to gossip with others."

- "My parents are old-school in their being—while I can say things to my mom, I can't share anything with my Dad."

- "I feel like I'm more disconnected from my father due to his working schedule."

- "I'm too different from my parents; lack of understanding."

- "My father never had the time nor the empathy to have productive conversations."

- "They have their own beliefs which are different from mine."

- "I can talk to my parents about some things, but if I feel like the emotional harm or backlash is too great, then I won't start the conversation. It is difficult to communicate with them."

As you can see, you are not alone. All families struggle with communicating with each other. It just takes time and practice. Keep at it because your parents and guardians do unconditionally love you—whether they know how to say it to you or not.

If any information in this playbook is upsetting, please talk to a parent/guardian, school counselor, teacher, or medical professional.
This book is sold with the understanding that the publisher and the author are not engaged in rendering medical, legal, or other professional advice or services.
If professional assistance is required, the services of a competent professional should be sought.

• Caregiver •

Brain Power

According to Platek et al. (2009), when comparing family faces to friend faces, the **Posterior Cingulate Cortex** and **Cuneus** are activated in the brain. Also, familiar family faces activate the Anterior Medial Substrates (**Anterior Cingulate Cortex** and **Medial Prefrontal Cortex**) areas in the brain.

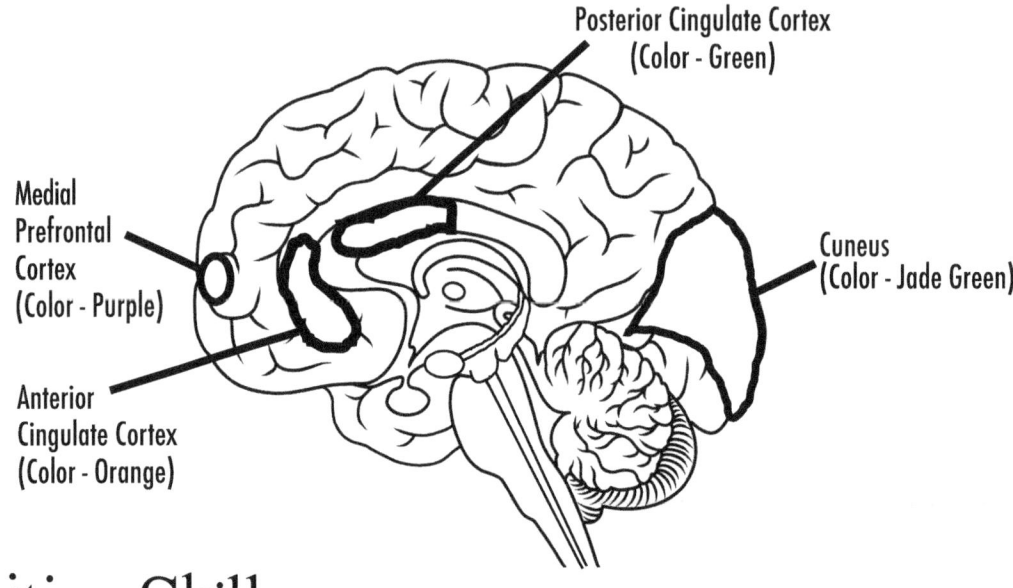

Cognitive Skills

Step #1: Expressive Writing to Overcome

_____
(Write a "Caregiver Topic" causing you distress.)

#1 Stop and Acknowledge - What are you thinking/feeling?
_____
_____

#2 Question and Tweak - What facts back up these thoughts?
_____
_____

#3 Balance and Thrive - Change your negative thought to this positive thought:
_____
_____

#4 Create your "I Am Statement" in overcoming this obstacle.
_____

Cognitive Skills

(Write a "Caregiver Topic" causing you distress.)

INSTRUCTIONS for Steps #2 and #3:
On the line above, write the "Caregiver Topic" causing you stress. Next, On the "Feelings Thermometer," color up to the point of your distress (from 1 to 5) and write a phrase on the matching line describing how you are feeling about this topic. Now that you know how you feel, move to Step #3 and write ten steps to overcome this fear. You can find tips below with a "possible scenario" to get you started.

Step #2: Gauging Your Feelings

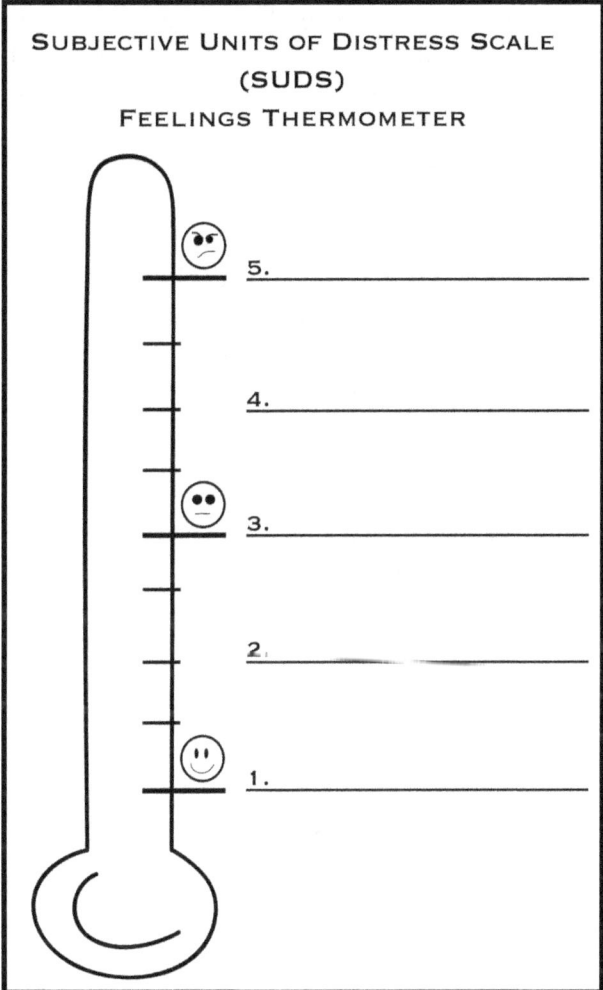

Step #3: Overcoming Obstacles

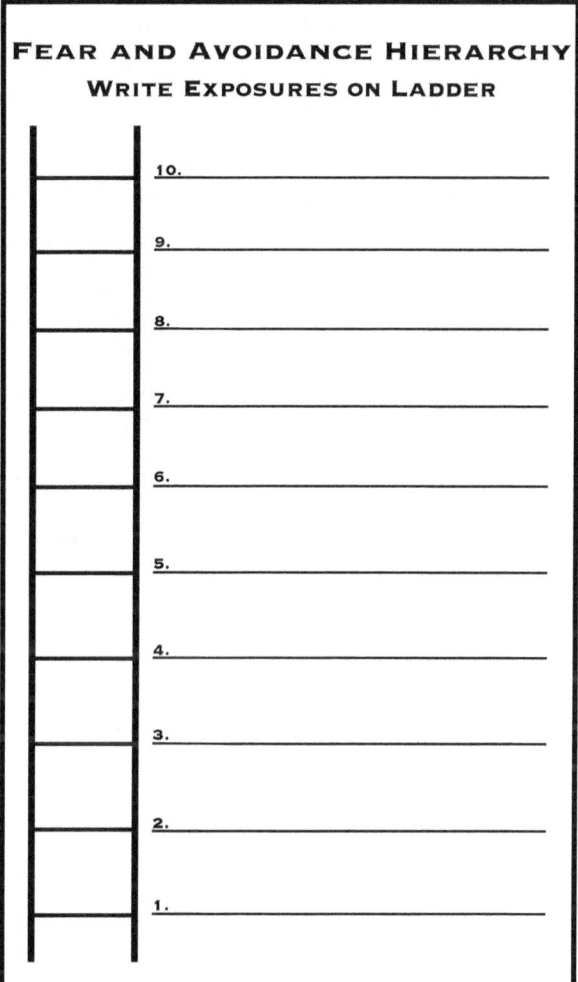

How You May Feel About Your Family:
5. Extreme anxiety/I'm afraid my parents will yell at me.
4. High anxiety/I don't feel like I can talk to my parents.
3. Moderately anxious/I am scared to talk to my family.
2. Mild anxiety/My thoughts spiral when I try talking to my dad.
1. No anxiety/I think I can to talk to my parents about anything.

Thoughts on Overcoming Family Fears:
10. I am confident to talk to my parents.
9. I will practice things to say to my parents.
8. I will journal ideas on how to express how I feel.
7. I will do breathing exercises to help me relax.
6. I will practice "I am" statements to increase my confidence.
5. I will work with a counselor to help give me pointers.
4. I will join a study group and identify what I still need to learn.
3. I will watch online videos with lessons about famiy drama.
2. I will watch a movie about family vacations.
1. I will listen to an upbeat song about loving families.

Communication Skills

Communication is key between you and your caregiver. As you get older and start to spend more time away from home—either at school with your friends or with after-school activities. As a family, you need to focus on setting up times to catch up with each other. One way to connect is to have set times and locations to get together (i.e., family dinner). Have some talking points prepared such as "Good thing, Bad thing," (also known as "Roses and Thorns") to help get the conversation rolling. This is an excellent activity because it gets everyone in the family involved—with a chance to talk while forming the habit of sharing not only any problems, but also good things that happened that day.

The goal for every family is that all communication comes from a place of **"Unconditional Love"** and **"Feeling Respected."** If your "Preferred Methods of Communication" is **"Spending Time Together"** or **"Hugs"** make sure to communicate this with your parents to make sure they know how important this is to you. Also, if one of your top communication methods is **"Compliments and Praise,"** then this is another important thing for them to know because yelling at you would be devastating. From a parent's perspective, many Moms might say that **"Helping Hand"** is their preferred method of communication because most Moms have multiple "balls in the air" at all times. Until they receive a **"Helping Hand,"** they likely will not have the time or energy to give you the **"Spending Time Together"** you are wanting to receive.

After completing the Reflections Publishing Communication Assessment on **page 10**, you can take a screenshot of your results and use it as talking points for a family activity. You can explain each of the "Preferred Methods of Communication" to your family members and you can conduct a live assessment with them.

Mindfulness Skills

This mindfulness technique is an excellent way to improve family connections.

"Gratitude Circle" Mindfulness Exercise

1. Find a place where all family members can get in a comfortable position with no distractions.
2. Begin taking long deep breaths to help center your thoughts and focus on the present moment.
3. Start this exercise by explaining the exercise so everyone understands they are each going to share an example of something they are grateful for and brings them joy.
4. During this exercise, everyone will practice active listening, showing interest, and providing the person talking their full attention.
5. Continue this exercise with no judgment as each person speaks.
6. At the end of the exercise, take time to sit and reflect about each person and what they are grateful for in their life—remembering the positive thoughts and emotions that each person choose to share with the group.

Well-Being Habit Tracker:

1. Fill out each Well-Being Habit Tracker category below.
2. When completed, check the box and note your subjective well-being from 1-10.

☐ **Sleep:** How many hours? _____ **Morning Light Exposure:** ☐ Well-Being Rating: _____

☐ **Exercise:** Length/Type? _____ Well-Being Rating: _____

☐ **Mindfulness:** Length/Type? _____ Well-Being Rating: _____

☐ **Nature:** Time spent/Activity outside? ____ / _____ Well-Being Rating: _____

☐ **Hydration:** I drank ☐☐☐☐☐☐ 8 oz. glasses of water. Well-Being Rating: _____

☐ **Nutrition:** Number of healthy meals or calories consumed? _____ Well-Being Rating: _____

☐ **Social Fitness:** Time spent/Activity? ____ / _____ Well-Being Rating: _____

☐ **Caring:** Act(s) of service? _____ Well-Being Rating: _____

☐ **Gratitude:** I am grateful for _____ Well-Being Rating: _____

☐ **Happiness:** _____ brought me joy! Well-Being Rating: _____

☐ **Laughter:** I laughed about _____

☐ **Smile:** I made someone smile by _____

☐ **Music:** I sang or listened to this song to motivate me and boost my mood and well-being:
_____

© 2024 Reflections Publishing LLC. All rights reserved.

Anxiety-Buster To-Do List:

1 Big Task - Let's Go!

☐ _____

2 Medium Tasks - Let's Do This!

☐ _____

☐ _____

3 Small Tasks - You Got This!

☐ _____

☐ _____

☐ _____

© 2024 Reflections Publishing LLC. All rights reserved.

• Friendships •

Who is in Your Friendship Bucket?

4II4U:

Did you know that having just one loyal friend provides a resistance and buffer to life stressors?

Friendship Bucket Activity Instructions:

Think about your group of friends. Put your friends into one of the buckets on the following page:

"24/7 Friend" Bucket
- I can share and trust intimate thoughts and feelings with this person.
- This individual is always a loyal, reliable, trustworthy friend—24 hours a day, 7 days a week.
- This person has a positive influence on me.
- I feel good about myself after spending time with this friend.
- This friend is happy for me when good things come my way.

"Common Interest Friend" Bucket
- I enjoy this person's company, but we do not share secrets or intimate thoughts and feelings.
- This friend is someone you likely met playing on the same sports team or extracurricular activity.

"Friend for a Season" Bucket
- I used to be really close friends with this person, but we have grown apart.
- I continue to have a friendly relationship with them.

"Peer Pressure Friend" Bucket
- This person has gotten you to do things you know are not morally correct.
- This individual encourages you to exclude others.

Knowing confidently who your true friends are is a gift. By identifying your friends as "24/7 Friends," "Common Interest Friends," "Friends for a Season," or "Peer Pressure Friends," you are identifying where to invest your time and energy in friendships. Being upset about a friendship that is no longer fruitful is a waste of your time and energy. It is okay to be friends with someone for "Just a Season." Some people come and go in our lives for a purpose or life lesson, and even though it may be hurtful when the friendship fizzles, it is okay to classify them as a "Friend for a Season."

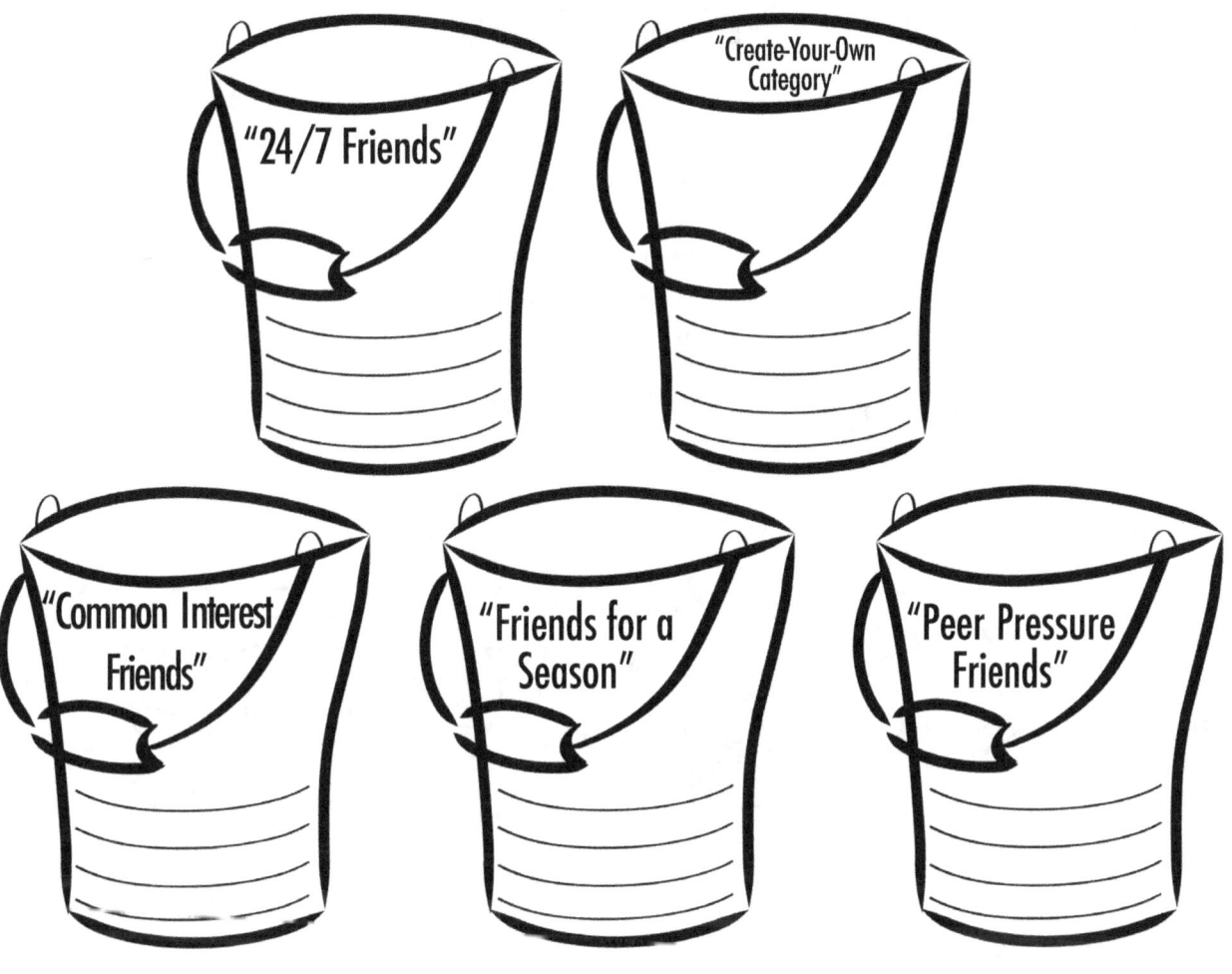

Friendship Checklist

Having trouble placing friends in these buckets? Here are some things to look for in a good friend:

☐ My friends are people who are my friend "24/7."
☐ My friends are honest, respectful, and loyal to me.
☐ My friends support me and my personal goals.
☐ My friends stand up for me in difficult situations.
☐ My friends are helpful and kind.
☐ I feel comfortable being myself when I am around my group of friends.
☐ I feel good about myself after being with my friends.
☐ I do not act differently when I am with my group of friends.
☐ My friends are nice to everyone and do not exclude others.

If any information in this playbook is upsetting, please talk to a parent/guardian, school counselor, teacher, or medical professional.
This book is sold with the understanding that the publisher and the author are not engaged in rendering medical, legal, or other professional advice or services.
If professional assistance is required, the services of a competent professional should be sought.

• Friendships •

Brain Power

According to Becht et al. (2020), having just one good, reliable friend can provide a buffer of protection in your brain. This childhood best friend can provide you with the developmental resilience you need to achieve your goals and develop strong social connections with your peers. Supportive friendships lead to more resilient brain functioning, which is highlighted below—affecting their neurodevelopmental trajectories within the social-cognitive realm.

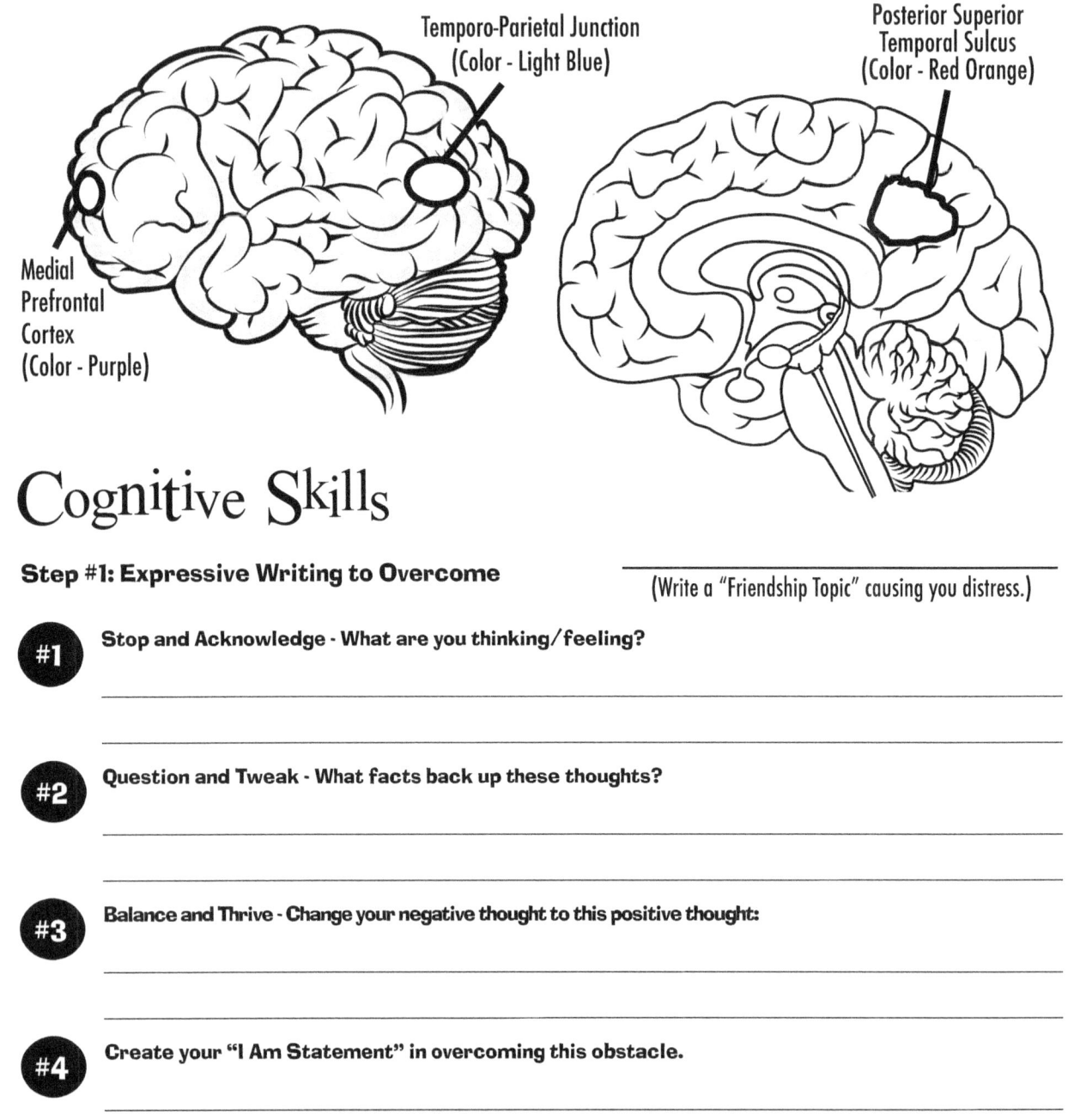

Temporo-Parietal Junction (Color - Light Blue)

Posterior Superior Temporal Sulcus (Color - Red Orange)

Medial Prefrontal Cortex (Color - Purple)

Cognitive Skills

Step #1: Expressive Writing to Overcome

_____
(Write a "Friendship Topic" causing you distress.)

#1 **Stop and Acknowledge** - What are you thinking/feeling?
_____
_____

#2 **Question and Tweak** - What facts back up these thoughts?
_____
_____

#3 **Balance and Thrive** - Change your negative thought to this positive thought:
_____
_____

#4 **Create your "I Am Statement"** in overcoming this obstacle.
_____

Cognitive Skills

_____

(Write a "Friendship Topic" causing you distress.)

INSTRUCTIONS for Steps #2 and #3:
On the line above, write the "Friendship Topic" causing you stress. Next, On the "Feelings Thermometer," color up to the point of your distress (from 1 to 5) and write a phrase on the matching line describing how you are feeling about this topic. Now that you know how you feel, move to Step #3 and write ten steps to overcome this fear. You can find tips below with a "possible scenario" to get you started.

Step #2: Gauging Your Feelings

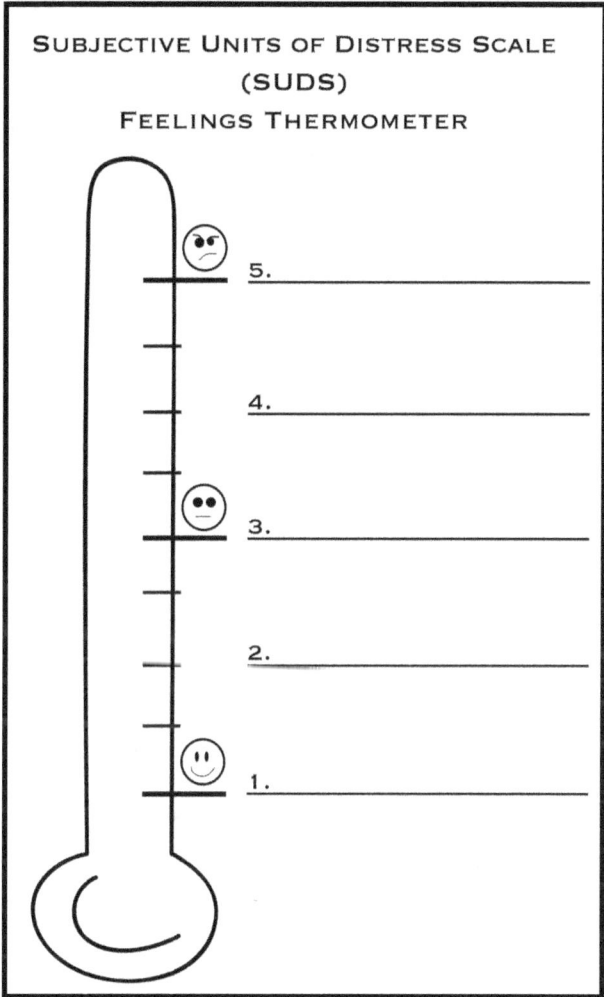

Step #3: Overcoming Obstacles

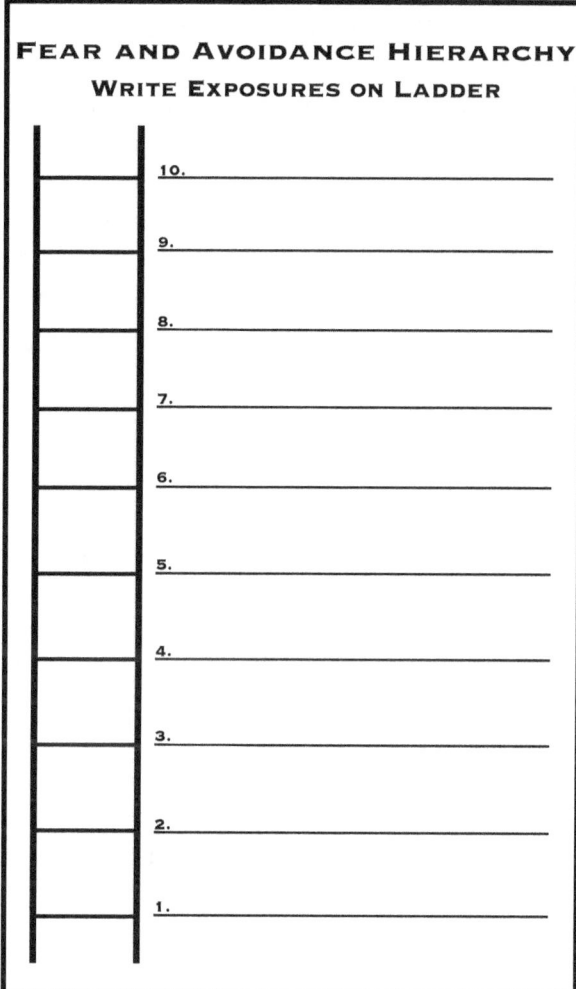

How you May Feel About Friendships:
5. Extreme anxiety/I don't think anyone is my friend.
4. High anxiety/My heart is racing because I don't trust people.
3. Moderately anxious/I think people are critiquing me.
2. Mild anxiety/I am pretty sure my friends are trustworthy.
1. No anxiety/I think everyone is my friend.

Overcoming Fear of New Friendships:
10. I will attend the end-of-year party for my grade.
9. I will share some personal information with a new friend.
8. I will meet a friend for coffee before school.
7. I will start a study group with some potential new friends.
6. I will ask someone in math class a homework question.
5. I will ask a new person to be my partner at practice warm-up.
4. I will say hello to everyone at school.
3. I will watch online videos about friendship.
2. I will watch a movie about middle/high school friendships.
1. I will listen to an upbeat song about friendship.

Communication Skills

Taking the Reflections Publishing Communication Assessment is critical to developing solid friendships because it lets you know your preferences and how your friends like to communicate. For example, you might have a female friend who, even if you remember to text her on her birthday, may be extremely hurt because she communicates through the action of gift-giving (**"Token of Friendship/Gift-Giving"**).

- If you pay attention to how people communicate with you (verbally or through their actions,) this is likely their "Preferred Method of Communication."

Looking through the lens of friendship, when we feel used or misunderstood, we can quickly deplete our energy supply. However, when we are with supportive friends, then they re-energize us. These are the types of friendships we want to have in our lives.

Mindfulness Skills

This mindfulness technique can deepen your ability to connect and have compassion towards your friends. This exercise provides you with practice to develop empathy and a loving attitude while nurturing and strengthening your relationships.

"Loving-Kindness" Mindfulness Meditation Exercise

1. Get in a comfortable position that is quiet with no distractions and close your eyes.
2. Begin taking long deep breaths and imagine any stress in your body exiting with each exhaled breath.
3. Direct loving and kind thoughts toward yourself, repeating positive affirmations such as: "May I be happy. May I be healthy. May I be safe. May I be at peace."
4. Now picture your friend and say the same above phrases about them.
5. Next picture loved ones and say the same above phrases about them too.
6. Repeat steps 3-5 above and when your mind wanders, gently bring your focus back to the exercise with no judgment.
7. In closing this meditative exercise, take several deep breaths bringing your awareness back to present.

Well-Being Habit Tracker:

1. **Fill out each Well-Being Habit Tracker category below.**
2. **When completed, check the box and note your subjective well-being from 1-10.**

- ☐ **Sleep:** How many hours? _____ **Morning Light Exposure:** ☐   Well-Being Rating: _____
- ☐ **Exercise:** Length/Type? _____   Well-Being Rating: _____
- ☐ **Mindfulness:** Length/Type? _____   Well-Being Rating: _____
- ☐ **Nature:** Time spent/Activity outside? ____ / _____   Well-Being Rating: _____
- ☐ **Hydration:** I drank ▢▢▢▢▢▢▢▢ 8 oz. glasses of water.   Well-Being Rating: _____
- ☐ **Nutrition:** Number of healthy meals or calories consumed? _____   Well-Being Rating: _____
- ☐ **Social Fitness:** Time spent/Activity? ____ / _____   Well-Being Rating: _____
- ☐ **Caring:** Act(s) of service? _____   Well-Being Rating: _____
- ☐ **Gratitude:** I am grateful for _____   Well-Being Rating: _____
- ☐ **Happiness:** _____ brought me joy!   Well-Being Rating: _____
- ☐ **Laughter:** I laughed about _____
- ☐ **Smile:** I made someone smile by _____
- ☐ **Music:** I sang or listened to this song to motivate me and boost my mood and well-being: _____

© 2024 Reflections Publishing LLC. All rights reserved.

Anxiety-Buster To-Do List:

1 Big Task - Let's Go!

- ☐ _____

2 Medium Tasks - Let's Do This!

- ☐ _____
- ☐ _____

3 Small Tasks - You Got This!

- ☐ _____
- ☐ _____
- ☐ _____

© 2024 Reflections Publishing LLC. All rights reserved.

• Peer Pressure •

Peer pressure is a challenge for all teenagers, and this section will reiterate and incorporate concepts discussed in the "What's Your Legacy? - Core Values" section. Peer Pressure is something that everyone deals with at some point in their life and it tests an individual's core beliefs and values. One of the best things you can do to combat peer pressure is to really work on building up your self-esteem and confidence. Teenagers who typically cave into peer pressure have low self-esteem and a tendency to do or say anything to fit into their peer group.

Here are some things to think about to help you when you are struggling on how to stand up for yourself—especially when someone is trying to get you to do something that you know in your heart is wrong.

1. If you know your core values and have a strong belief system, then it makes it easier to say "no" in pressure situations. Focusing on creating a strong sense of self and knowing who you are and what you stand for makes it much easier to say "no."

2. Have a game plan in place so when people try to get you to do something unwanted, then you can have a witty comeback that redirects your entire friend group to a more desired activity.

3. Choose your friends carefully. People who are your true friends will not try to force you to do something you do not want to do.

4. Make decisions and choices that you will not regret later. Ask any adult and they can tell you stories about classmates who made poor decisions. A bad choice or decision lasts a lifetime, and do not let anyone convince you otherwise.

5. Stay in a safe environment that will not place you in a possible bad situation.

6. A friend who has your back 24 hours a day/7 days a week (a 24/7 friend) will always support you and your morals. Their values will align with your own, so you never have to defend yourself. A true and loyal friend will always support and respect your choices and understand that your choices and decisions have a consequence for any action you perform.

List all of the ways you have experienced peer pressure:

_____
_____
_____
_____
_____
_____
_____
_____
_____

- **Doodle or Draw how you feel when you experience peer pressure:**

PEER PRESSURE

If any information in this playbook is upsetting, please talk to a parent/guardian, school counselor, teacher, or medical professional.
This book is sold with the understanding that the publisher and the author are not engaged in rendering medical, legal, or other professional advice or services.
If professional assistance is required, the services of a competent professional should be sought.

• Peer Pressure •

Brain Power

The influence of peer feedback and peer pressure on how to think shows up in activated clusters in the **Ventrolateral Prefrontal Cortex**, **Medial Prefrontal Cortex**, **Superior Temporal Gyrus/Sulcus**, and **Occipital Cortex**.

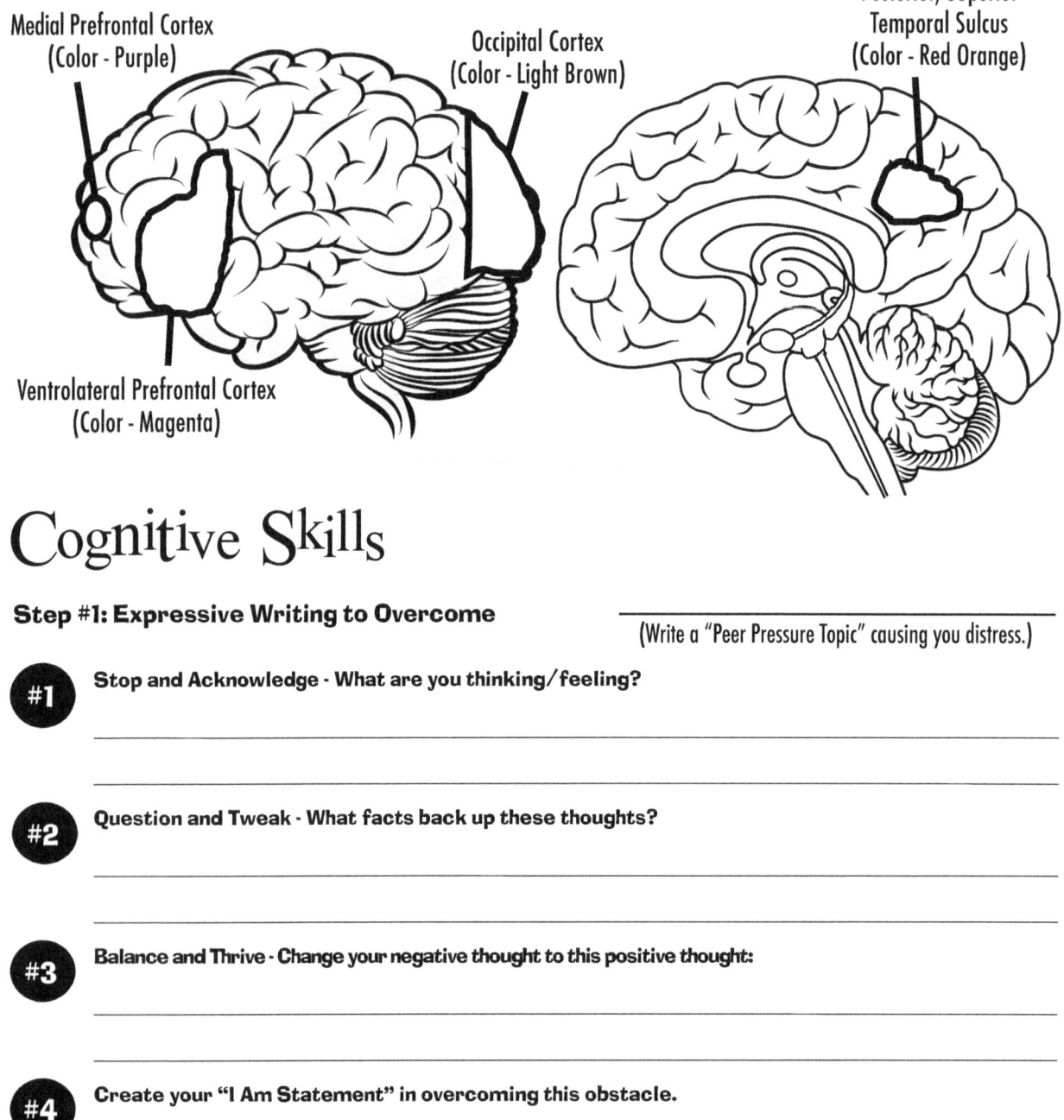

Medial Prefrontal Cortex (Color - Purple)
Occipital Cortex (Color - Light Brown)
Posterior, Superior Temporal Sulcus (Color - Red Orange)
Ventrolateral Prefrontal Cortex (Color - Magenta)

Cognitive Skills

Step #1: Expressive Writing to Overcome

(Write a "Peer Pressure Topic" causing you distress.)

#1 Stop and Acknowledge - What are you thinking/feeling?
___

#2 Question and Tweak - What facts back up these thoughts?
___

#3 Balance and Thrive - Change your negative thought to this positive thought:
___

#4 Create your "I Am Statement" in overcoming this obstacle.
___

-142-

Cognitive Skills

(Write a "Peer Pressure Topic" causing you distress.)

INSTRUCTIONS for Steps #2 and #3:
On the line above, write the "Peer Pressure Topic" causing you stress. Next, On the "Feelings Thermometer," color up to the point of your distress (from 1 to 5) and write a phrase on the matching line describing how you are feeling about this topic. Now that you know how you feel, move to Step #3 and write ten steps to overcome this fear. You can find tips below with a "possible scenario" to get you started.

Step #2: Gauging Your Feelings

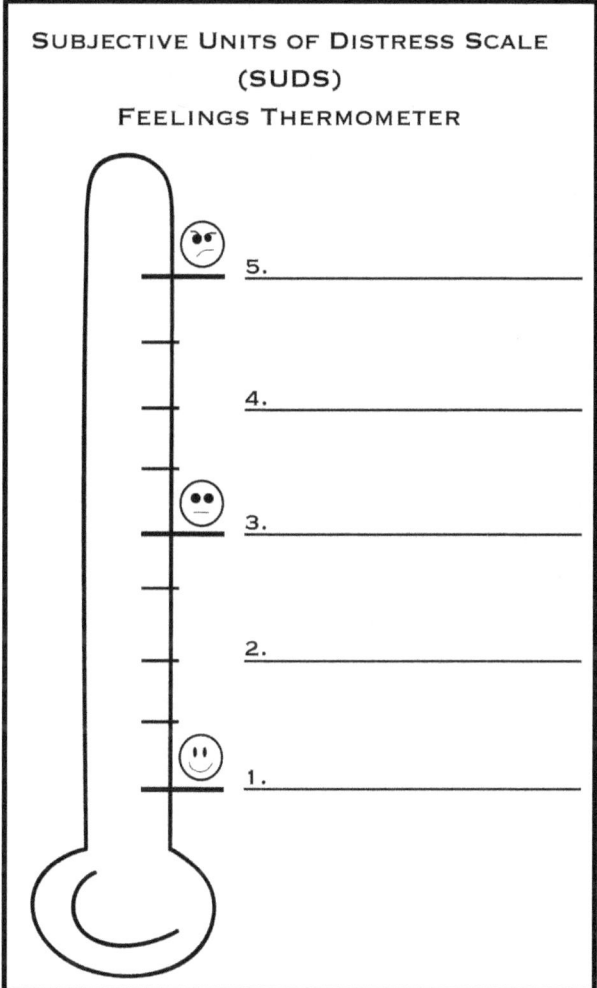

Step #3: Overcoming Obstacles

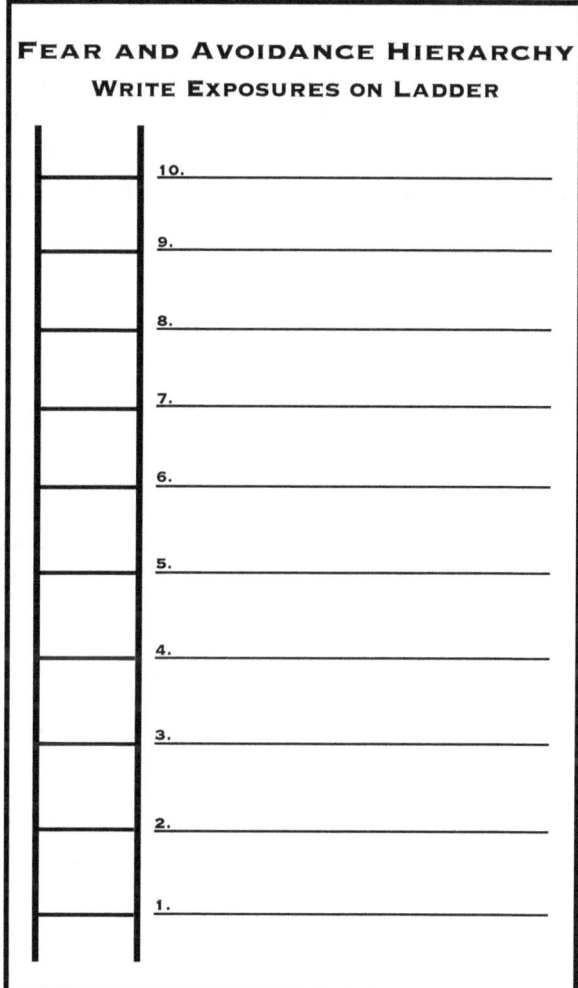

Possible Ideas on Feeling Peer Pressure:
5. Extreme anxiety/I am feeling emotional turmoil.
4. High anxiety/I feel overwhelmed by the pressure.
3. Moderately anxious/I'm feeling pressured to go along with friends.
2. Mild anxiety/I'm having trouble staying true to my values.
1. No anxiety/I haven't encountered a peer pressure situation.

Ideas on Overcoming Peer Pressure:
10. I am confident in handling peer pressure.
9. I will talk to my parents about helping with pressure.
8. I will do role playing for peer presssure.
7. I will do the breathing exercise that helps me to relax.
6. I will practice "I am" statements to increase my confidence.
5. I will work with a counselor to help with peer pressure.
4. I will join a study group and identify what I still need to learn.
3. I will watch online videos with lessons about peer pressure.
2. I will watch a movie about middle/high school pressure.
1. I will listen to an upbeat song about peer pressure.

Communication Skills

When you feel you are in a peer pressure situation, make sure to be assertive and clearly communicate your plans so there is no miscommunication. You can express your opinion regarding a situation you do not want to participate in, but just do so in a respectful manner. Again, knowing your core values and beliefs are helpful in these situations because your mind is already prepared to state your decision, without hesitation or wavering.

Never feel bad setting clear boundaries with your friends and making decisions that are the right decisions for you. You get to make your own choices and that goes both ways. Even when you may not agree with someone else's decisions or choices, you do not get to make decisions for them. Unless that person is a harm to themselves or others, only communicate on your own behalf.

Practice writing your own "Go-To Phrase" to stand up for yourself: _____
_____.

Mindfulness Skills

This mindfulness technique called STOP is effective with your age group. By utilizing this STOP exercise in peer pressure stiuations, you give yourself some separation and space from the stressful situation you are facing. The exercise gives you time to pause and reflect and think about the consequence of the decisions and/or actions you are about to make.

"STOP" Mindfulness Exercise

1. **S**TOP: When you feel or anticipate peer pressure mounting in your friend group, then take a moment to stop and pause regarding what you are about to do and give yourself a mental break to assess the situation.

2. **T**ake slow and deep breaths—breathing deeply through your nose on the inhale and breathing slowly out your mouth on the exhale.

3. **O**bserve everything around you with no judgement—your thoughts, feelings, and emotions. Acknowledge these thoughts and feelings, but remember that a thought or feeling is not a command or something you have to do just because it crossed your mind.

4. **P**roceed mindfully and make a conscious decision about how you want to respond. Do not give into external pressures and make decisions that align with your priorities, core values, and belief system.

Well-Being Habit Tracker:

1. **Fill out each Well-Being Habit Tracker category below.**
2. **When completed, check the box and note your subjective well-being from 1-10.**

- ☐ **Sleep:** How many hours? _____ **Morning Light Exposure:** ☐ Well-Being Rating: _____
- ☐ **Exercise:** Length/Type? _____ Well-Being Rating: _____
- ☐ **Mindfulness:** Length/Type? _____ Well-Being Rating: _____
- ☐ **Nature:** Time spent/Activity outside? ____ / _____ Well-Being Rating: _____
- ☐ **Hydration:** I drank ☐☐☐☐☐☐☐☐ 8 oz. glasses of water. Well-Being Rating: _____
- ☐ **Nutrition:** Number of healthy meals or calories consumed? _____ Well-Being Rating: _____
- ☐ **Social Fitness:** Time spent/Activity? ____ / _____ Well-Being Rating: _____
- ☐ **Caring:** Act(s) of service? _____ Well-Being Rating: _____
- ☐ **Gratitude:** I am grateful for _____ Well-Being Rating: _____
- ☐ **Happiness:** _____ brought me joy! Well-Being Rating: _____
- ☐ **Laughter:** I laughed about _____
- ☐ **Smile:** I made someone smile by _____
- ☐ **Music:** I sang or listened to this song to motivate me and boost my mood and well-being: _____

© 2024 Reflections Publishing LLC. All rights reserved.

Anxiety-Buster To-Do List:

1 Big Task - Let's Go!
- ☐ _____

2 Medium Tasks - Let's Do This!
- ☐ _____
- ☐ _____

3 Small Tasks - You Got This!
- ☐ _____
- ☐ _____
- ☐ _____

© 2024 Reflections Publishing LLC. All rights reserved.

Section Ten

The Resilience Game Plan Post-Assessment

• *The Resilience Game Plan* Post-Assessment •

- **STEP #1:** Take this Post-Assessment after completing *The Resilience Game Plan*.
- **STEP #2:** Rank your Subjective Well-Being (from 1-10) and then ***For every "Yes" response, write an "X" on the right-hand line.**

Subjective Well-Being: (Rank from 1-10)

1. How satisfied are you with your life? (1 Extremely Unsatisfied - to - 10 Extremely Satisfied) _____
2. What are your feelings about people or situations in your life? (1 Extreme Anxiety - to - 10 Extremely Peaceful) _____
3. Do you feel your life has meaning and purpose? (1 Extremely Disagree - to - 10 Extremely Agree) _____

WHAT'S YOUR GAME PLAN? • WARM-UP

Academic Pressures:

1. Do you feel you belong and are connected at your school?
   ☐ Yes - I belong to teams/clubs   ☐ No - I feel like an outsider   *** (If "Yes," write "X" here:)** _____
2. Do you find your schoolwork engaging and interesting?
   ☐ Yes - I am learning for the "love of learning"   ☐ No - I am a "robo-learner"/only learn for tests _____
3. Do you find your schoolwork meaningful and relevant to real life?
   ☐ Yes - I am learning life-long skills   ☐ No - I am a "robo-learner"/only learn for tests _____
4. Do you feel respected and valued at school?
   ☐ Yes   ☐ No _____
5. Do you have a close connection to at least one teacher at school?
   ☐ Yes - list name: _____   ☐ No _____

Habit Formation: New Habits and Breaking Old Habits:

1. Do you have habits you want to break? If Yes, list: _____ _____
2. Do you have new habits you want to form? If Yes, list: _____ _____

What's Your Legacy? Knowing Your Core Values:

1. How do you want to be remembered after you graduate? List: _____

Who Are Your Personal "Cheerleaders," Coaches, and/or Mentors:

1. Do you have a mentor/cheerleader in your life?
   ☐ Yes - list name: _____   ☐ No _____

WHAT'S YOUR GAME PLAN? • LIFE CHOICES

Self and Identity: List Your Peer Friend Group: _____

1. Do you associate your identity with your peer group? If "Yes," list your friend group on the line above and put "X" here: _____

Social Media:

1. Do you feel good about yourself after spending time on Social Media (e.g., Instagram, Snapchat, and TikTok)?
   ☐ Yes - I feel good about myself.   ☐ No - I feel worse about myself _____

Time Management - Life Balance:

1. Do you think you have a good life balance?
   ☐ Yes   ☐ Average   ☐ No _____

WHAT'S YOUR GAME PLAN? + LIFE CRISES

Abuse - Domestic, Physical, and Verbal:

1. Do you have a concern of feeling unsafe at school and home?
   ☐ Yes - List location: _____ ☐ No _____

2. Do you feel anxious at home (i.e., not enough food or do not feel protected)?
   ☐ Yes - List concern: _____ ☐ No _____

Anxiety:

1. Do you consider yourself an anxious person? If yes, list things that make you feel anxious:
   ☐ Yes - List: _____ ☐ No _____

Depression:

1. Do you feel depressed or down? If yes, list why you may feel this way or what makes you depressed:
   ☐ Yes - List: _____ ☐ No _____

Substance Abuse - Alcohol and Drugs:

1. Do either you, a friend, or a family member abuse alcohol and drugs?
   ☐ Yes - List: _____ ☐ No _____

Self-Harm:

1. Have you ever wanted to hurt yourself?
   ☐ Yes - List how you would hurt yourself: _____ ☐ No _____

WHAT'S YOUR GAME PLAN? + RELATIONSHIPS

Bullying/Cyberbullying:

1. Have you ever been bullied or been the recipient of cyberbullying?
   ☐ Yes - List situation: _____ ☐ No _____

Family or Guardian:

1. How would you rate your relationship with your family or guardian?
   ☐ Good ☐ Average ☐ Bad - List situation: _____

Friendship:

1. Are you in a peer-pressuring and/or non-supportive friend group?
   ☐ Yes - List your friends: _____ ☐ No _____

Peer Pressure:

1. Have you ever been put in a peer pressure situation?
   ☐ Yes - List situation: _____ ☐ No _____

List Your Stress Level Today (1 = not very stressed and 10 = very stressed) **(1-10)** _____

© 2023 Reflections Publishing LLC. All rights reserved.
This book is sold with the understanding that the publisher and the author are not engaged in rendering medical, legal, or other professional advice or services.
If professional assistance is required, the services of a competent professional should be sought.

Section Eleven

4114U

•

Appendix

- Depression Game Plan - 152
- Nutrition Game Plan - 153
- Brain Power Color Chart - 154

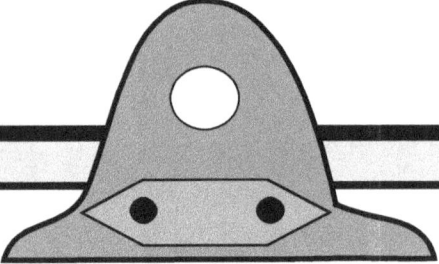

• Depression Game Plan •

Many people are struggling and not feeling like they did before the pandemic occurred. For some individuals, puberty triggers new feelings including depression, so be kind to yourself during these years. There are many ways to help you start feeling better, but know that people cannot read your mind; you need to communicate how you are feeling. **If you are in a downward spiral or experiencing an emergency, seek help immediately from a parent/guardian, school counselor, or medical professional.**

- Here is a checklist of things to discuss with your parent/guardian or medical professional:

- ☐ It is normal to experience a "Natural Depression"—where you may not feel like yourself for up to one year after a loved one has passed away. Share any losses, major changes, or trauma with your doctor that might affect how you feel.

- ☐ Sometimes your gut microbiome and the gut-brain axis can get out of sync, so have your doctor do a test for 16S rRNA gene sequencing. Also, try eating a Mediterranean diet which is known to help get your gut healthy.

- ☐ Ask your doctor to conduct a Pharmacogenetic (PGx) (Genomind™) or Psychotropic (GeneSight®) test to assess your genetics to create your personal therapeutic game plan. These tests identify potential gene-drug interactions and how your body metabolizes medicine.

- ☐ Ask your doctor to order an MTHFR blood test as this gene is often linked to depression.

- ☐ Check into Cognitive Behavior Therapy (CBT) or iCBT, as it is known to help treat depression.

- ☐ Pet therapy is notorious for assisting individuals who are depressed or suffering from post traumatic stress.

- ☐ Go outside, get grounded, and exercise every day—it is the best known therapy for depression.

- ☐ Socialize and find those 24/7 friends to reduce depression.

Just remember that doctors and educators went into their area of practice because they love to work with and help adolescents, so do not hesitate to talk to them and ask for assistance—whether medically or academically.

© 2024 Reflections Publishing LLC. All rights reserved.
This book is sold with the understanding that the publisher and the author are not engaged in rendering medical, legal, or other professional advice or services. If professional assistance is required, the services of a competent professional should be sought.

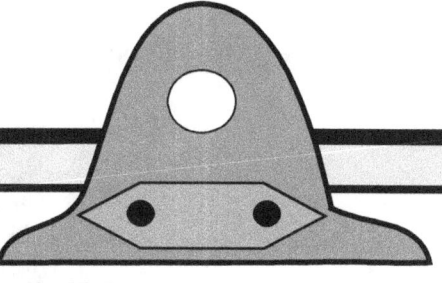

Date:

• Nutrition Game Plan •

Time:	Place:	Thoughts/Feelings:	Food:	# of Healthy Meals or Daily Calories:
Breakfast:				
Snack:				
Lunch:				
Snack:				
Dinner:				
Snack:				
Hydration:	I drank _____ 8 oz glasses of water.			

© 2024 Reflections Publishing LLC. All rights reserved.

NUTRITION GAME PLAN

• Brain Power Color Chart •

Instructions: Fill in the boxes with the color indicated. These colors match the markings in the Brain Power section.

☐ **Red – Amygdala**
Processes emotions and certain types of learning and memory (Bear, Connors, & Paradiso, 2007).

☐ **Red Orange – Posterior Superior Temporal Sulcus**
Plays a "role in detecting, predicting, and reasoning about social actions and the intentions underlying actions" (Allison et al., 2000).

☐ **Orange – Anterior Cingulate Cortex**
"Complex cognitive functions, such as empathy, impulse control, emotion, and decision-making" (Neuroscientifically Challenged, 2023).

☐ **Peach – Nucleus Accumbens**
Believed to "play an important role in motivation, reward, and addiction" (Neuroscientifically Challenged, 2023).

☐ **Pink – Dorsal Anterior Cingulate Cortex**
Known for conflict monitoring, error processing, accomplishing tasks, and reaching goals (Encyclopedia of Neuroscience, 2009).

☐ **Magenta – Ventromedial Prefrontal Cortex**
May reflect heightened sensitivity to threats and safety conditions (Britton et al., 2013).

☐ **Purple – Medial Prefrontal Cortex**
Long-term assessments of your environmental experiences are stored here (Bonnici et al., 2012).

☐ **Light Purple – Ventral Striatum**
Believed "to be involved in reward processing" (Neuroscientifically Challenged, 2023).

☐ **Blue – Hypothalamus**
Processes your body temperature, ability to sleep, and need to eat and drink (Bear, Connors, & Paradiso, 2007).

☐ **Sky Blue – Insula**
Believed "to play a role in a number of functions: self-awareness, perception, and cognition" (Neuroscientifically Challenged, 2023).

☐ **Light Blue – Temporo-Parietal Junction**
"Involved specifically in reasoning about the contents of another person's mind"—theory of mind (Saxe & Kanwisher 2003).

☐ **Aqua – Lateral Occipital Cortex**
"Known to be involved in visual object perception" (i.e., face-processing) (Nagy, Greenlee, & Kovács, 2012).

☐ **Golden Yellow – Cerebellum**
"Role in memory, cognition, emotion, coordination, balance, posture, & smooth motor movements" (Neuroscientifically Challenged, 2023).

☐ **Yellow – Dorsolateral Prefrontal Cortex**
Plays a role in impulse control (Bonnici et al., 2012).

☐ **Yellow Green – Medial Parietal**
Plays a role in "memory recall, visual scene processing, navigation, and default mode network (Silson et al., 2019).

☐ **Green – Posterior Cingulate Cortex**
Internally-generated thought processes and self-directed cognitions (Leech & Sharp, 2014).

☐ **Jade Green – Precuneus**
Believed involvement "ranging from memory to consciousness" (Neuroscientifically Challenged, 2023).

☐ **Navy Blue – Thalamus**
"Plays important roles in consciousness and arousal" (Neuroscientifically Challenged, 2023).

☐ **Burgandy – Superior Temporal Sulcus**
"Hub for social and cognition perception of faces..others' actions, mental states, and language" (Deen et al., 2015).

☐ **Brown – Orbitalfrontal Cortex**
Believed "to be involved in decision-making and emotional processing" (Neuroscientifically Challenged, 2023).

☐ **Light Brown – Occipital Cortex**
"Retinotopic organization of spatial frequency processing (Sasaki et al., 2001).

☐ **Tan – Putamen**
Involved in motor control (Bear, Connors, & Paradiso, 2007).

☐ **Gray – Hippocampus**
Plays a role in learning (Bear, Connors, & Paradiso, 2007); short-term memories are embedded here (Bonnici et al., 2012).

☐ **Black – Sugenual Cingulate**
"Critical brain region in emotion processing and the pathogenesis of mood disorders" (Mayberg et al., 2005).

Section Twelve

4114U

•

Notes

• Section Three: How *The Resilience Game Plan* Will Benefit You •

Developing a Growth Mindset

12 *when you develop a growth mindset, you will learn at a young age that through your hard work and determination, you can achieve a stronger academic performance and gain more confidence in your abilities*: Haimovitz, K., & Dweck, C. S. (2017). The origins of children's growth and fixed mindsets: New research and a new proposal. *Child Development, 88*(6), 1849–1859. https://doi.org/10.1111/cdev.12955

12 *Evidence-based research conducted by Carol Dweck indicates that the earlier you can create a foundation of a growth mindset along with positive thinking, the sooner you are setting yourself up for a life of success and healthy emotional and social well-being*: Campbell, J. A., & Løkken, I. M. (2023). Inside out: A scoping review on optimism, growth mindsets, and positive psychology for child well-being in ECEC. *Education Sciences, 13*(1), 29. https://doi.org/10.3390/educsci13010029; Dweck, C. (2017). *Mindset: Changing the way you think to fulfill your potential*. Random House.

12 *Researchers coined the concept of developmental resilience as they discovered that resilient children all seem to possess the following factors*: Siegler, R., Saffron, J. R., Gershoff, E. T., Eisenberg, N., & Leaper, C. (2020). *How Children Develop* (6th ed.). Worth Publishers.

12 *1. Personal traits (e.g., compassionate to others, confidence in achieving goals, and intelligence)*
    2. Responsive and supportive caregiver: Masten, A., Best, K., & Garmezy, N. (1990). Resilience and development: Contributions from the study of children who overcome adversity. *Development and Psychopathology, 2*(4), 425-444. doi:10.1017/S0954579400005812; Samcroff, A. J. (1998). Environmental risk factors in infancy. *Pediatrics, 102*(5 Suppl E):1287–1292.

13 *If you never fail at something when you are young, the research indicates you are more likely not to know how to cope when you struggle with something as an adolescent, young adult, and even during your adult years*: Campbell, J. A., & Løkken, I. M. (2023). Inside out: A scoping review on optimism, growth mindsets, and positive psychology for child well-being in ECEC. *Education Sciences, 13*(1), 29. https://doi.org/10.3390/educsci13010029

13 *the smartest children in the world in elementary school, do not always end up the smartest adults*: Siegler, R. S. (1992). The Other Alfred Binet. *Developmental Psychology, 28*(2), 179–190. https://doi.org/10.1037/0012-1649.28.2.179

• Section Five: Playbook Strategy #1: Understanding Brain Power •

20 *Early adolescence through young adulthood is a sensitive period where social and environmental stressors can potentially alter a developing brain*: Selemon, L. D., & Zecevic, N. (2015). Schizophrenia: A tale of two critical periods for prefrontal cortical development. *Translational Psychiatry, 5*(8), e623–e623. https://doi.org/10.1038/tp.2015.115

20 *Harvard scientists David Hubel and Torsten Wiesel named this brain process* **plasticity**, *which occurs when your brain is molded like plastic based on your life experiences*: Hubel, D., & Wiesel, T. (2012). David Hubel and Torsten Wiesel. *Neuron (Cambridge, Mass.), 75*(2), 182–184. https://doi.org/10.1016/j.neuron.2012.07.002; Jensen, F. E., & Nutt, A. E. (2015). *The teenage brain: A neuroscientist's survival guide to raising adolescents and young adults*. Harper, an imprint of HarperCollinsPublishers.

20 *Eagleman coined the phrase* **livewire** *in place of* **plasticity** *because the brain is constantly changing and the word plasticity, possibly meaning, occurring once and molded for good*: Eagleman, D. (2020). *Livewired: The inside story of the ever-changing brain* (1st ed.). Pantheon Books.

Human Brain Anatomy:

21 *During your teenage years, your brain is only 80 percent developed—wiring together from the bottom up and from the back to the front. This explains why teens struggle with decision-making and making good choices, as the Frontal Lobe area is the last to develop. The synapses strengthen as brain cells in neural pathways and synapses are actively repeated*: Jensen, F. E., & Nutt, A. E. (2015). *The teenage brain: A neuroscientist's survival guide to raising adolescents and young adults*. Harper, an imprint of HarperCollinsPublishers.

• Section Five: Playbook Strategy #2: Learning Cognitive Skills •

22 *Of those thoughts, 80 percent are negative, and 95 are repetitive. Unless we make a point to retrain our brains, negative thoughts will consume our lives. Cognitive Behavior Specialists have even created a term called Automatic Negative Thoughts (ANT)*: National Science Foundation. (2012). *Bothered by negative, unwanted thoughts? Just throw them away.* NewsRX LLC.

22 *The good news is that evidence-based research supports the theory that we can all build new "brain pathways"*

22 *and stop these negative and ruminating thoughts*: Harper, N. J., Fernee, C. R., & Gabrielsen, L. E. (2021). Nature's role in outdoor therapies: An umbrella review. *International Journal of Environmental Research and Public Health, 18*(10), 5117. https://doi.org/10.3390/ijerph18105117

22 *techniques assist in building these new brain pathways*: Sperling, J. (2021). *Find your fierce: How to put social anxiety in its place.* Magination Press.

22 *Concepts such as: determining your values; setting your goals; understanding your emotions; identifying anxiety in your body and the cause; matching your thoughts to feelings; recording your thoughts, feelings, actions, and behaviors; and practicing mindfulness behaviors until they are habits*: Sperling, J. (2021). *Find your fierce: How to put social anxiety in its place.* Magination Press.

22 *the benefit of learning these Cognitive Skills techniques is that when you feel depressed or anxious, The RGP strategies will teach you to automatically replace negative thoughts with more productive, positive, and beneficial cognitions*: Rohde, P., Stice, E., Shaw, H., & Gau, J. M. (2015). Effectiveness trial of an indicated ognitive-behavioral group adolescent depression prevention program versus bibliotherapy and brochure control at 1- and 2-year follow-up. *Journal of Consulting and Clinical Psychology, 83*(4), 736–747. https://doi.org/10.1037/ccp0000022

23 *creating an "I Am Statement" is a self-affirmation that can provide a barrier to harmful or threatening experiences, lower your feelings of stress, and improve your physical and mental well-being. Through "I Am Statements," these affirmations can elevate a student's academic performance. When you look through the lens of personally adopting a growth mindset, you are expanding your mind—academically, behaviorally, and emotionally*. Cascio, C. N., O'Donnell, M. B., Tinney, F. J., Lieberman, M. D., Taylor, S. E., Strecher, V. J., & Falk, E. B. (2016). Self-affirmation activates brain systems associated with self-related processing and reward and is reinforced by future orientation. *Social Cognitive and Affective Neuroscience, 11*(4), 621–629. https://doi.org/10.1093/scan/nsv136

23 *these self-affirmations have potentially long-lasting effects as they can replace negative, ruminating thoughts by creating an adaptive, positive feedback loop in your self-related processing and reward pathways in your brain*: Cohen, G. L., & Sherman, D. K. (2014). The Psychology of change: Self-affirmation and social psychological intervention. *Annual Review of Psychology, 65*(1), 333–371. https://doi.org/10.1146/annurev-psych-010213-115137; Memarian, N., Torre, J. B., Haltom, K. E., Stanton, A. L., & Lieberman, M. D. (2017). Neural activity during affect labeling predicts expressive writing effects on well-being: GLM and SVM approaches. *Social Cognitive and Affective Neuroscience, 12*(9), 1437–1447. https://doi.org/10.1093/scan/nsx084

Step #2: Gauging Your Emotions

25 *gauge your feelings on the provided Subjective Units of Distress Scale (SUDS) "Feelings Thermometer"....step back and acknowledge, and rate your level of anxiety/distress*: Abramowitz, J. S., Deacon, B. J., & Whiteside, S. P. H. (2019). *Exposure therapy for anxiety: Principles and practice.* Guilford Press.

Step #3: Overcoming Obstacles

26 *your "Fear and Avoidance Hierarchy Ladder." This framework provides an exposure and response prevention (ERP) plan that identifies what will personally help you to work through your specific fears. As you build this framework, you must turn your focus inward as you self-assess what is triggering you and the baby steps you will need to take to overcome the situation*: Langley, A. K., Bergman, L., McCracken, J., & Piacentini, J. C. (2004). Impairment in childhood anxiety disorders: Preliminary examination of the child anxiety impact scale–parent version. *Journal of Child and Adolescent Psychopharmacology, 14*(1), 105–114. http://doi.org/10.1089/104454604773840544

26 *You will create a fear hierarchy of graduated exposures—starting with your least to most feared stimuli. You will then systematically progress up your graduated exposure list—moving up the ladder, rung-by-rung until you reach the top step. At this point, you will have overcome your fear and anxiety*: Hagopian, L. P., & Jennett, H. K. (2008). Behavioral assessment and treatment of anxiety in individuals with intellectual disabilities and autism. *Journal of Developmental Physical and Disabilities 20,* 467–483. https://doi.org/10.1007/s10882-008-9114-8

• Section Four: Playbook Strategy #3: Learning Communication Skills•

27 *The goal is to equip you with adaptive communication skills to make sure you have healthy and meaningful relationships in your life*: Kanine, R. M., Bush, M. L., Davis, M., Jones, J. D., Sbrilli, M. D., & Young, J. F. (2023). Depression in pediatric primary care: Implementation and outcomes of interpersonal psychotherapy—Adolescent Skills Training. *Child Psychiatry and Human Development, 54*(1), 96–108. DOI: https://doi.org/10.1007/s10578-021-01222-6

27 *Communication plays a key role in interpersonal problem-solving skills and these skills can improve relationships and deter the development of depressive symptoms in adolescents*: Young, J. F., Mufson, L., & Schueler, C. M. (2016). *Preventing adolescent depression: Interpersonal psychotherapy–adolescent skills training.* Oxford University Press

- **Feeling Respected**

27 *When used as a noun, respect can mean when a person shows respect to another person or as a verb when you respect someone. Respect is also used in deference to an elder or to be polite; however, respect can run much deeper on a fundamental human level. True respect should lead us to oppose discrimination against other individuals (i.e., age, gender, sexuality, race or religion). Respect can stand for not silencing or insulting another human being—even if we fundamentally disagree with them*: Isaacs, D. (2020). Respect. *Journal of Pediatrics and Child Health, 56*(2), 189–190. https://doi-org.ezp-prod1.hul.harvard.edu/10.1111/jpc.14663

- **Helping Hand**

28 *experience increased well-being. For males, this includes experiencing positive social relations, the feeling of purpose/meaning in life, and self-acceptance. For females, this also includes pro-social interactions, a sense of purpose/meaning in life, and better overall health*: Schwartz, C. E., Keyl, P. M., Marcum, J. P., & Bode, R. (2009). Helping others shows differential benefits on health and well-being for male and female teens. *Journal of Happiness Studies, 10*(4), 431–448. https://doi.org/10.1007/s10902-008-9098-1

28 *By cultivating a civic responsibility at a young age, you lay a framework for yourself of compassion and sensitivity towards others. By learning compassionate skills at a young age, you are preparing yourself to be a future problem solver in our multifaceted, diverse, and complicated world*: Stapleton, B. (2009). Connecting with kids: Lending a helping hand. *Parenting for High Potential, 21*.

- **Hugs**

28 *The power of physical touch or a hug can fill a person's love tank*: Wang, Y., Zhao, T., Zhang, Y., Li, S., & Cong, X. (2021). Positive effects of kangaroo mother care on long-term breastfeeding rates, growth, and neurodevelopment in preterm infants. *Breastfeeding Medicine, 16*(4), 282–291. https://doi.org/10.1089/bfm.2020.0358

- **Spending Time Together**

28 *Analyzing research from the American Time Use Survey, Price (2008) also discovered that the quality of time between a parent and child decreases as a child gets older; hence, these findings significantly correlate the birth order and a child's outcome. Furthermore, in a family with two children, research shows that the first-born child receives 40 percent more time than the second-born child*: Price, J. (2008). Parent-child quality time: Does birth order matter? *The Journal of Human Resources, 43*(1), 240–265. https://www.jstor.org/stable/40057344

- **Token of Friendship/Gift-Giving**

29 *Note: Since close relationships are linked to an individual's sense of self, you (as the gift giver) are motivated to purchase a gift that you know your friend wants to receive; however, you can experience internal conflict when buying a gift that differs from your own personal identity and self-concept*: Ward, M. K., & Broniarczyk, S. M.. (2011). It's not me, it's you: How gift giving creates giver identity threat as a function of social closeness. *The Journal of Consumer Research, 38*(1), 164-181. https://www.jstor.org/stable/10.1086/658166

29 *Knowing and understanding the internal battle a purchaser experiences can explain how this can elevate a person's inner need to validate oneself with material items*: Ward, M. K., & Broniarczyk, S. M. (2011). It's not me, it's you: How gift giving creates giver identity threat as a function of social closeness. *The Journal of Consumer Research, 38*(1), 164–181. https://www.jstor.org/stable/10.1086/658166

- **Unconditional Love**

29 *Some may question if unconditional love is actually a form of communication, but functional neuroimaging scans prove this as true. Comparing romantic to maternal love in the brain, they discovered that by researching overlapping regions in the brain's reward system, this also proved unconditional love to be a form of communication. Their findings showed a significant activation location in the experimental condition compared to the control condition. Additionally, Beauregard et. al., (2008) findings indicated that regions of the brain such as "the Middle Insula, Superior Parietal Lobule, Right Periaqueductal Gray, Right Globus Pallidus (Medial), Right Caudate Nucleus (Dorsal Head), Left Ventral Tegmental Area and Left Rostro-Dorsal Anterior Cingulate Cortex" all indicate that "unconditional love" is mediated by a distinct neural network relative to that mediating other emotions. This network contains cerebral structures known to be involved in romantic love or maternal love. Some of these structures represent key components of the brain's reward system*: Beauregard, M., Courtemanche, J., Paquette, V., & St-Pierre, É. L. (2009). The neural basis of unconditional love. *Psychiatry Research: Neuroimaging, 172*(2), 93–98. https://doi.org/10.1016/j.pscychresns.2008.11.003

• Section Five: Playbook Strategy #4: Learning Mindfulness Skills •

30   *In this section, for each life topic, you will find a specific mindfulness meditation technique to help you work through the difficult life topic you are navigating. Mindfulness techniques are considered a state of consciousness where you will focus on a moment-to-moment awareness of your internal and external state (e.g., emotions, physical sensations, and thoughts) in a non-judgmental way*: Brown, K. W., & Ryan, R. M. (2003). The benefits of being present. *Journal of Personality and Social Psychology, 84*(4), 822–848. https://doi.org/10.1037/0022-3514.84.4.822

30   *These three components **intention**, **attention**, and **attitude***: Zoogman, S., Goldberg, S. B., Hoyt, W. T., & Miller, L. (2015). Mindfulness interventions with youth: A meta-analysis. *Mindfulness, 6*(2), 290–302. https://doi.org/10.1007/s12671-013-0260-4

• Section Five: Playbook Strategy #5: Developing New Habits •

Well-Being Habit Tracker

• Sleep

34   *Sleep is one of the most important things we do all day, and getting a good night's sleep is critical to your health. According to neuroscientist and author Dr. Frances E. Jensen, sleep is as important as the air you breathe and the food you eat and helps you to manage your stress levels*: Jensen, F. E., & Nutt, A. E. (2015). *The teenage brain: A neuroscientist's survival guide to raising adolescents and young adults*. Harper, an imprint of HarperCollinsPublishers.

34   *research indicates that when you get a good night's sleep, everything you learned that day gets stored in your working memory for you to access during your test...Make sure you get at least 8 hours of sleep*: Jensen, F. E., & Nutt, A. E. (2015). *The teenage brain: A neuroscientist's survival guide to raising adolescents and young adults*. Harper, an imprint of HarperCollinsPublishers.

34   *expose yourself to bright morning light...to help you wake up and start your day*. Crowley, S. J., & Eastman, C. I. (2017). Human adolescent phase response curves to bright white light. *Journal of Biological Rhythms, 32*(4), 334–344. https://doi.org/10.1177/0748730417713423

34   *Many years ago, people lived outdoor lifestyles where sleep, moods, and circadian rhythmic cycles aligned with natural light cycles. For increased well-being, identify activities in nature during daylight hours to help your mood and sleep*: Jensen, F. E., & Nutt, A. E. (2015). *The teenage brain: a neuroscientist's survival guide to raising adolescents and young adults*. Harper, an imprint of HarperCollinsPublishers.

• Exercise

35   *Through evidence-based research, PA is strongly linked to well-being*: Taylor, L., De Neve, J., DeBurst, L., & Khanna, D. (2022). *Well-being in education in childhood and adolescence*. International Baccalaureate Organization.

35   *PA is known to improve physical health which improves your neurocognitive health*: Stillman, C. M., Cohen, J., Lehman, M. E., & Erickson, K. I. (2016). Mediators of physical activity on neurocognitive function: A review at multiple levels of Analysis. *Frontiers in Human Neuroscience, 10*, 626–626. https://doi.org/10.3389/fnhum.2016.00626

35   *PA as "any bodily movement produced by skeletal muscles that requires energy expenditure"*: World Health Organization (2010). Global Recommendations on Physical Activity for Health. WHO Press.

35   *any activity that raises the heart rate above resting levels*: Caspersen, C. J., Powell, K. E., & Christenson, G. M. (1985). Physical activity, exercise, and physical fitness: Definitions and distinctions for health-related research. *Public Health Reports (1974), 100*(2), 126–131.

35   *continued research in this area supports not only a positive relationship between PA and cognitive functions, but also academic achievement. When you get PA, your neurocognitive brain function is enhance, specifically your executive functions (EF), which is a set of top-down mental processes that allows for controlled and goal-directed behavior*: Miyake, A, Friedman, N. P., Emerson, M. J., Witzki, A. H., Howerter, A, Wager, T. D. (2000) The unity and diversity of executive functions and their contributions to complex "frontal lobe" tasks: A latent variable analysis. *Cognitive Psychology, 41*, 49–100. https://doi.org/10.1006/cogp.1999.0734 PMID: 10945922

35   *The research findings show significant benefits in a decrease of anxiety and depression when a consistent and ongoing training program is conducted (i.e., exercising over 30 minutes a day versus only working out for a couple of days). Moreover, after intense aerobic exercise (i.e., between 30 to 70 percent of maximal heart rate), a reduction in an individual's anxiety and depression is achieved*: Weinberg, R. S., & Gould, D. (2015). *Foundations of sport and exercise psychology, 6th Edition*. Human Kinetics.

35	*Even participating in an anaerobic activity, such as stretching has a significant, positive impact on a person's mood*: Berger, B., & Motl, R. (2001). Physical activity and quality of life. In eds R. N. Singer, H. A. Hausenblas, & C. M. Janelle (Eds.), *Handbook of sport psychology* (2nd ed., pp.636–670). Wiley.
35	*Getting outside and moving your body everyday in a natural environment can provide psychological restoration; as well as strong long-term health outcomes*: Hartig, T., & Staats, H. (2006). The need for psychological restoration as a determinantof environmental preferences. *Journal of Environmental Psychology, 26*(3), 215–226. https://doi.org/10.1016/j.jenvp.2006.07.007
35	*Sweating/perspiring is how our body regulates its temperature*: Mahlouji, M., Vaghasloo, M. A, Dadmehr, M., Rezaeizadeh, H., Nazem, E., & Tajadini, H. (2023). Sweating as a preventive care and treatment strategy in traditional Persian medicine. *Galen Medical Journal, 9*, e2003. https://doi.org/10.31661/gmj.v9i.2003
35	*and plays a role in preventing diseases*: Balchin, R., Linde, J., Blackhurst, D., Rauch, H. L., & Schönbächler, G. (2016). Sweating away depression? The impact of intensive exercise on depression. *Journal of Affective Disorders, 200*, 218–221. https://doi.org/10.1016/j.jad.2016.04.030
35	*When you exercise, more sweat is needed to cool your body, and your muscles heat up. When you exercise for longer periods, work out more intensely, or work out in a hot environment (e.g., hot weather or a hot yoga class), your sweat loss may cause a water/electrolyte imbalance in your body*: Baker, L. B. (2017). Sweating rate and sweat sodium concentration in athletes: A review of methodology and intra/interindividual variability. *Sports Medicine, 47* (Suppl. 1), 111–128. https://doi.org/10.1007/s40279-017-0691-5
35	*Sweat consists of sodium, potassium, calcium, and magnesium, which are electrolytes*: Schiefermeier-Mach, N., Egg, S., Erler, J., Hasenegger, V., Rust, P., König, J., Purtscher, A. E. (2020). Electrolyte intake and major food sources of sodium, potassium, calcium and magnesium among a population in western Austria. *Nutrients, 12*(7), 1956. DOI: 10.3390/nu12071956
35	*drinking electrolytes (e.g., electrolyte hydration mix or sports drink)*: Fan, P. W., Burns, S. F., & Lee, J. K. W. (2020). Efficacy of ingesting an oral rehydration solution after exercise on fluid balance and endurance performance. *Nutrients, 12*(12), 3826. https://doi.org/10.3390/nu12123826
35	*replenish your body with foods such as fruits..., vegetables..., legumes..., and calcium-rich foods...*: Schiefermeier-Mach, N., Egg, S., Erler, J., Hasenegger, V., Rust, P., König, J., Purtscher, A. E. (2020). Electrolyte intake and major food sources of sodium, potassium, calcium and magnesium among a population in western Austria. *Nutrients, 12*(7), 1956. DOI: 10.3390/nu12071956
35	*Sweating contains numerous health benefits (i.e., it removes waste products, maintains your body's health, and keeps your body temperature balanced)*: Mahlouji, M., Vaghasloo, M. A, Dadmehr, M., Rezaeizadeh, H., Nazem, E., & Tajadini, H. (2023). Sweating as a preventive care and treatment strategy in traditional Persian medicine. *Galen Medical Journal, 9*, e2003. https://doi.org/10.31661/gmj.v9i.2003

- **Mindfulness**

36	*Through mindfulness practice, individuals can cultivate a heightened focus on the present moment, leading to the development of positive qualities such as joy and compassion. This practice enhances attention, emotions, and behavioral self-regulation skills*: Crane, R. S., Brewer, J., Feldman, C., Kabat-Zinn, J., Santorelli, S., Williams, J. M. G., & Kuyken, W. (2017). What defines mindfulness-based programs? The warp and the weft. *Psychological Medicine, 47*(6), 990–999. https://doi.org/10.1017/S0033291716003317
36	*improved well-being*: Zhou, W., & McLellan, R. (2024). The effectiveness of taught, self-help mindfulness-based interventions on Chinese adolescents' well-being, mental health, prosocial and difficult behavior, and coping strategy. *Applied Psychology: Health and Well-Being, 16*(3), 1024–1045. https://doi.org/10.1111/aphw.12517
36	*Christine O'Shaughnessy, who leads mindfulness meditation workshops at Harvard University, considers mindfulness a fitness routine to keep your brain healthy. Mindfulness keeps your mind on track by being aware when your mind wanders. Mindfulness is the power of your breath and connecting that breath to your body as you breathe in and out. O'Shaughnessy offers a Mindfulness app called Present-Guided Meditation with several free meditation sessions*: Mineo, L. (2018, April 17). Less stress clearer thoughts with mindfulness meditation. Harvard Gazette. https://news.harvard.edu/gazette/story/2018/04/less-stress-clearer-thoughts-with-mindfulness-meditation/
36	*Harvard researchers discovered that practicing mindfulness 20 minutes a day will help you to be more focused, creative, productive, and less anxious*: Gillett, R. (2014, September 5). *The new habit challenge: Meditate for 20*

36   *minutes a day*. Fast Company. https://www.fastcompany.com/3035250/the-new-habit-challenge-meditate-for-20-minutes-a-day#:~:text=Just%2020%20minutes%20a%20day,not%20to%20mention%20less%20anxious.

36   *"Lakhiani says for most people, 15 to 20 minutes will give you just the changes that you need. You can take a one- to three-minute dip into peacefulness, and you can see remarkable results. The biggest benefits are going to happen in the first few minutes"*: Onque, R. (2023, May 20). *This is the perfect amount of time to meditate, says mindfulness expert: It's when 'the biggest benefits happen.* CNBC.com. https://www.cnbc.com/2023/05/20/world-meditation-day-the-ideal-length-to-meditate-from-an-expert.html#:~:text="For%20most%20people%2C%2015%20to,in%20the%20first%20few%20minutes."

36   *In a neuroscience-based mindfulness intervention program called Training for Awareness, Resilience, and Action (TARA), two different studies with 14- to 18-year-olds who participated in a 12-week group TARA training of mindfulness, yoga, and other therapy techniques showed significant improvements. In the smaller study, the depressed adolescents experienced decreased depressive and anxiety symptoms, along with improved sleep. In the other larger TARA study, the healthy control group reported increased emotional well-being, less anxiety, improved sleep quality, and positive changes within the inner white matter structural brain connectivity and outer gray matter volume*: Tymofiyeva, O., Henje, E., Yuan, J. P., Huang, C.-Y., Connolly, C. G., Ho, T. C., Bhandari, S., Parks, K. C., Sipes, B. S., Yang, T. T., & Xu, D. (2021). Reduced anxiety and changes in amygdala network properties in adolescents with training for awareness, resilience, and action (TARA). *NeuroImage Clinical, 29*, 102521. https://doi.org/10.1016/j.nicl.2020.102521; Tymofiyeva, O., Sipes, B. S., Luks, T., Hamlat, E. J., Samson, T. E., Hoffmann, T. J., Glidden, D. V., Jakary, A., Li, Y., Ngan, T., Henje, E., & Yang, T. T. (2024). Interoceptive brain network mechanisms of mindfulness-based training in healthy adolescents. *Frontiers in Psychology, 15*, 1410319. https://doi.org/10.3389/fpsyg.2024.1410319

- **Nature**

37   *Furthermore, spending at least 120 minutes a week in nature or getting outside is associated with positive correlations for both health and well-being*: White, M. P., Alcock, I., Grellier, J., Wheeler, B. W., Hartig, T., Warber, S. L., Bone, A., Depledge, M. H., & Fleming, L. E. (2019). Spending at least 120 minutes a week in nature is associated with good health and wellbeing *Scientific Reports, 9*(1), 7730–11. https://doi.org/10.1038/s41598-019-44097-3

37   *If you can develop a strong connection to nature, you will experience a strong physical and mental (i.e., reduced anxiety, depression, and stress) well-being*: Oh, R. R. Y., Fielding, K. S. S., Chang, C.-C., Nghiem, L. T. P., Tan, C. L. Y., Quazi, S. A., Shanahan, D. F., Gaston, K. J., Carrasco, R. L., & Fuller, R. A. (2021). Health and wellbeing benefits from nature experiences in tropical settings depend on strength of connection to nature. *International Journal of Environmental Research and Public Health, 18*(19), 10149. https://doi.org/10.3390/ijerph181910149

37   *go outside and take advantage of the natural healing power of the earth and place your bare feet on the concrete, dirt, grass, gravel, or wet sand. A study published in the European Biology and Bioelectromagnetics Journal, discovered that if you get grounded every day, it will calm your busy mind and reduce stress and tension. It shifts your nervous system from a stressed out state to a much calmer state of mind*: Mousa, H. A.-L. (2022). Prevention and treatment of COVID-19 infection by earthing. *Biomedical Journal. 46*(1), 60–69. https://doi.org/10.1016/j.bj.2022.08.002

37   *If you think of your body as a continuous semiconducting fabric, when you ground it, this negative charge soaks into every part of your body (i.e., interiors of the cell and its nuclei). When these moving electrons are grounded, they quickly neutralize the positive charges in your body.*: Oschman, J. L. (2022). Illnesses in technologically advanced societies due to lack of grounding (Earthing). *Biomedical Journal.* https://doi.org/10.1016/j.bj.2022.10.004

- **Hydration**

38   *Our bodies are comprised of 60% water, so it just makes common sense that if we sweat every day, we would need to replenish our bodies with water*: Laja Garcia, A. I., de Lourdes Smaniego-Vaesken, M., Partearroyo, T., & Varela-Moreiras, G. (2019). Adaptation and validation of the hydration status questionnaire in a Spanish adolescent-young population: A cross sectional study. *Nutrients, 11*(3), 565. https://doi.org/10.3390/nu11030565; Shirreffs, S. M. (2003). Markers of hydration status. *European Journal of Clinical Nutrition, 57* (Suppl. 2), S6–S9. https://doi.org/10.1038/sj.ejcn.1601895

38   *Maintaining hydration is significantly associated with a person's excellent physical condition*: Cheuvront S. N., Carter, R. III, & Sawka, M. N. (2003). Fluid balance and endurance performance. *Current Sports Medicine Reports, 2*(4), 202–208. https://journals.lww.com/acsm-csmr/Abstract/2003/08000/Fluid_Balance_and_Endurance_Exercise_Performance.6.aspx

38 *cognitive performance*: Suhr, J. A., Patterson, S. M., Austin, A. W., & Heffner, K. L. (2010). The relation of hydration status to declarative memory and working memory in older adults. *The Journal of Nutrition, Health & Aging, 14*, 840–843. https://doi.org/10.1007/s12603-010-0108-8

38 *With the brain comprised of 70% water (compared to 60% in the human body), staying hydrated is essential, as an adequately hydrated brain is known via brain imaging to improve mood, enhance memory, and decrease anxiety symptoms*: Benton, D., Cousins, A., & Young, H. (2019). Small differences in everyday hydration status influence mood. *Current Developments in Nutrition, 3*(Suppl. 1), nzz051.P04-134-19. https://doi.org/10.1093/cdn/nzz051.P04-134-19 Benton, D., & Young, H. A. (2015). Do small differences in hydration status affect mood and mental performance? *Nutrition Reviews, 73*(Suppl. 2), 83–96. https://doi.org/10.1093/nutrit/nuv045; Vian, J., Pereira, C., Chavarria, V., Kohler, C., Stubbs, B., Quevedo, J., King, S. W., Carvalho, A. F., Berk, M., & Fernandes, B. S. (2017). The renin-angiotensinsystem: a possible new target for depression. *BMC Medicine, 15*(144). https://doi.org/10.1186/s12916-017-0916-3

- **Nutrition**

38 *When adolescents do not eat a proper nutritious diet, then cognition is impaired, working memory is compromised, and social cues and empathy are lacking. Tthis causes a higher-level of anxiety and bad decisions to be made:* Olivo, G., Gaudio, S., & Schioth, H. B. (2019). Brain and cognitive development in adolescents with anorexia nervosa: A systematic review of fMRI studies. *Nutrients, 11*(8), 1907. https://doi.org/10.3390/nu11081907

38 *As your body grows, focus on eating a whole-food diet rich in vitamins and nutrients*: Pawelski, P. S., & Pawelski, J. (2024, April 17). *Why Aren't Today's Youth Happy? A recent happiness report finds a steep drop in happiness among today's youth*. Psychology Today. Happiness. https://www.psychologytoday.com/us/blog/happy-together/202404/why-arcnt-todays-youth-happy

- **Social Fitness**

39 *discuss several longitudinal studies that also report significant findings of the importance of human connections. These studies report that if people live lonely lives, then they also have a shorter life expectancy. In fact, Great Britain is addressing this public health concern in their country by appointing a Minister of Loneliness*: Waldinger, R. J. & Schulz, M. S. (2023). *The good life: Lessons from the world's longest scientific study of happiness.* Simon & Schuster.

39 *social relationships in your life have short- and long term effects on your physical and mental health—both good and bad. They also state that the social skills you develop during your childhood years have a cumulative effect into your adult years*: Umberson, D., & Montez, J. K. (2010). Social relationships and health: A flashpoint for health policy. *Journal of Health and Social Behavior, 51*(Suppl. 1), S54–S66. https://doi.org/10.1177/0022146510383501

- **Caring**

40 *prosocial behavior (compassion and social trust)*: Krekel, C., De Neve, J.-E., Fancourt, D., & Layard, R. (2021). A local community course that raises wellbeing and pro-sociality: Evidence from a randomised controlled trial. Journal of Economic Behavior and Organization, 188, 322–336. https://doi.org/10.1016/j.jebo.2021.05.021

- **Gratitude**

40 *Gratitude is an emotion and attribute that, when practiced daily, is strongly correlated to your overall health and well-being*: Dickens, L. R. (2017). Using Gratitude to Promote Positive Change: A Series of Meta-Analyses Investigating the Effectiveness of Gratitude Interventions. *Basic and Applied Social Psychology, 39*(4), 193–208. https://doi.org/10.1080/01973533.2017.1323638; Karns, C. M., Moore, W. E., & Mayr, U. (2017). The cultivation of pure altruism via gratitude: A functional MRI study of change with gratitude practice. *Frontiers in Human Neuroscience, 11*, 599–599. https://doi.org/10.3389/fnhum.2017.00599

40 *Incorporating the daily practice of gratitude helps you open your eyes to all of the positive aspects of your life*: Wood, A. M., Froh, J. J., & Geraghty, A. W. A. (2010). Gratitude and well-being: A review and theoretical integration. *Clinical Psychology Review, 30*(7), 890–905. https://doi.org/10.1016/j.cpr.2010.03.005

40 *In a study with teenagers and young adults, MRI imaging captured the practice of gratitude journaling in the ventromedial prefrontal cortex and nucleus accumbens areas, considered "value-sensitive" and reward systems cortical brain regions. Researchers discovered these brain changes lead to more prosocial behaviors and moral emotions known to increase your well-being*: Karns, C. M., Moore, W. E., & Mayr, U. (2017). The cultivation of pure altruism via gratitude: A functional MRI study of change with gratitude practice. *Frontiers in Human Neuroscience, 11*, 599–599. https://doi.org/10.3389/fnhum.2017.00599

- **Happiness**

40 *self-assess your well-being; you are reliable and capable of addressing these questions*: Diener, E. (2000). Subjective well-being: The science of happiness and a proposal for a national index. *The American Psychologist, 55*(1), 34–43. https://doi.org/10.1037/0003-066X.55.1.34; Diener, E., Kahneman, D., & Helliwell, J. (2010). *International Differences in Well-Being* (1st ed.). Oxford University Press New York. https://doi.org/10.1093/acprof:o- so/9780199732739.001.0001; Diener, E., Lucas, R. E., & Oishi, S. (2002). Subjective well-being: The science of happiness and life satisfaction. In C. R. Snyder & S. J. Lopez (Eds.), Handbook of positive psychology (pp. 463–73). Oxford University Press; Diener, E., & Suh, E. M. (Eds.). (2003). Culture and subjective well-being. MIT press.; Diener, E., Suh, E. M., Lucas, R. E., & Smith, H. L. (1999). Subjective well-being: Three decades of progress. *Psychological Bulletin, 125*(2), 276–302. https://doi.org/10.1037/0033-2909.125.2.276

40 *known to affect your happiness into adulthood*: Huotari, P., Nupponen, H., Mikkelsson, L., Laakso, L., & Kujala, U. (2011). Adolescent physical fitness and activity as predictors of adulthood activity. *Journal of Sports Sciences, 29*(11), 1135–1141. https://doi.org/10.1080/02640414.2011.585166; Kjønniksen, L., Torsheim, T., & Wold, B. (2008). Tracking of leisure-time physical activity during adolescence and young adulthood: a 10-year longitudinal study *International Journal of Behavioral Nutrition and Physical Activity, 5*(1): 1–11. https:// doi.org/10.1186/1479-5868-5-69; Mäkelä, S., Aaltonen, S., Korhonen, T., Rose, R. J., & Kaprio, J. (2017). Diversity of leisure-time sport activities in adolescence as a predictor of leisure-time physical activity in adulthood. *Scandinavian Journal of Medicine & Science in Sports, 27*(12), 1902–1912. https://doi.org/10.1111/sms.12837; Sacker, A., & Cable, N. (2006). Do adolescent leisure-time physical activities foster health and well-being in adulthood? Evidence from two British birth cohorts. *European Journal of Public Health, 16*(3), 331–335. https://doi.org/10.1093/eurpub/cki189

40 *continue setting high goals, which can lead to a better job and increased income* De Neve, J.-E., & Oswald, A. J. (2012). Estimating the influence of life satisfaction and positive affect on later income using sibling fixed effects. *PNAS Proceedings of the National Academy of Sciences of the United States of America, 109*(49), 19953–19958. https://doi.org/10.1073/pnas.1211437109; Lyubomirsky, S., King, L., & Diener, E. (2005). The benefits of frequent positive affect: Does happiness lead to success? *Psychological Bulletin, 131*(6), 803–855. DOI: 10.1037/0033-2909.131.6.803

40 *identifying carefree activities at your age is important. Having hobbies and interests can help you lead a well-balanced life*: Csikszentmihalyi, M., & Hunter, J. (2003). Happiness in everyday life: The uses of experience sampling. *Journal of Happiness Studies, 4*(2), 185–199. https://doi.org/10.1023/A:1024409732742; Kim, E.-J., Kang, H.-W., & Park, S.-M. (2024). Determinants of the happiness of adolescents: A leisure perspective. *PloS One, 19*(4), e0301843–e0301843. https://doi.org/10.1371/journal.pone.0301843

40 *physical and social activity*: Asquith, S. L., Wang, X., Quintana, D. S., & Abraham, A. (2022). The role of personality traits and leisure activities in predicting wellbeing in young people. *BMC Psychology, 10*(1), 249–249. https://doi.org/10.1186/s40359-022-00954-x; Ito, E., Walker, G. J., Mitas, O., & Liu, H. (2019). Cultural similarities and differences in the relationship between types of leisure activity and happiness in Canadian, Chinese, and Japanese university students. *World Leisure Journal, 61*(1), 30–42. https://doi.org/10.1080/16078055.2018.1535449; Tukel, Y. (2020). *The study of the relationships among participation in recreation activities, life satisfaction and happiness in university students. In international society for technology, education, and science*. International Society for Technology, Education, and Science.

40 *volunteering*: Hernantes, N., Pumar-Méndez, M. J., López-Dicastillo, O., Iriarte, A., & Mujika, A. (2020). Volunteerism as adolescent health promotion asset: a scoping review. *Health Promotion International, 5*(3), 610–623. https://doi.org/10.1093/heapro/daz026; Piliavin, J. A., & Siegl, E. (2015). Health and well-being consequences of formal volunteering. In *the Oxford handbook of prosocial behavior. Oxford University Press.* https://doi.org/10.1093/oxfordhb/9780195399813.013.024; Ranapurwala, S. I., Casteel, C., & Peek-Asa, C. (2016). Volunteering in adolescence and young adulthood crime involvement: a longitudinal analysis from the add health study. *Injury Epidemiology, 3*(1), 26–26. https://doi.org/10.1186/s40621-016-0091-6; Schreier, H. M. C., Schonert-Reichl, K. A., & Chen, E. (2013). Effect of volunteering on risk factors for cardiovascular disease in adolescents: A randomized controlled trial. *JAMA Pediatrics, 167*(4), 1–6. https://doi.org/10.1001/jamapediatrics.2013.1100

40 *outdoor activities*: Bailey, A. W., & Fernando, I. K. (2012). Routine and project-based leisure, happiness, and meaning in life. *Journal of Leisure Research, 44*(2), 139–154. https://doi.org/10.1080/00222216.2012.11950259; Benita, F., Bansal, G., & Tunçer, B. (2019). Public spaces and happiness: Evidence from a large-scale field experiment. *Health & Place,*

56, 9–18. https://doi.org/10.1016/j.healthplace.2019.01.014; Weng, P.-Y., & Chiang, Y.-C. (2014). Psychological restoration through indoor and outdoor leisure activities. *Journal of Leisure Research, 46*(2), 203–217. https://doi.org/10.1080/00222216.2014.11950320

• Laughter

41   *Laughter is a known thing to have physiological, psychological, social, spiritual, and quality-of-life benefits. In contrast, as found in other areas of medicine, no adverse effects are known. The therapeutic efficacy of laughter is typically induced by external stimuli (i.e., a display of positive emotion, or self-induced laughter). Since the brain cannot distinguish between internal versus external stimuli, similar benefits are assumed to be achieved with both factors. Researchers continue to monitor laughter as a healing agent since it possesses many positive and quantifiable effects on an individual's health*: Mora-Ripoll, R. (2010). The therapeutic value of laughter in medicine. *Alternative Therapies in Health and Medicine, 16*(6), 56–64.

• Music

41   *Going back to the prehistoric era, music has always played a vital role in expressing emotion (i.e., compassion and fear), as well as serving relaxation and healing purposes. Hippocrates, the founding father of rational medicine, and Plato are known to utilize music to soothe patients*: Nobakht, N., Kamgar, M., Bilder, R. M., & Nobakht, E. (2022). Music for health: From ear to kidney. *Clinical Journal of the American Society of Nephrology, 17*(9), 1410–1412. https://doi.org/10.2215/CJN.04320422

41   *A learned, cognitive response validates the effectiveness of music; the associated learning process can get rooted in your memory*: Clements-Cortes, A., & Bartel, L. (2018). Are we doing more than we know? Possible mechanisms of response to music therapy. *Frontiers in Medicine, 5*, 255–255. https://doi.org/10.3389/fmed.2018.00255

41   *music increases dopamine and serotonin levels in the brain*: Moraes, M. M., Rabelo, P. C. R., Pinto, V. A., Pires, W., Wanner, S. P., Szawka, R. E., & Soares, D. D. (2018). Auditory stimulation by exposure to melodic music increases dopamine and serotonin activities in rat forebrain areas linked to reward and motor control. *Neuroscience Letters, 673*, 73–78. https://doi.org/10.1016/j.neulet.2018.02.058 2018

41   *Listening to music is known to reach a cellular and epigenetic level in the human body*: Nair, P. S., Raijas, P., Ahvenainen, M., Philips, A. K., Ukkola-Vuoti, L., & Järvelä, I. (2021). Music-listening regulates human microRNA expression. *Epigenetics, 16*(5), 554–566. https://doi.org/10.1080/15592294.2020.1809853

• Section Six: What's Your Game Plan - Warm-up •

• Academic Pressures

Study tips:

45   *When taking notes, writing in red and blue colors can enhance your cognitive skills (e.g., concentration and attention span) while also increasing your brain function (i.e., learning new information while embedding it into your working memory to encode, store, and retrieve this new information). Also, the color red is known to enhance your performance on simple, detail-oriented tasks; in contrast, blue improves performance on simple and difficult, detail-oriented tasks, as well as on creative tasks*: Xia, T., Song, L., Wang, T. T., Tan, L., & Mo, L. (2016). Exploring the effect of red and blue on cognitive task performances. *Frontiers in Psychology, 7*, 784–784. https://doi.org/10.3389/fpsyg.2016.00784

45   *Another concept you should implement is **Repeated Reading** (RR). This reading strategy can improve your reading fluency by reading and/or listening to a passage to help you comprehend the text*: Guerin, A., & Murphy, B. (2015). Repeated reading as a method to improve reading fluency for struggling adolescent readers. *Journal of Adolescent & Adult Literacy, 58*(7), 551–560. https://doi.org/10.1002/jaal.395

45   *free voluntary reading (i.e., reading all genres) is a wonderful way to increase your ability to read, write, spell, and comprehend. In addition to improving your math skills, reading a lot of the style you want to write in is also an effective writing method*: Krashen, S. D. (1993). *The power of reading: Insights from the research*. Libraries Unlimited.

48   *A breathing technique to help you relax before taking a test is called Alternate Nostril Breathing. This method is known to be good for your heart (i.e., reduce your heart rate and lower blood pressure), lungs (i.e., improve lung function), and brain (i.e., sympathetic stress)*: Nestor, J., Levin, C. J., & Swoap, S. J. (2019). The impact of deep breathing and alternate nostril breathing on heart rate variability: A human physiology laboratory. *Advances in Physiology Education, 43*(3), 270–276. https://doi.org/10.1152/advan.00019.2019

• Section Seven: What's Your Game Plan - Life Choices •

• Social Media - Setting Boundaries

76 *According to the Child Mind Institute, teenagers and young adults are the individuals who are the most avid and intense users of social media. The concern about too much screen time for this age group is that while your brain is forming, social media can negatively impact your self-esteem and trigger self-harm ideation. The research conducted by the Child Mind Institute continues that too much screen time is also associated with not getting enough sleep, developing anxiety, and also linked to the onset of mental health symptoms. Also, the Child Mind Institute 2017 indicates that teenagers and young adults who are constantly using social media are increasing their chances of developing depression from between 13 to 66 percent*: Miller, C. (2023, August 8). *Does Social Media Use Cause Depression?: How heavy Instagram and Facebook use may be affecting kids negatively*. Child Mind Institute. https://childmind.org/article/is-social-media-use-causing-depression/

78 *A research study analyzing social feedback processing in adolescents highlighted increased brain activity in the Dorsal Medial Prefrontal Cortex, Anterior Cingulate Cortex, and Bilateral Insula areas. The report emphasized that neuroimaging captured how females in their late adolescent years change their behavior based on feedback from their peers. The findings indicated a significant association between media-by-peer interactions and a female's future interpretation of an ideal female body*: Van der Meulen, M., Veldhuis, J., Braams, B. R., Peters, S., Konijn, E. A., & Crone, E. A. (2017). Brain activation upon ideal-body media exposure and peer feedback in late adolescent girls. *Cognitive, Affective, & Behavioral Neuroscience, 17*(4), 712–723. https://doi.org/10.3758/s13415-017-0507-y

• Time Management - Life Balance

84 *The Posterior Cingulate Cortex (PCC) mediates the students' internally generated thought processes they experience during emotional and social events. The PCC also includes self-directed cognitions and future planning, which is helpful with time management skills*: Leech, R., & Sharp, D. J. (2014). The role of the posterior cingulate cortex in cognition and disease. *Brain, 137*(1), 12–32.

• Section Eight: What's Your Game Plan - Life Crises •

• Anxiety

96 *Researchers who study test anxiety among adolescents, found that mandala coloring was linked to an increased state of mindfulness and decreased test anxiety*: Carsley, D., & Heath, N. L. (2019). Evaluating the effectiveness of a mindfulness coloring activity for test anxiety in children. *The Journal of Educational Research, 112*(2), 143–151. https://doi.org/10.1080/00220671.2018.1448749; Rose, S. E., & Lomas, M. H. R. (2020). The potential of a mindfulness-based coloring intervention to reduce test anxiety in adolescents. *Mind, Brain and Education, 14*(4), 335–340. https://doi.org/10.1111/mbe.12255 Rose & Lomas, 2020).

98 *Anxiety is a state where your sympathetic nervous system is stuck. In a research article about adolescents suffering from anxiety, the Anterior Cingulate Cortex region of the brain had hypo-activation in anxious adolescents and adults. "The unique U-shaped pattern of activation in the Ventromedial Prefrontal Cortex in many anxious adolescents may reflect heightened sensitivity to threat and safety conditions"*: Britton, J. C., Grillon, C., Lissek, S., Norcross, M. A., Szuhany, K. L., Chen, G., Ernst, M., Nelson, E. E., Leibenluft, E., Shechner, T., & Pine, D. S. (2013). Response to learned threat: An fMRI study in adolescent and adult anxiety. *The American Journal of Psychiatry, 170*(10), 1195–1204. https://doi.org/10.1176/appi.ajp.2013.12050651

• Depression

104 *In a 1,100-participant study of patients diagnosed with depression, fMRI scans were taken, and researchers noted similarities in the brain and categorized their depressive symptoms into four biotypes: the Insula, Orbitofrontal Cortex, Ventromedial Prefrontal Cortex, and multiple subcortical areas (i.e., Corpus Callosum, Hippocampus, Amygdala, Thalamus, and Putamen)*: Drysdale, A. T., Grosenick, L., Downar, J., Dunlop, K., Mansouri, F., Meng, Y., Fetcho, R. N., Zebley, B., Oathes, D. J., Etkin, A., Schatzberg, A. F., Sudheimer, K., Keller, J., Mayberg, H. S., Gunning, F. M., Alexopoulos, G. S., Fox, M. D., Pascual-Leone, A., Voss, H. U., Casey, B. J., Dubin, M. J., & Liston, C. (2017). Resting-state connectivity biomarkers define neurophysiological subtypes of depression. *Natural Medicine, 23*, 28–38. https://doi.10.1038/nm.4246

- **Self-Harm**

108 *nonsuicidal self-injury (NSSI) a current crisis*: Wester, K. L., Wachter Morris, C., & Williams, B. (2017). Nonsuicidal self-injury in the schools: A tiered prevention approach for reducing social contagion. *Professional School Counseling, 21*, 142–151. https://doi.org/10.5330/1096-2409-21.1.142

108 *Research indicates that self-harm ideation can potentially pass in fifteen minutes*: Zuromski, K. (2020, November 9). *Assessing and Intervening on Imminent Risk* [Lecture]. PSYC E-1247: The Psychology of Self-Harm, Harvard University, Boston, MA, United States.

- **Substance Abuse - Alcohol and Drugs**

114 *research on cannabis is indicating that teenagers with no family history are developing schizophrenia due to daily cannabis use. It is becoming such a pandemic that my Harvard Psychopharmacology instructor was approved to teach a class on this subject*: Boomhower, S. (2020, July 30). *Substance Abuse* [Lecture]. PSYC E-1410: Psychopharmacology, Harvard University, Boston, MA, United States.

115 *reports that the brain may continue to develop until age 30*: Edwards, S. (2010, August 9). *Deciphering the teenage brain*. Harvard Medical School. News and Research. https://hms.harvard.edu/news/deciphering-teen age-brain#:~:text=The%20maturing%20of%20the%20forward, be%20complete%20until%20age%2030.

115 *neuroscience research stating we may need to reconsider the age at which a child becomes an adult*: Johnson, S. (2022, January 31). *Big Think: Neuropsych*. Why is 18 the age of adulthood if the brain can take 30 years to mature? https://bigthink.com/neuropsych/adult-brain/

115 *we are undergoing a major public health crisis. Curran et al. (2016) report the known crisis is that some individuals are at even more risk of adverse effects of consuming weed—developing symptoms of: psychotic illness, cognitive impairment and long-term addiction*: Curran, H. V., Freeman, T. P., Mokrysz, C., Lewis, D. A., Morgan, C. J. A., & Parsons, L. H. (2016). Keep off the grass? Cannabis, cognition and addiction. *Nature Reviews. Neuroscience, 17*(5), 293–306. https://doi.org/10.1038/nrn.2016.28

115 *The Koob and Volkow Model of Addiction explains how the three stages of weed addiction affect three major neurocircuits in the brain*: Zehra, A., Burns, J., Liu, C., K., Manza, P., Wiers, C. E., Volkow, N. D., & Wang, G.-J. (2018). Cannabis addiction and the brain: A review. *Journal of Neuroimmune Pharmacology, 13*(4), 438–452. DOI: 10.1007/s11481-018-9782-9

115 *Weed contains 100 unique ingredients called cannabinoids, and the two most prominent ingredients are Delta9-tetrahydrocannabinol (Δ^9-THC) and cannabidiol (CBD), which tend to have adverse effects on the developing human brain behavior. Research indicates that Δ^9-THC impairs learning, produces psychosis-like effects and increases anxiety*: Curran, H. V., Freeman, T. P., Mokrysz, C., Lewis, D. A., Morgan, C. J. A., & Parsons, L. H. (2016). Keep off the grass? Cannabis, cognition and addiction. *Nature Reviews. Neuroscience, 17*(5), 293–306. https://doi.org/10.1038/nrn.2016.28

116 *The term "amotivation syndrome" gets used in individuals because positron emission tomography (PET) shows proof that adolescents who heavily consume weed during their key formative brain development years (i.e., puberty through at least the age of 25-years-old) and used on a regular basis, show a reduction in the Striatal Dopamine Synthesis*: Meier, M. H., Caspi, A., Ambler, A., Harrington, H., Houts, R., Keefe, R. S. E., McDonald, K., Ward, A., Poulton, R., & Moffitt, T. E. (2012). Persistent cannabis users show neuropsychological decline from childhood to midlife. *Proceedings of the National Academy of Sciences, 109*(40), E2657–E2664. https://doi.org/10.1073/pnas.1206820109

• Section Nine: What's Your Game Plan - Relationships •

- **Friendships**

136 *This childhood best friend can provide you with the developmental resilience you need to achieve your goals and develop strong social connections with your peers*: Sameroff, A. J. (1998). Environmental risk factors in infancy. *Pediatrics, 102*(5 Suppl. E),1287–1292.

136 *Supportive friendships lead to more resilient brain functioning*: van Harmelen, A.-L. van, Kievit, R. A., Ioannidis, K., Neufeld, S., Jones, P. B., Bullmore, E., Dolan, R., Fonagy, P., & Goodyer, I. (2017). Adolescent friendships predict later resilient functioning across psychosocial domains in a healthy community cohort. *Psychological Medicine, 47*(13), 2312–2322. https://doi.org/10.1017/S0033291717000836

- **Peer Pressure**

142 *peer feedback and peer pressure on how to think shows up in activated clusters in the Ventrolateral Prefrontal Cortex, Medial Prefrontal Cortex, Superior Temporal Gyrus and Sulcus, and Occipital Cortex*: Wikman, P., Moisala, M., Ylinen, A., Lindblom, J., Leikas, S., Salmela-Aro, K., Lonka, K., Güroğlu, B., & Alho, K. (2022). Brain responses to peer feedback in social media are modulated by valence in late adolescence. *Frontiers in Behavioral Neuroscience, 16*, 790478–790478. https://doi.org/10.3389/fnbeh.2022.790478

• Section Eleven: 4114U - Appendix •

- **Depression Game Plan**

152 *It is normal to experience a "Natural Depression"—where you may not feel like yourself for up to one year after a loved one has passed away. Share any losses, major changes, or trauma with your doctor that might affect how you feel*: Keyes, K. M., Pratt, C., Galea, S., McLaughlin, K. A., Koenen, K. C., & Shear, M. K. (2014). The burden of loss: unexpected death of a loved one and psychiatric disorders across the life course in a national study. *American Journal of Psychiatry, 171*(8), 864–871. https://doi.org/10.1176/appi.ajp.2014.13081132

152 *Sometimes your gut microbiome and the gut-brain axis can get out of sync*: Simkin, D. R. (2019). Microbiome and mental health, specifically as it relates to adolescents. *Current Psychiatry Reports, 21*(9), 93–12. https://doi.org/10.1007/s11920-019-1075-3

152 *have your doctor do a test for 16S rRNA gene sequencing*: Choi, J. G., Huh, E., Kim, N., Kim, D.-H., & Oh, M. S. (2019). High-throughput 16S rRNA gene sequencing reveals that 6-hydroxydopamine affects gut microbial environment. *PloS One, 14*(8), e0217194–e0217194. https://doi.org/10.1371/journal.pone.0217194

152 *try eating a Mediterranean diet which is known to help get your gut healthy*: Latorre-Pérez, A., Hernández, M., Iglesias, J. R. Morán, J., Pascual, J., Porcar, M., Vilanova, C., & Collado, L. (2021). The Spanish gut microbiome reveals links between between microorganisms and Mediterranean diet. *Scientific Reports 11*, 21602. https://doi.org/10.1038/s41598-021-01002-1

152 *Ask your doctor to conduct a Pharmacogenetic (PGx) (Genomind™) or Psychotropic (GeneSight®) test to assess your genetics to create your personal therapeutic game plan—these tests identify potential gene-drug interactions and how your body metabolizes medicine*: Krause, D. S., & Dowd, D. (2022). Use of a consultation service following pharmacogenetic testing in psychiatry. *Pharmacogenomics, 23*(5), 327–333. https://doi.org/10.2217/pgs-2021-0121

152 *Ask your doctor to order an MTHFR blood test as this gene is often linked to depression*: Peerbooms, O., Rutten, B. P. F., Collip, D., Lardinois, M., Lataster, T., Thewissen, V., Rad, S. M., Drukker, M., Kenis, G., van Os, J., Myin-Germeys, I., & Van Winkel, R. (2011). Evidence that interactive effects of COMT and MTHFR moderate psychotic response to environmental stress. *Acta Psychiatrica Scandinavica, 125*(3), 247–256. https://doi.org/10.1111/j.1600-0447.2011.01806.x

152 *Cognitive Behavior Therapy (CBT) OR iCBT, as it is known to help treat depression*: Purdie, D. R., Federman, M., Chin, A., Winston, D., Bursch, B., Olmstead, R., Bulut, Y., & Irwin, M. R. (2022). Hybrid delivery of mindfulness meditation and perceived stress in pediatric resident physicians: A randomized clinical trial of in-person and digital mindfulness meditation. *Journal of Clinical Psychology in Medical Settings*. https://doi.org/10.1007/s10880-022-09896-3

152 *Pet therapy is notorious for assisting individuals who are depressed or suffering from post traumatic stress*: Purewal, R., Christley, R., Kordas, K., Joinson, C., Meints, K., Gee, N., & Westgarth, C. (2017). Companion animals and child/adolescent development: A systematic review of the evidence. *International Journal of Environmental Research and Public Health, 14*(3), 234. https://doi.org/10.3390/ijerph14030234; Rhoades, H., Winetrobe, H., & Rice, E. (2015). Pet ownership among homeless youth: Associations with mental health, service utilization and housing status. *Child Psychiatry and Human Development, 46*(2), 237–244. https://doi.org/10.1007/s10578-014-0463-5

152 *Go outside and get grounded*: Sinatra, S. T., Oschman, J. L., Chevalier, G., & Sinatra, D. (2017). Electric nutrition: The surprising health and healing benefits of biological grounding (Earthing). *Alternative Therapies in Health and Medicine, 23*(5), 8–16.

152 *and exercise every day—it is the best known therapy for depression*: Serrander, M., Bremander, A., Jarbin, H., & Larsson, I. (2021). Joy of living through exercise-a qualitative study of clinically referred adolescents' experiences of moderate to vigorous exercise as treatment for depression. *Nordic Journal of Psychiatry, 75*(8), 574–581. https://doi.org/10.1080/08039488.2021.1909128; Wang, X., Cai, Z.-D., Jiang, W.-T., Fang, Y.-Y., Sun, W.-X., Wang, X. (2022). Systematic review and meta-analysis of the effects of exercise on depression in adolescents. *Child Adolescent Psychiatry Mental Health 16*(16). https://doi.org/10.1186/s13034-022-00453-2

152 *Socialize and find those 24/7 friends to reduce depression*: Adams, R. E., Santo, J. B., & Bukowski, W. M. (2011). The presence of best friend buffers the effects of negative experiences. *Developmental Psychology, 47*(6), 1786–1791. https://doi.org/10.1037/a0025401

• Section Thirteen: 4114U - Glossary of Terms •

170 **automatic negative thoughts (ANT):** *"thoughts that are instantaneous, habitual, and nonconscious"*: (APA Dictionary of Psychology)

170 **correlation:** *When you observe a relationship between naturally-occurring variables versus cause and effect variables—as found in an experimental study*: (Field, 2018). *A correlation is a predictable relationship between two variables*: (Arnett, 2018); *thus, these variables are predictor and outcome variables in correlational studies. The stronger the correlation between the variables, the better you can predict the relationship. Correlational studies are not experimental, as there is no cause and effect relationship; however, a prediction can be made about one variable from the other one in correlational research*: (Field, 2018).

170 **cortisol:** *a hormone produced by the adrenal gland and released when stressed. Too much cortisol in the brain can affect your immune system and blood pressure; when you are constantly stressed, the excess cortisol will damage and kill neurons and become toxic in your hippocampus*: (Bear, Connors, & Paradiso, 2007).

170 **dopamine:** *Neurotransmitter activating brain functions: motivation, the reward center, and motor control*: (Purves et al., 2018).

170 **fMRI functional magnetic resonance imaging:** *This is a brain-scanning technique that measures blood flow and can safely and painlessly observe brain functioning while an individual performs a task*: (Purves et al., 2018).

170 **gray-matter:** *The outermost layer of the brain* (Arnett, 2018) *and located in the cortex. Contains neurons and unmyelineated axons*: (Arnett, 2018). *Gray-matter volume peaks in females at age 11 and males around age 14 and then declines*: (Jensen & Nutt, 2015). *Research supports doing mindfulness exercises every day has shown to increase the gray matter in the brain*: (Mineo, 2018, April 17).

170 **habitual explanatory style:** *In psychology, this term is used to describe how an individual can have a habitual way of thinking (i.e., negative or positive, pessimistic or optimistic)*: (Campbell & Løkken, 2023).

170 **impairment:** *Weakness or damage in a body's typical physiological or psychological function*: (APA Dictionary of Psychology)

170 **melatonin:** *The brain's pineal gland generates this hormone which regulates your circadian sleep rhythm*: (Jensen & Nutt, 2015).

170 **prefrontal cortex:** *Located in the frontal lobe and this part of the brain is responsible for social behavior, decision-making tasks, and personality*: (Purves et al., 2018).

170 **ruminating:** *Repetitive and obsessive thoughts*: (APA Dictionary of Psychology)

170 **significant effect:** *When you have thirty or more participants in a research study, you have statistical power. When you have a study with statistical power and the majority of the results are positive, then you can claim the result have a significant effect*: (Field, 2018).

170 **stimuli:** *A behaviorist defines consciousness as an observable response to a stimulus. It is a message coming in from the outside world to somewhere in your inside world and the person is then able to indicate that the message was received. An example would be a whisper in your ear, saying if you can hear me, blink your eyes*: (Caine, 2021).

170 **THC (tetrahydrocannabinol):** *THC is known for cannabis' addictive mind-altering psychoactive properties and damaging effects on brain dopaminergic function*: (Zehra at al., 2018). *The psychoactive properties of THC have triggered learning impairment and produced psychosis-like episodes and anxiety attacks in humans*: (Curran et al., 2016).

172 **variables:** *In an experiment, this is an element that can be changed, manipulated, and measured*: (Field, 2018).

172 **ventral tegmental area (VTA):** *Part of the brain's dopamine system responsible for drug and alcohol addiction. Many neurons are connected in the VTA which operates your reward circuitry cycle*: (Jensen & Nutt, 2015).

172 **white-matter:** *The white matter supports the connections between brain regions and consists of mylenated axons*: (Arnett, 2018). *The matter increases into (the 30's) early adulthood*: (Giedd et al., 1999). *Imaging studies in heavy cannabis users showed reductions in the white-matter, along with deficits when measurements of neurocognitive tests were performed*: (Curran et al., 2016).

Section Thirteen

4114U

•

Glossary of Terms

• 4114U - Glossary of Terms •

- **aberration:** Negative changes or alterations in the brain; not normal brain development.
- **automatic negative thoughts (ANT):** "thoughts that are instantaneous, habitual, and nonconscious."
- **correlation:** When you observe a relationship between naturally-occurring variables versus cause and effect variables. A correlation is a predictable relationship between two variables; thus, these variables are predictor and outcome variables in correlational studies. The stronger the correlation between the variables, the better you can predict the relationship. Correlational studies are not experimental, as there is no cause and effect relationship; however, a prediction can be made about one variable from the other variable in correlational research.
- **cortisol:** A hormone produced by the adrenal gland and released when stressed. Too much cortisol in the brain can affect your immune system and blood pressure: when you are constantly stressed the excess cortisol will damage and kill neurons and become toxic in your hippocampus.
- **dopamine:** Neurotransmitter activating brain functions: motivation, the reward center and motor control.
- **fMRI functional magnetic resonance imaging:** A brain-scanning technique that measures blood flow and can safely and painlessly observe brain functioning while an individual performs a task.
- **gray-matter:** The outermost layer of the brain and located in the cortex. Contains neurons and unmyelineated axons. Gray-matter volume peaks in females at age 11 and males around age 14 and then declines. Research supports doing mindfulness exercises every day has shown to increase the gray matter in the brain.
- **habitual explanatory style:** In psychology, this term is used to describe how an individual can have a habitual way of thinking (i.e., negative or positive, pessimistic or optimistic).
- **impairment:** Weakness or damage in a body's typical physiological or psychological function.
- **melatonin:** The brain's pineal gland generates this hormone which regulates the circadian sleep rhythm.
- **prefrontal cortex:** Located in the frontal lobe and this part of the brain is responsible for social behavior, decision-making tasks, and personality.
- **ruminating:** Repetitive and obsessive thoughts—like you are stuck in a hamster wheel.
- **significant effect:** When you have thirty or more participants in a research study, you have statistical power. When you have a study with statistical power and the majority of the results are positive, then you can claim the results have a significant effect.
- **stimuli:** A behaviorist defines consciousness as an observable response to a stimulus. It is a message coming in from the outside world to somewhere in your inside world and the person is then able to indicate that the message was received. An example would be a whisper in your ear, saying if you can hear me, blink your eyes.
- **THC (tetrahydrocannab**inol): THC is known for cannabis' addictive mind-altering psychoactive properties that damage effects on the brain's dopaminergic function. The psychoactive properties of THC impairs learning and produces psychosis-like episodes and anxiety attacks in humans.
- **variables**: In an experiment, this is an element that can be changed, manipulated, and measured.
- **ventral tegmental area (VTA):** Part of the brain's dopamine system responsible for drug and alcohol addiction. Many neurons are connected in the VTA which operates your reward circuitry cycle.
- **white-matter:** The white matter supports the connections between brain regions and consists of mylenated axons; the matter increases into (the 30's) early adulthood. Imaging studies in heavy cannabis users showed reductions in the white-matter, along with deficits when measurements of neurocognitive tests were performed.

Section Fourteen

4114U

•

Resources

• 4114U - Resources •

Phone Numbers to Call or Text for Help with Trained Professionals:

- **988 Suicide and Crisis Hot Line:** Call 9-8-8
  Nacional de Prevención del Suicidio: Llamar 1-888-628-9454

- **All Emergencies:** Call 9-1-1

- **Call Blackline:** Call or text 1-800-604-5841
  Peer support, counseling, and reporting maltreatment for Black, Brown, Indigenous, and people of all color

- **Crisis Text Line:** Text HOME to 741741
  Confidential peer support for teens and young adults needing help, resource referrals, or information regarding how to have a healthy relationship and dating abuse in the US

- **Love is Respect:** Text LOVEIS to 22522 or Call 1-866-331-9474

- **National Alliance on Mental Illness HelpLine:** Call 1-800-950-6264 or text: HELP4U to 435748
  Peer support line and resource referrals

- **The National Sexual Assault Telephone Hotline (RAINN):** Call 1-800-656-4673

- **SAMHSA National Helpline:** Call 1-800-622-HELP (4357)
  Substance Abuse and Mental Health Services Administration for treatment referrals

- **The Trevor Project:** Call at 1-866-488-7386 or Text 'START' to 678-678
  Counselors trained with the focus on suicide prevention among lesbian, gay, bisexual, transgender, queer, and questioning youth

Websites:

- **Action for Happiness**
  https://actionforhappiness.org

  For all ages: Available as a cell phone App too. The mission of Action for Happiness is to help people create a happier world, with a culture that prioritizes happiness and kindness.

- **Cyberbullying Research Center**
  https://cyberbullying.org/category/resources/students

  For ages 11 +: This website is filled with pdf files of ways to identify, prevent, respond to cyberbullying.

- **Earthing**
  https://www.earthing.com

  For all ages: Backed in research, this company creates awareness and designs grounding products to help people stay connected with the earth to achieve, maintain, and restore their natural state of health.

- **Feelings Word List by Wasatch Family Therapy**
  https://wasatchfamily therapy.com/blog/archives/27325

  For all ages: There are lots of emotions you can feel and experience. By learning to name and identify your emotions, this will help you to move through the situation in which you feel stuck.

- **Find a Therapist**
  https://www.psychologytoday.com/us/therapists

  For all ages: This website provides assistance in helping you to find a therapist in the U.S.

- **Genomind™**
  https://www.genomind.com

  For all ages: Genomind™ states that they turn "genetic data into actionable treatment insights that can help you narrow down medication choices and personalize dosing."

- **GenoSight®**
  https://www.genosight.com

  For all ages: GeneSight® states that their "Psychotropic test is a genetic test that shows your provider how your genes may affect medication outcomes. The GeneSight test may reveal which medications to treat depression, anxiety, ADHD, and other mental health conditions require dose adjustments, be less likely to work, or have an increased risk of side effects based on your DNA. The test is a simple cheek swab taken in your healthcare provider's office or can be sent by your doctor to be taken in the convenience of your home."

- **Love is Respect**
  https://www.loveisrespect.org

  For ages 11+: This website helps you look outside of your emotional feelings toward someone and focus on how they are treating you and help you to set boundaries.

- **TeenSource**
  https://www.teensource.org

  For ages 11+: The TeenSource website is packed with resources for preteens and teenagers to assist them with daily life topics.

- **The Cool Spot**
  http:/www.thecoolspot.gov/

  For ages 11 +: The Cool Spot is designed to educate teenagers about alcohol and how to resist peer pressure.

- **The Hotline**
  https://www.thehotline.org

  For ages 11+: The Hotline is a National Domestic Abuse Hotline where you or someone you care about can reach out if abuse is occuring.

Section Fifteen

4114U

•

References

• 4114U - References •

Abel, E. L., & Kruger, M. L. (2010). Smile intensity in photographs predicts longevity. *Psychological Science, 21*(4), 542–544. https://doi.org/10.1177/0956797610363775

Abramowitz, J. S., Deacon, B. J., & Whiteside, S. P. H. (2011). *Exposure therapy for anxiety: Principles and practice.* Guilford Press.

Adams, R. E., Santo, J. B., & Bukowski, W. M. (2011). The presence of best friend buffers the effects of negative experiences. *Developmental Psychology, 47*(6), 1786–1791. https://doi.org/10.1037/a0025401

Allen, M. W. (2016). CCAF and interactive instruction. In *Michael Allen's guide to e-learning* (pp. 235–265). John Wiley & Sons, Inc. https://doi.org/10.1002/9781119176268.ch12

American Psychiatric Association. (2013). *Diagnostic and statistical manual of mental disorders* (5th ed.).

Andersen, S. L., & Teicher, M. H. (2008). Stress, sensitive periods and maturational events in adolescent depression. *Trends in Neurosciences, 31*(4), 183–191. https://doi.org/10.1016/j.tins.2008.01.004

APA Dictionary of Psychology. (2023). https://dictionary.apa.org

Archambeau, S. (2020). *Unapologetically ambitious: Take risks, break barriers, and create success on your own terms.* Grand Central Publishing.

Asquith, S. L., Wang, X., Quintana, D. S., & Abraham, A. (2022). The role of personality traits and leisure activities in predicting wellbeing in young people. *BMC Psychology, 10*(1), 249–249. https://doi.org/10.1186/s40359-022-00954-x

Baker, L. B. (2017). Sweating rate and sweat sodium concentration in athletes: A review of methodology and intra/interindividual variability. *Sports Medicine, 47*(Suppl. 1), 111–128. https://doi.org/10.1007/s40279-017-0691-5

Balchin, R., Linde, J., Blackhurst, D., Rauch, H. L., & Schönbächler, G. (2016). Sweating away depression? The impact of intensive exercise on depression. *Journal of Affective Disorders, 200,* 218–221. https://doi.org/10.1016/j.jad.2016.04.030

Banks, B., & Connell, L. (2023). Multi-dimensional sensorimotor grounding of concrete and abstract categories. *Philosophical Transactions of the Royal Society of London. Series B. Biological Sciences, 378*(1870), 20210366. https://doi.org/10.1098/rstb.2021.0366

Bass, R. (2022). *The teens' workbook to self regulate: empowering teenagers to handle emotions with success through coping strategies and CBT exercises.* RBG Publishing.

Battistella, G., Fornari, E., Annoni, J. M., Haithem Chtioui, H., Dao, K., Fabritius, M., Favrat, B., Mall, J-F., Maeder, P., & Giroud, C. (2014). Long-term effects of cannabis on brain structure. *Neuropsychopharmacology, 39,* 2041–2048. https://doi.org/10.1038/npp.2014.67

Baer, R. A. (2003). Mindfulness training as a clinical intervention: A conceptual and empirical review. *Clinical Psychology: Science and Practice, 10,* 125–143.

Baer, R. A., Smith, G. T., Hopkins, J., Krietemeyer, J., & Toney, L. (2006). Using self-report assessment methods to explore facets of mindfulness. *Assessment, 13*(1), 27–45. DOI: https://doi.org/10.1177/1073191105283504

Bailey, A. W., & Fernando, I. K. (2012). Routine and project-based leisure, happiness, and meaning in life. *Journal of Leisure Research, 44*(2), 139–154. https://doi.org/10.1080/00222216.2012.11950259

Beauregard, M., Courtemanche, J., Paquette, V., & St-Pierre, É. L. (2009). The neural basis of unconditional love. *Psychiatry Research: Neuroimaging, 172*(2), 93–98. https://doi.org/10.1016/j.pscychresns.2008.11.003

Bear, M. F., Connors, B. W., & Paradiso, M. A. (2007). *Neuroscience: Exploring the brain* (3rd ed.). Lippincott Williams & Wilkins.

Becht, A. I., Wierenga, L. M., Mills, K. L., Meuwese, R., van Duijvenvoorde, A., Blakemore, S. J., Güroğlu, B., Crone, E. A. (2021). Beyond the average brain: Individual differences in social brain development are associated with friendship quality. *Social Cognitive and Affective Neuroscience, 16*(3), 292–301.

Beck, A. T., Steer, R., & Garbin, M. (1988). Psychometric properties of the Beck depression inventory - 25 years of evaluation. *Clinical Psychology Review, 8*(1), 77–100. https://doi.org/10.1016/0272-7358(88)90050-5

Behan. (2020). The benefits of meditation and mindfulness practices during times of crisis such as COVID-19. *Irish Journal of Psychological Medicine, 37*(4), 256–258. https://doi.org/10.1017/ipm.2020.38

Benedetti, F., Bollettini, I., Radaelli, D., Poletti, S., Locatelli, C., Falini, A., Smeraldi, E., & Colombo, C. (2014). Adverse childhood experiences influence white matter microstructure in patients with bipolar disorder. *Psychological Medicine, 44*(14), 3069–3082. https://doi.org/10.1017/S0033291714000506

Benita, F., Bansal, G., & Tunçer, B. (2019). Public spaces and happiness: Evidence from a large-scale field experiment. *Health & Place, 56,* 9–18. https://doi.org/10.1016/j.healthplace.2019.01.014

Benton, D., Cousins, A., & Young, H. (2019). Small differences in everyday hydration status influence mood. *Current Developments in Nutrition, 3*(Suppl. 1), nzz051.P04-134-19. https://doi.org/10.1093/cdn/nzz051.P04-134-19

Benton, D., & Young, H. A. (2015). Do small differences in hydration status affect mood and mental performance? *Nutrition Reviews, 73*(Suppl. 2), 83–96. https://doi.org/10.1093/nutrit/nuv045

Berger, B., & Motl, R. (2001). Physical activity and quality of life. In eds R. N. Singer, H. A. Hausenblas, & C. M. Janelle (Eds.), *Handbook of sport psychology* (2nd ed., pp.636–670). Wiley.

Black, D. S., O'Reilly, G. A., Olmstead, R., Breen, E. C., & Irwin, M. R. (2015). Mindfulness meditation and improvement in sleep quality and daytime impairment among older adults with sleep disturbances: A randomized clinical trial. *JAMA Internal Medicine, 175*(4), 494–501. https://doi.org/10.1001/jamainternmed.2014.8081

Birmaher, B., & Brent, D. (2007). Practice parameter for the assessment and treatment of children and adolescents with depressive disorders. *Journal of the American Academy of Child and Adolescent Psychiatry, 46*(11), 1503–1526. https://doi.org/10.1097/chi.0b013e318145ae1c

Bitsko, R. H., Claussen, A. H., Lichstein, J., Black, L. I., Everett Jones, S., Danielson, M. L., Hoenig, J. M., Davis Jack, S. P., Brody, D. J., Gyawali, , S., Maenner, M. J., Warner, M., Holland, K. M., Perou, R., Crosby, A. E., Blumberg, S. J., Avenevoli, S., Kaminski, J.cW., Ghandour, R. M. (2022) Mental health surveillance among children—United States, 2013–2019. *CDC: Morbidity and Mortality Weekly Report Suppl 2022, 71*(Suppl. 2), 1–42. http://dx.doi.org/10.15585/mmwr.su7102a1

Bjork, E. L, & Bjork, R. A. (2011). *Making things hard on yourself, but in a good way: Creating desirable difficulties to enhance learning. In: Psychology and the real world: Essays illustrating fundamental contributions to society.* Worth Publishers.

Bonnici, H. M., Chadwick, M. J., Lutti, A., Hassabis, D., Weiskopf, N., & Maguire, E. A. (2012). Detecting representations of recent and remote Autobiographical memories in vmPFC and hippocampus. *The Journal of Neuroscience, 32*(47), 16982–16991. https://doi.org/10.1523/JNEUROSCI.2475-12.2012

Boomhower, S. (2020, July 30). *Substance Abuse* [Lecture]. PSYC E-1410: Psychopharmacology, Harvard University, Boston, MA, United States.

Bossong, M. G., & Niesink, R. J. (2010). Adolescent brain maturation, the endogenous cannabinoid system and the neurobiology of cannabis-induced schizophrenia. *Progress in Neurobiology, 92*, 370–385. https://doi.org/10.1016/j.pneurobio.2010.06.010

Boyatzis, R. E., & Akrivou, K. (2006). The ideal self as the driver of intentional change. *The Journal of Management Development, 25*(7), 624–642. https://doi.org/10.1108/02621710610678454

Boyatzis, R. E. (2008). Leadership development from a complexity perspective. *Consulting Psychology Journal, 60*(4), 298–313. https://doi.org/10.1037/1065-9293.60.4.298

Bousman, C. A., Bengesser, S. A., Aitchison, K. J., Amare, A. T., Aschauer, H., Baune, B. T., Asl, B. B., Bishop, J. R., Burmeister, M., Chaumette, B., Chen, L.-S., Cordner, Z. A., Deckert, J., Degehardt, F., DeLisi, L. E., Folkersen, L., Kennedy, J. L., Klein, T. E., McClay, J. L., McMahon, F. J., Musil, R., Saccone, N. L., Sangkuhl, K., Stowe, R. M., Tan, E.-C., Tiwari, A. K., Zai, C. C., Zai, G., Zhang, J., Gaedigk, A., Müller, D. J. (2020). Review and consensus on pharmacogenomic testing in psychiatry. *Pharmacopsychiatry, 54*(1), 5–17. https://doi.org/10.1055/a-1288-1061

Britton, J. C., Grillon, C., Lissek, S., Norcross, M. A., Szuhany, K. L., Chen, G., Ernst, M., Nelson, E. E., Leibenluft, E., Shechner, T., & Pine, D. S. (2013). Response to learned threat: An fMRI study in adolescent and adult anxiety. *The American Journal of Psychiatry, 170*(10), 1195–1204. https://doi.org/10.1176/appi.ajp.2013.12050651

Brown, K. W., & Ryan, R. M. (2003). The benefits of being present. *Journal of Personality and Social Psychology, 84*(4), 822–848. https://doi.org/10.1037/0022-3514.84.4.822

Brown, K. W., Ryan, R. M., & Creswell, J. D. (2007). Mindfulness: Theoretical foundations and evidence for its salutary effects. *Psychological Inquiry, 18*, 211–237. DOI: https://doi.org/10.1080/10478400701598298

Bueno-Notivol, J., Gracia-García, P., Olaya, B., Lasheras, I., López-Antón, R., & Santabárbara, J. (2021). Prevalence of depression during the COVID-19 outbreak: A meta-analysis of community-based studies. *International Journal of Clinical and Health Psychology, 21*(1), 100196. https://doi.org/10.1016/j.ijchp.2020.07.007

Burke Harris, N. (2018). *The deepest well: Healing the long-term effects of childhood adversity.* Houghton Mifflin Harcourt.

Burns, D. D. (1999). *The feeling good handbook.* Penguin.

Cai, L.-F., Wang, S.-B., Hou, C.-L., Li, Z.-B., Liao, Y.-J., & Jia, F.-J. (2022). Association between non-suicidal self-injury and gut microbial characteristics in chinese adolescent. *Neuropsychiatric Disease and Treatment, 18*, 1315–1328. https://doi.org/10.2147/NDT.S360588

Caine, B. (2021, September 18). *Introduction to Neuroscience* [Lecture]. PSYC E-1415: Dopamine, Harvard University, Boston, MA, United States.

Campbell, J. A., & Løkken, I. M. (2023). Inside out: A scoping review on optimism, growth mindsets, and positive psychology for child well-being in ECEC. *Education Sciences, 13*(1), 29. https://doi.org/10.3390/educsci13010029

Cameron, I. M., Crawford, J. R., Lawton, K., & Reid, I. C. (2008). Psychometric comparison of PHQ-9 and HADS for measuring depression severity in primary care. *British Journal of General Practice, 58*(546), 32–36. https://doi.org/10.3399/bjgp08X263794

Carsley, D., & Heath, N. L. (2019). Evaluating the effectiveness of a mindfulness coloring activity for test anxiety in children. *The Journal of Educational Research, 112*(2), 143–151. https://doi.org/10.1080/00220671.2018.1448749

Cascio, C. N., O'Donnell, M. B., Tinney, F. J., Lieberman, M. D., Taylor, S. E., Strecher, V. J., & Falk, E. B. (2016). Self-affirmation activates brain systems associated with self-related processing and reward and is reinforced by future orientation. *Social Cognitive and Affective Neuroscience, 11*(4), 621–629. https://doi.org/10.1093/scan/nsv136

Caspi, A., Sugden, K., Poulton, R., Moffitt, T. E., Taylor, A., Craig, I. W., Harrington, H., McClay, J., Mill, J., Martin, J., & Braithwaite, A. (2003). Influence of life stress on depression: Moderation by a polymorphism in the 5-HTT gene. *Science, 301*(5631), 386–389. https://doi.org/10.1126/science.1083968

Casu, M. A., Pisu, C., Sanna, A., Tambaro, S., Spada, G. P., Mongeau, R., & Pani, L. (2005). Effect of delta9-tetrahydrocannabinol on phosphorylated CREB in rat cerebellum: an immunohistochemical study. *Brain Research,1048(1-2)*, 41–47. https://doi.org/10.1016/j.brainres.2005.04.053

Cawley, A., & Tejeiro, R. (2024). Brief Virtual Reality Mindfulness is More Effective than Audio Mindfulness and Colouring in Reducing Stress in University Students. *Mindfulness, 15*(2), 272–281. https://doi.org/10.1007/s12671-024-02306-9

Challenge Success. (2021, February 15). *Kids under pressure: A look at student well-being and engagement during the pandemic.* https://challengesuccess.org/wp-content/uploads/2021/02/CS-NBC-Study-Kids-Under-Pressure-PUBLISHED.pdf

Chattopadhyay, S., Tait, R., Simas, T., van Nieuwenhuizen, A., Hagan, C. C., Holt, R. J., Graham, J., Sahakian, B. J., Wilkinson, P. O., Goodyer, I. M., & Suckling, J. (2017). Cognitive behavioral therapy lowers elevated functional connectivity in depressed adolescents. *EBioMedicine 17*, 216–222. http://dx.doi.org/10.1016/j.ebiom.2017.02.010

Cheuvront, S. N., Carter, R., III, & Sawka, M. N. (2003). Fluid balance and endurance performance. *Current Sports Medicine Reports, 2*(4): 202–208.

Choi, J. G., Huh, E., Kim, N., Kim, D.-H., & Oh, M. S. (2019). High-throughput 16S rRNA gene sequencing reveals that 6-hydroxydopamine affects gut microbial environment. *PloS One, 14*(8), e0217194–e0217194. https://doi.org/10.1371/journal.pone.0217194

Churcher, K., Downs, E., & Tewksbury, D. (2014). "Friending" Vygotsky: A social constructivist pedagogy of knowledge building through classroom social media use. *The Journal of Effective Teaching, 14*(1), 33.

Clear. J., (2018). *Atomic habits: Tiny changes, remarkable results: An easy & proven way to build good habits & break bad ones.* Avery, an imprint of Penguin Random House.

Clements-Cortes, A., & Bartel, L. (2018). Are We Doing More Than We Know? Possible Mechanisms of Response to Music Therapy. *Frontiers in Medicine, 5*, 255–255. https://doi.org/10.3389/fmed.2018.00255

Cohen, G. L., & Sherman, D. K. (2014). The Psychology of change: Self-affirmation and social psychological intervention. *Annual Review of Psychology, 65*(1), 333–371. https://doi.org/10.1146/annurev-psych-010213-115137

Cohen-Cory, S. (2002). The developing synapse: Construction and modulation of synaptic structures and circuits. *Science, 298*, 770–776. DOI: 10.1126/science.1075510

Colarossi, L. G., & Eccles, J. S. (2003). Differential effects of support providers on adolescents' mental health. *Social Work Research, 27*(1), 19–30. https://doi.org/10.1093/swr/27.1.19

Cole, J., Costafreda, S. G., McGuffin, P., & Fu, C. H. (2011). Hippocampal atrophy in first episode depression: A meta-analysis of magnetic resonance imaging studies. *Journal of Affective Disorders, 134*(1), 483–487. https://doi.org/10.1016/j.jad.2011.05.057

Cole, M. (1986). The zone of proximal development: where culture and cognition. *Culture, communication, and cognition: Vygotskian perspectives, 146*.

Conner, J. O., & Pope, D. C. (2013). Not just robo-students: Why full engagement matters and how schools can promote it. *Journal of Youth and Adolescence, 42*(9), 1426–1442. https://doi.org/10.1007/s10964-013-9948-y

Crane, R. S., Brewer, J., Feldman, C., Kabat-Zinn, J., Santorelli, S., Williams, J. M. G., & Kuyken, W. (2017). What defines mindfulness-based programs? The warp and the weft. *Psychological Medicine, 47*(6), 990–999. https://doi.org/10.1017/S0033291716003317

Crowley, S. J., & Eastman, C. I. (2017). Human adolescent phase response curves to bright white light. *Journal of Biological Rhythms, 32*(4), 334–344. https://doi.org/10.1177/0748730417713423

Csikszentmihalyi, M., & Hunter, J. (2003). Happiness in everyday life: The uses of experience sampling. *Journal of Happiness Studies, 4*(2), 185–199. https://doi.org/10.1023/A:1024409732742

Curran, H. V., Freeman, T. P., Mokrysz, C., Lewis, D. A., Morgan, C. J. A., & Parsons, L. H. (2016). Keep off the grass? Cannabis, cognition and addiction. *Nature Reviews. Neuroscience, 17*(5), 293–306. https://doi.org/10.1038/nrn.2016.28

De Neve, J.-E., & Oswald, A. J. (2012). Estimating the influence of life satisfaction and positive affect on later income using sibling fixed effects. *PNAS Proceedings of the National Academy of Sciences of the United States of America, 109*(49), 19953–19958. https://doi.org/10.1073/pnas.1211437109

Diamond A. (2013). Executive functions. *Annual Review of Psychology, 64*, 135–68. DOI: 10.1146/annurev-psych-113011-143750

Di Consiglio, M., Merola, S., Pascucci, T., Violani, C., & Couyoumdjian, A. (2021). The impact of COVID-19 pandemic on Italian university students' mental health: Changes across the waves. *International Journal of Environmental Research and Public Health, 18*(18), 9897. https://doi.org/10.3390/ijerph18189897

Dickens, L. R. (2017). Using gratitude to promote positive change: A series of meta-analyses investigating the effectiveness of gratitude interventions. *Basic and Applied Social Psychology, 39*(4), 193–208. https://doi.org/10.1080/01973533.2017.1323638

Diener, E. (2000). Subjective well-being: The science of happiness and a proposal for a national index. *The American Psychologist, 55*(1), 34–43. https://doi.org/10.1037/0003-066X.55.1.34

Diener, E., Kahneman, D., & Helliwell, J. (2010). *International Differences in Well-Being* (1st ed.). Oxford University Press New York. https://doi.org/10.1093/acprof:o- so/9780199732739.001.0001

Diener, E., Lucas, R. E., & Oishi, S. (2002). Subjective well-being: The science of happiness and life satisfaction. In C. R. Snyder & S. J. Lopez (Eds.), Handbook of positive psychology (pp. 463–73). Oxford University Press.

Diener, E., & Suh, E. M. (Eds.). (2003). Culture and subjective well-being. MIT Press.

Diener, E., Suh, E. M., Lucas, R. E., & Smith, H. L. (1999). Subjective well-being: Three decades of progress. *Psychological Bulletin, 125*(2), 276–302. https://doi.org/10.1037/0033-2909.125.2.276

Dirksen, J. (2016). *Design for how people learn (1st edition)*. New Riders.

Donahue, D. (2021, February 15). NBC News: 'TODAY,' 'NBC Nightly News,' MSNBC, NBCNews.com, NBC News NOW & 'StayTuned'. *Kids under pressure: A look at student well-being and engagement during the pandemic.* New York, NY: National Broadcasting Service. https://press.nbcnews.com/2021/02/15/student-stress-is-up-engagement-with-learning-is-down-according-to-new-research-study-by-nbc-news-challenge-success/

Dong, C., Chen, J., Harrington, A., Vinod, K. Y., Hegde, M. L., & Hegde, V. L. (2019). Cannabinoid exposure during pregnancy and its impact on immune function. *Cellular and Molecular Life Sciences: CMLS, 76*(4), 729–743. https://doi.org/10.1007/s00018-018-2955-0

Drysdale, A. T., Grosenick, L., Downar, J., Dunlop, K., Mansouri, F., Meng, Y., Fetcho, R. N., Zebley, B., Oathes, D. J., Etkin, A., Schatzberg, A. F., Sudheimer, K., Keller, J., Mayberg, H. S., Gunning, F. M., Alexopoulos, G. S., Fox, M. D., Pascual-Leone, A., Voss, H. U., Casey, B. J., Dubin, M. J., & Liston, C. (2017). Resting-state connectivity biomarkers define neurophysiological subtypes of depression. *Natural Medicine, 23*, 28–38. https://doi.10.1038/nm.4246

Dweck, C. (2017) *Mindset: Changing the way you think to fulfill your potential*. Random House.

Dzulkifli, M. A., & Mustafar, M. F. (2013). The Influence of colour on memory performance: A review. *The Malaysian Journal of Medical Sciences, 20*(2), 3–9.

Eagleman, D. (2020). *Livewired: The inside story of the ever-changing brain* (1st ed.). Pantheon Books.

Edwards, S. (2010, August 9). *Deciphering the teenage brain*. Harvard Medical School. News and Research. https://hms.harvard.edu/news/deciphering-teenage-brain#:~:text=The%20maturing%20of%20the%20forward,be%20complete%20until%20age%2030.

Egger, F., Benzing, V., Conzelmann, A., & Schmidt, M. (2019). Boost your brain, while having a break! The effects of long-term cognitively engaging physical activity breaks on children's executive functions and academic achievement. *PLoS ONE 14*(3), e0212482. https://doi.org/10.1371/journal.pone.0212482

Ellis, R., Seal, M. L., Adamson, C., Beare, R., Simmons, J. G., Whittle, S., & Allen, N. B. (2016). Brain connectivity networks and longitudinal trajectories of depression symptoms in adolescence. *Psychiatry Research Neuroimaging, 260*, 62–69. https://doi.org/10.1016/j.pscychresns.2016.12.010

English, T., & Chen, S. (2011). Self-concept consistency and culture: The differential impact of two forms of consistency. *Personality & Social Psychology Bulletin, 37*(6), 838–849. https://doi.org/10.1177/0146167211400621

Erickson, K. I., Banducci, S. E., Weinstein, A. M., MacDonald, A. W., Ferrell, R. E., Halder, I., Flory, J. D., & Manuck, S. B. (2013). The brain-derived neurotrophic factor Val66Met polymorphism moderates an effect of physical activity on working memory performance. *Psychological Science, 24*(9), 1770–1779. https://doi.org/10.1177/0956797613480367

Fadda, R., Rapinett, G., Grathwohl, D., Parisi, M., Fanari, R., Calò, C. M., & Schmitt, J. (2012). Effects of drinking supplementary water at school on cognitive performance in children. *Appetite, 59*(3), 730–737. https://doi.org/10.1016/j.appet.2012.07.005

Falk, E., & Scholz, C. (2018). Persuasion, influence, and value: Perspectives from communication and social neuroscience. *Annual Review of Psychology, 69*(1), 329–356. https://doi.org/10.1146/annurev-psych-122216-011821

Fan, P. W., Burns, S. F., & Lee, J. K. W. (2020). Efficacy of ingesting an oral rehydration solution after exercise on fluid balance and endurance performance. *Nutrients, 12*(12), 3826. https://doi.org/10.3390/nu12123826

Faraci, P., Bottaro, R., Valenti, G. D., & Craparo, G. (2022). Psychological well-being during the second wave of COVID-19 pandemic: The mediation role of generalized anxiety. *Psychology Research and Behavior Management, 15*, 695–709. https://doi.org/10.2147/PRBM.S354083

Feiring, C., Taska, L., & Lewis, M. (1999). Age and gender differences in children's and adolescents' adaptation to sexual abuse. *Child Abuse & Neglect, 23*(2), 115–128. https://doi.org/10.1016/S0145-2134(98)00116-1

Field, A. (2018). *Discovering Statistics Using IBM SPSS Statistics* (5th ed.). Sage Publications, Inc.

Fogg, B. J., (2019). *Tiny habits: The small changes that change everything*. Houghton Mifflin Harcourt.

Food and Nutrition Board. (1980). *Recommended dietary allowances* (9th ed.). National Academy Press.

Gericke, F., Ebert, D. D., Breet, E., Auerbach, R. P., & Bantjes, J. (2021). A qualitative study of university students' experience of internet-based CBT for depression. *Counselling and Psychotherapy Research, 21*(4), 792–804. https://doi.org/10.1002/capr.12465

Giedd, J. N., Blumenthal, J., & Jeffries, N. O. (1999). Brain development during childhood and adolescence: A longitudinal MRI study. *Nature Neuroscience, 2*, 861–863. https://doi.org/10.1038/13158

Gillett, R. (2014, September 5). *The new habit challenge: Meditate for 20 minutes a day*. Fast Company. https://www.fastcompany.com/3035250/the-new-habit-challenge-meditate-for-20-minutes-a-day#:~:text=Just%2020%20minutes%20a%20day,not%20to%20mention%20less%20anxious.

Gillies, D., Christou, M. A., Dixon, A. C., Featherston, O. J., Rapti, I., Garcia-Anguita, A., Villasis-Keever, M., Reebye, P., Christou, E., Al Kabir, N., & Christou, P. A. (2018). Prevalence and characteristics of self-harm in adolescents: Meta-analyses of community-based studies 1990–2015. *Journal of the American Academy of Child & Adolescent Psychiatry, 57*(10), 733–741. https://doi.org/10.1016/j.jaac.2018.06.018

Goodyer, T. S., Byford, S., Dubicka, B., Hill, J., Kelvin, R., Reynolds, S., Roberts, C., Senior, R., Suckling, J., Wilkinson, P., Target, M., & Fonagy, P. (2011). Improving mood with psychoanalytic and cognitive therapies (IMPACT): A pragmatic effectiveness superiority trial to investigate whether specialized psychological treatment reduces the risk for relapse in adolescents with moderate to severe unipolar depression: Study protocol for a randomized controlled trial. *Trials, 12*(1), 175. https://doi.org/10.1186/1745-6215-12-175

Gordon, J. S., Sbarra, D., Armin, J., Pace, T. W. W., Gniady, C., & Barraza, Y. (2021). Use of a guided imagery mobile app (see me serene) to reduce COVID-19–related stress: Pilot feasibility study. *JMIR Formative Research, 5*(10), e32353–e32353. https://doi.org/10.2196/32353

Gould, M. S., Lake, A. M., Kleinman, M., Galfalvy, H., & McKeon, R. (2022). Third-party callers to the national suicide prevention lifeline: Seeking assistance on behalf of people at imminent risk of suicide. *Suicide & Life-Threatening Behavior, 52*(1), 37–48. https://doi.org/10.1111/sltb.12769

Gould, M. S., Lake, A. M., Munfakh, J. L., Galfalvy, H., Kleinman, M., Williams, C., Glass, A., & McKeon, R. (2016). Helping callers to the national suicide prevention lifeline who are at imminent risk of suicide: Evaluation of caller risk profiles and interventions implemented. *Suicide & Life-Threatening Behavior, 46*(2), 172–190. https://doi.org/10.1111/sltb.12182

Gratzer, D., & Khalid-Khan, F. (2016). Internet-delivered cognitive behavioural therapy in the treatment of psychiatric illness. *Canadian Medical Association Journal, 188*(4), 263–272. https://doi.org/10.1503/cmaj.150007

Greenberg, P. E., Fournier, A.-A., Sisitsky, T., Pike, C. T., & Kessler, R. C. (2015). The economic burden of adults with major depressive disorder in the United States (2005 and 2010). *Journal Clinical Psychiatry 76*, 155–162. https://doi.10.4088/JCP.14m09298

Greene, T., Bell, P., & Boyer, W. (1983). Coloring the environment–Hue, arousal, and boredom. *Bulletin of the Psychonomic Society, 21*(4), 253–254. https://doi.org/10.3758/BF0333470

Guerin, A., & Murphy, B. (2015). Repeated reading as a method to improve reading fluency for struggling adolescent readers. *Journal of Adolescent & Adult Literacy, 58*(7), 551–560. https://doi.org/10.1002/jaal.395

Hagopian, L. P., & Jennett, H. K. (2008). Behavioral assessment and treatment of anxiety in individuals with intellectual disabilities and autism. *Journal of Developmental Physical and Disabilities 20*, 467–483. https://doi.org/10.1007/s10882-008-9114-8

Haimovitz, K., & Dweck, C. S. (2017). The origins of children's growth and fixed mindsets: New research and a new proposal. *Child Development, 88*(6), 1849–1859. https://doi.org/10.1111/cdev.12955

Hamermesh, D., Frazis, H., & Stewart, J. (2005). Data Watch: The American Time Use Survey. *Journal of Economic Perspectives. 19*(1), 221–232.

Harper, N. J., Fernee, C. R., & Gabrielsen, L. E. (2021). Nature's role in outdoor therapies: An umbrella review. *International Journal of Environmental Research and Public Health, 18*(10), 5117. https://doi.org/10.3390/ijerph18105117

Hartig, T., & Staats, H. (2006). The need for psychological restoration as a determinant of environmental preferences. *Journal of Environmental Psychology, 26*(3), 215–226. https://doi.org/10.1016/j.jenvp.2006.07.007

Heath, C., & Heath, D., (2010). *Switch: how to change things when change is hard*. Broadway Books.

Hebb, D. (1949). *The organisation of behaviour*. John Wiley and Sons.

Helliwell, J. F., Layard, R., Sachs, J. D., De Neve, J.-E., Aknin, L. B., & Wang, S. (Eds.). (2024). *World Happiness Report 2024*. University of Oxford: Wellbeing Research Centre.

Henderson, C., Noblett, J., Parke, H., Clement, S., Caffrey, A., Gale-Grant, O., Schulze, B., Druss, B., & Thornicroft, G. (2014). Mental health-related stigma in health care and mental health care settings. *The Lancet. Psychiatry, 1*(6), 467–482. https://doi.org/10.1016/S2215-0366(14)00023-6

Hernantes, N., Pumar-Méndez, M. J., López-Dicastillo, O., Iriarte, A., & Mujika, A. (2020). Volunteerism as adolescent health promotion asset: a scoping review. *Health Promotion International, 35*(3), 610–623. https://doi.org/10.1093/heapro/daz026

Hogg, M. A. (2012). *Social identity and the psychology of groups*. In Leary, M. R., & Tangney, J. P. Handbook of self and identity (2nd ed.). Guilford Press.

Hölzel, B. K., Lazar, S. W., Gard, T., Schuman-Olivier, Z., Vago, D. R., & Ott, U. (2011). How does mindfulness meditation work? Proposing mechanisms of action from a conceptual and neural perspective. *Perspectives on Psychological Science, 6*(6), 537–559. https://doi.org/10.1177/1745691611419671

Hubel, D., & Wiesel, T. (2012). David Hubel and Torsten Wiesel. *Neuron, 75*(2), 182–184. https://doi.org/10.1016/j.neuron.2012.07.002

Huotari, P., Nupponen, H., Mikkelsson, L., Laakso, L., & Kujala, U. (2011). Adolescent physical fitness and activity as predictors of adulthood activity. *Journal of Sports Sciences, 29*(11), 1135–1141. https://doi.org/10.1080/02640414.2011.585166

Insel, C. B., Garvey, M., Heinssen, R., Pine, D. S., Quinn, K., Sanislow, C., & Wang, P. (2010). Research domain criteria (RDoC): Toward a new classification framework for research on mental disorders. *The American Journal of Psychiatry, 167*(7), 748–751. https://doi.org/10.1176/appi.ajp.2010.09091379

Isaacs, D. (2020). Respect. *Journal of Pediatrics and Child Health, 56*(2), 189–190. https://doi-org.ezp-prod1.hul.harvard.edu/10.1111/jpc.14663

Ito, E., Walker, G. J., Mitas, O., & Liu, H. (2019). Cultural similarities and differences in the relationship between types of leisure activity and happiness in Canadian, Chinese, and Japanese university students. *World Leisure Journal, 61*(1), 30–42. https://doi.org/10.1080/16078055.2018.1535449

Izard, C. E. (1971). *The face of emotion*. Appleton-Century-Crofts.

Jack, A. I., Boyatzis, R. E., Khawaja, M. S., Passarelli, A. M., & Leckie, R. L. (2013). Visioning in the brain: An fMRI study of inspirational coaching and mentoring. *Social Neuroscience, 8*(4), 369–384. https://doi.org/10.1080/17470919.2013.808259

Jensen, F. E., & Nutt, A. E. (2015). *The teenage brain: A neuroscientist's survival guide to raising adolescents and young adults*. Harper, an imprint of HarperCollinsPublishers.

John-Steiner, V., & Mahn, H. (1996). Sociocultural approaches to learning and development: A Vygotskian framework. *Educational Psychologist, 31*(3-4), 191–206. https://doi.org/10.1207/s15326985ep3103&4_4

Johnson, S. (2022, January 31). *Why is 18 the age of adulthood if the brain can take 30 years to mature?* Big Think. Neuropsych. https://bigthink.com/neuropsych/adult-brain/

Kaczmarek, L. D., Behnke, M., Kashdan, T. B., Kusiak, A., Marzec, K., Mistrzak, M., & Włodarczyk, M. (2018). Smile intensity in social networking profile photographs is related to greater scientific achievements. *The Journal of Positive Psychology, 13*(5), 435–439. https://doi.org/10.1080/17439760.2017.1326519

Kamin, M. L., & Dweck, C. S. (1999). Person versus process praise and criticism: Implications for contingent self-worth and coping. *Developmental Psychology, 35*(3), 835–847. https://doi.org/10.1037/0012-1649.35.3.835

Kandel, E. R., Schwartz, J. H., Jessell, T. M. (2000). *Principles of neural science* (4th ed.). McGraw-Hill, Health Professions Division.

Kanine, R. M., Bush, M. L., Davis, M., Jones, J. D., Sbrilli, M. D., & Young, J. F. (2023). Depression prevention in pediatric primary care: Implementation and outcomes of interpersonal psychotherapy—adolescent skills training. *Child Psychiatry and Human Development, 54*(1), 96–108. https://doi.org/10.1007/s10578-021-01222-6

Karns, C. M., Moore, W. E., & Mayr, U. (2017). The cultivation of pure altruism via gratitude: A functional MRI study of change with gratitude practice. *Frontiers in Human Neuroscience, 11*, 599–599. https://doi.org/10.3389/fnhum.2017.00599

Keyes, K. M., Pratt, C., Galea, S., McLaughlin, K. A., Koenen, K. C., & Shear, M. K. (2014). The burden of loss: Unexpected death of a loved one and psychiatric disorders across the life course in a national study. *American Journal of Psychiatry, 171*(8), 864–871. https://doi.org/10.1176/appi.ajp.2014.13081132

Kim, E.-J., Kang, H.-W., & Park, S.-M. (2024). Determinants of the happiness of adolescents: A leisure perspective. *PloS One, 19*(4), e0301843–e0301843. https://doi.org/10.1371/journal.pone.0301843

Kim, T. H., Jeong, G. W., Baek, H. S., Kim, G. W., Sundaram, T., Kang, H. K., Lee, S. W., Kim, H.-J., & Song, J.-K.c(2010). Human brain activation in response to visual stimulation with rural and urban scenery pictures: A functional magnetic resonance imaging study. *The Science of the Total Environment, 408*(12), 2600–2607. https://doi.org/10.1016/j.scitotenv.2010.02.025

Kobak, K. A., Mundt, J. C., & Kennard, B. (2015). Integrating technology into cognitive behavior therapy for adolescent depression: A pilot study. *Annals of General Psychiatry, 14*(37), 37. https://doi.org/10.1186/s12991-015-0077-8

Kolb, D. A. (1984). *Experiential learning: Experience as the source of learning and development*. Prentice-Hall.

Krashen, S. D. (1993). *The power of reading: Insights from the research*. Libraries Unlimited.

Krause, D. S., & Dowd, D. (2022). Use of a consultation service following pharmacogenetic testing in psychiatry. *Pharmacogenomics, 23*(5), 327–333. https://doi.org/10.2217/pgs-2021-0121

Krusemark, E. A., Novak, L. R., Gitelman, D. R., Li, W. (2013). When the sense of smell meets emotion: anxiety-state-dependent olfactory processing and neural circuitry adaptation. *The Journal of Neuroscience 33*(39):15324–15332. DOI: 10.1523/JNEUROSCI.1835-13.2013

Kuntz, L. (2022). New 988 Suicide Hotline Hope or Hype? *The Psychiatric Times, 39*(7), 1.

Kjønniksen, L., Torsheim, T., & Wold, B. (2008). Tracking of leisure-time physical activity during adolescence and young adulthood: a 10-year longitudinal study. *International Journal of Behavioral Nutrition and Physical Activity, 5*(1): 1–11. https:// doi.org/10.1186/1479-5868-5-69

Lacagnina, S. (2019). Epigenetics. *American Journal of Lifestyle Medicine, 13*(2), 165–169. https://doi.org/10.1177/1559827618817247

Laja Garcia, A. I., de Lourdes Samaniego-Vaesken, M., Partearroyo, T., & Varela-Moreiras, G. (2019). Adaptation and validation of the hydration status questionnaire in a Spanish adolescent-young population: A cross sectional study. *Nutrients, 11*(3), 565. https://doi.org/10.3390/nu11030565

Langley, A. K., Bergman, L., McCracken, J., & Piacentini, J. C. (2004). Impairment in childhood anxiety disorders: Preliminary examination of the child anxiety impact scale–parent version. *Journal of Child and Adolescent Psychopharmacology, 14*(1), 105–114. http://doi.org/10.1089/104454604773840544

LaBar, K. S., Gitelman, D. R., Parrish, T. B., & Mesulam, M.-M. (1999). Neuroanatomic overlap of working memory and spatial attention networks: A functional MRI comparison within subjects. *NeuroImage, 10*(6), 695–704. https://doi.org/10.1006/nimg.1999.0503

Latorre-Pérez, A., Hernández, M., Iglesias, J. R., Morán, J., Pascual, J., Porcar, M., Vilanova, C., & Collado, L. (2021).The Spanish gut microbiome reveals links between microorganisms and Mediterranean diet. *Scientific Reports 11*, 21602. https://doi.org/10.1038/s41598-021-01002-1

Laumann, K., Gärling, T., & Stormark, K. M. (2003). Selective attention and heart rate responses to natural and urban environments. *Journal of Environmental Psychology, 23*(2), 125-134. https://doi.org/10.1016/S0272-4944(02)00110-X

Layard, R. (2020). *Can we be happier? Evidence and Ethics*. Penguin Books.

Lee, G., Feng, H., Xu, S., Jin, N., & Huang, J. (2020). Arranging play activities with missing items to increase object-substitution symbolic play in children with autism spectrum disorder. *Disability and Rehabilitation, 43*(22), 3199–3211. https://doi:10.1080/ 09638288.2020.1734107

Lee, J., & Yoon, S. Y. (2017). The effects of repeated reading on reading fluency for student with reading disabilities. *Journal of Learning Disabilities, 50*(2), 213–224. https://doi.org/10.1177/0022219415605194

Leech, R., & Sharp, D. J. (2014). The role of the posterior cingulate cortex in cognition and disease. *Brain, 137*(1), 12–32.

Liu, Q., He, H., Yang, J., Feng, X., Zhao, F., & Lyu, J. (2020). Changes in the global burden of depression from 1990 to 2017: Findings from the global burden of disease study. *Journal of Psychiatric Research, 126*, 134–140. https://doi.org/10.1016/j.jpsychires.2019.08.002

Lopizzo, N., Marizzoni, M., Begni, V., Mazzelli, M., Provasi, S., Borruso, L., Riva, M. A., & Cattaneo, A. (2021). Social isolation in adolescence and long-term changes in the gut microbiota composition and in the hippocampal inflammation: Implications for psychiatric disorders. *Psychoneuroendocrinology, 133*, 105416. https://doi.org/10.1016/j.psyneuen.2021.105416

Lyubomirsky, S., King, L., & Diener, E. (2005). The benefits of frequent positive affect: Does happiness lead to success? *Psychological Bulletin, 131*(6), 803–855. DOI: 10.1037/0033-2909.131.6.803

Mäkelä, S., Aaltonen, S., Korhonen, T., Rose, R. J., & Kaprio, J. (2017). Diversity of leisure-time sport activities in adolescence as a predictor of leisure-time physical activity in adulthood. *Scandinavian Journal of Medicine & Science in Sports, 27*(12), 1902–1912. https://doi.org/10.1111/sms.12837

Mahlouji, M., Vaghasloo, M. A., Dadmehr, M., Rezaeizadeh, H., Nazem, E., & Tajadini, H. (2020). Sweating as a preventive care and treatment strategy in traditional Persian medicine. *Galen Medical Journal, 9*, e2003. https://doi.org/10.31661/gmj.v9i0.2003

Mandolesi, L., Polverino, A., Montuori, S., Foti, F., Ferraioli, G., Sorrentino, P., & Sorrentino, G. (2018). Effects of physical exercise on cognitive functioning and wellbeing: Biological and psychological benefits. *Frontiers in Psychology, 9*, 509–509. https://doi.org/10.3389/fpsyg.2018.00509

Mantler, A., & Logan, A. C. (2015). Natural environments and mental health. *Advances in Integrative Medicine, 2*(1), 5–12. https://doi.org/10.1016/j.aimed.2015.03.002

Masicampo, E. J., & Baumeister, R. F. (2011). Consider it done! Plan making can eliminate the cognitive effects of unfulfilled goals. *Journal of Personality and Social Psychology, 101*(4), 667–683. https://doi.org/10.1037/a0024192

Masten, A., Best, K., & Garmezy, N. (1990). Resilience and development: Contributions from the study of children who overcome adversity. *Development and Psychopathology, 2*(4), 425–444. doi:10.1017/S0954579400005812

McAdams, C. J., & Krawczyk, D. C. (2014). Who am I? How do I look? Neural differences in self-identity in anorexia nervosa. *Social Cognitive and Affective Neuroscience, 9*(1), 12–21. https://doi.org/10.1093/scan/nss093

Memarian, N., Torre, J. B., Haltom, K. E., Stanton, A. L., & Lieberman, M. D. (2017). Neural activity during affect labeling predicts expressive writing effects on well-being: GLM and SVM approaches. *Social Cognitive and Affective Neuroscience, 12*(9), 1437–1447. https://doi.org/10.1093/scan/nsx084

Mehta, R., & Zhu, R. (2009). Blue or red? Exploring the effect of color on cognitive task performances. *Science (American Association for the Advancement of Science), 323*(5918), 1226–1229. https://doi.org/10.1126/science.1169144

Miller, C. (2023, August 8). *Does Social Media Use Cause Depression?: How heavy Instagram and Facebook use may be affecting kids negatively*. Child Mind Institute. https://childmind.org/article/is-social-media-use-causing-depression/

Miller, P. (2016). *Theories of developmental psychology* (6th ed.). Worth Publishers.

Mineo, L. (2018, April 17). *Less stress clearer thoughts with mindfulness meditation*. Harvard Gazette. https://news.harvard.edu/gazette/story/2018/04/less-stress-clearer-thoughts-with-mindfulness-meditation/

Miyake, A, Friedman, N. P., Emerson, M. J., Witzki, A. H., Howerter, A, Wager, T. D. (2000) The unity and diversity of executive functions and their contributions to complex "frontal lobe" tasks: A latent variable analysis. *Cognitive Psychology, 41*, 49–100. https://doi.org/10.1006/cogp.1999.0734 PMID: 10945922

Mora-Ripoll, R. (2010). The therapeutic value of laughter in medicine. *Alternative Therapies in Health and Medicine, 16*(6), 56–64.

Moraes, M. M., Rabelo, P. C. R., Pinto, V. A., Pires, W., Wanner, S. P., Szawka, R. E., & Soares, D. D. (2018). Auditory stimulation by exposure to melodic music increases dopamine and serotonin activities in rat forebrain areas linked to reward and motor control. *Neuroscience Letters, 673*, 73–78. https://doi.org/10.1016/j.neulet.2018.02.058 2018

Mousa, H. A. L. (2016). Health effects of alkaline diet and water, reduction of digestive-tract bacterial load, and earthing. *Alternative Therapies in Health and Medicine, 22*(Suppl. 1), 24–33.

Mousa, H. A.-L. (2022). Prevention and treatment of COVID-19 infection by earthing. *Biomedical Journal. 46*(1), 60–69. https://doi.org/10.1016/j.bj.2022.08.002

Nair, P. S., Raijas, P., Ahvenainen, M., Philips, A. K., Ukkola-Vuoti, L., & Järvelä, I. (2021). Music-listening regulates human microRNA expression. *Epigenetics, 16*(5), 554–566. https://doi.org/10.1080/15592294.2020.1809853

National Science Foundation. (2012) *Bothered by negative, unwanted thoughts? Just throw them away*. NewsRX LLC.

Nestor, J., Levin, C. J., & Swoap, S. J. (2019). The impact of deep breathing and alternate nostril breathing on heart rate variability: A human physiology laboratory. *Advances in Physiology Education, 13*(3), 270–276

Neuroscientifically Challenged. (2023). https://neuroscientificallychallenged.com

Nock, M. K., Boccagno, C. E., Kleiman, E. M., Ramirez, F., & Wang, S. B. (2019). Suicidal and nonsuicidal self-injury. In M. J. Prinstein, E. A. Youngstrom, E. J. Mash, & R. A. Barkley (Eds.), Treatment of disorders in childhood and adolescence (pp. 258–277). The Guilford Press.

Nobakht, N., Kamgar, M., Bilder, R. M., & Nobakht, E. (2022). Music for health: From ear to kidney. *Clinical Journal of the American Society of Nephrology, 17*(9), 1410–1412. https://doi.org/10.2215/CJN.04320422

Nouretdinov, I., Costafreda, S. G., Gammerman, A., Chervonenkis, A., Vovk, V., Vapnik, V., & Fu, C. H. (2011). Machine learning classification with confidence: Application of transductive conformal predictors to MRI-based diagnostic and prognostic markers in depression. *NeuroImage, 56*(2), 809–813. https://doi.org/10.1016/j.neuroimage.2010.05.023

Ober, C., Sinatra, S. T., & Zucker, M. (2014). *Earthing: The most important health discovery ever!* (2nd ed.). Basic Health Publications.

Organisation for Economic Co-operation and Development (OECD). (2019). *OECD Future of Education and Skills: Conceptual Learning Framework: Skills for 2030*. https://www.oecd.org/education/2030-project/teaching-and-learning/learning/skills/Skills_for_2030_concept_note.pdf

Oh, R. R. Y., Fielding, K. S. S., Chang, C.-C., Nghiem, L. T. P., Tan, C. L. Y., Quazi, S. A., Shanahan, D. F., Gaston, K. J., Carrasco, R. L., & Fuller, R. A. (2021). Health and wellbeing benefits from nature experiences in tropical settings depend on strength of connection to nature. *International Journal of Environmental Research and Public Health, 18*(19), 10149. https://doi.org/10.3390/ijerph181910149

Office of the Surgeon General (OSG). (2021). *Protecting Youth Mental Health: The U.S. Surgeon General's Advisory*. US Department of Health and Human Services. https://www.hhs.gov/sites/default/files/surgeon-general-youth-mental-health-advisory.pdf

Olivo, G., Gaudio, S., & Schioth, H. B. (2019). Brain and cognitive development in adolescents with anorexia nervosa: A systematic review of fMRI studies. *Nutrients, 11*(8), 1907. https://doi.org/10.3390/nu11081907

Onque, R. (2023, May 20). *This is the perfect amount of time to meditate, says mindfulness expert: It's when 'the biggest benefits happen*. CNBC.com. https://www.cnbc.com/2023/05/20/world-meditation-day-the-ideal-length-to-meditate-from-an-expert.html#:~:text="For%20most%20people%2C%2015%20to,in%20the%20first%20few%20minutes."

Oschman, J. L. (2022). Illnesses in technologically advanced societies due to lack of grounding (Earthing). *Biomedical Journal*. https://doi.org/10.1016/j.bj.2022.10.004

Pan, Y. (2011). Content-based verbal working memory-driven capture of visual attention. *Journal of Zhejiang University. Sciences edition, 38*(6), 727–732. https://doi.org/10.3785/j.issn.1008-9497.2011.06.022

Patton, G. C., Hibbert, M. E., Carlin, J., Shao, Q., Rosier, M., Caust, J., & Bowes, G. (1996). Menarche and the onset of depression and anxiety in Victoria, Australia. *Journal of Epidemiology and Community Health, 50*(6), 661–666. https://doi.org/10.1136/jech.50.6.661

Paus, T., Zijdenbos, A., Worsley, K., Collins, D. L., Blumenthal, J., Giedd, J. N., Rapoport, J. L., & Evans, A. C. (1999). Structural maturation of neural pathways in children and adolescents: In vivo study. *Science, 283*, 1908–1911.

Pawelski, P. S., & Pawelski, J. (2024, April 17). *Why Aren't Today's Youth Happy? A recent happiness report finds a steep drop in happiness among today's youth.* Psychology Today. Happiness. https://www.psychologytoday.com/us/blog/happy-together/202404/why-arent-todays-youth-happy

Pechtel, P., Lyons, R., K., Anderson, C. M., & Teicher, M. H. (2014). Sensitive periods of amygdala development: The role of maltreatment in preadolescence. *NeuroImage, 97*, 236–244. https://doi.org/10.1016/j.neuroimage.2014.04.025

Peerbooms, O., Rutten, B. P. F., Collip, D., Lardinois, M., Lataster, T., Thewissen, V., Rad, S. M., Drukker, M., Kenis, G., van Os, J., Myin-Germeys, I., & Van Winkel, R. (2011). Evidence that interactive effects of COMT and MTHFR moderate psychotic response to environmental stress. *Acta Psychiatrica Scandinavica, 125*(3), 247–256. https://doi.org/10.1111/j.1600-0447.2011.01806.x

Pennebaker, J. W. (1993). Putting stress into words: Health, linguistic, and therapeutic implications. *Behaviour Research and Therapy, 31*(6), 539–548. https://doi.org/10.1016/0005-7967(93)90105-4

Pennebaker, J. W. (2018). Expressive writing in psychological science. *Perspectives on Psychological Science, 13*(2), 226–229. https://doi.org/10.1177/1745691617707315

Phillippo, K. L., Conner, J., Davidson, S., & Pope, D. (2017). A systematic review of student self-report instruments that assess student-teacher relationships. *Teachers College Record, 119*(8), 1–42. https://doi.org/10.1177/016146811711900801

Piliavin, J. A., & Siegl, E. (2015). Health and well-being consequences of formal volunteering. In *the Oxford handbook of prosocial behavior.* Oxford University Press. https://doi.org/10.1093/oxfordhb/9780195399813.013.024;

Pine, D. S., Cohen, P., Gurley, D., Brook, J., & Ma, Y. (1998). The risk for early-adulthood anxiety and depressive disorders in adolescents with anxiety and depressive disorders. *Archives of General Psychiatry 55,* 56–64. https://doi.org/10.1001/archpsyc.55.1.56

Platek, S. M., & Kemp, S. M. (2009). Is family special to the brain? An event-related fMRI study of familiar, familial, and self-face recognition. *Neuropsychologia, 47*(3), 849–858. https://doi.org/10.1016/j.neuropsychologia.2008.12.027

Pope, D., & Miles, S. (2022). A caring climate that promotes belonging and engagement. *Phi Delta Kappan, 103*(5), 8–12. https://doi.org/10.1177/00317217221079972

Price, J. (2008). Parent-child quality time: Does birth order matter? *The Journal of Human Resources, 43*(1), 240–265. https://www.jstor.org/stable/40057344

Purdie, D. R., Federman, M., Chin, A., Winston, D., Bursch, B., Olmstead, R., Bulut, Y., & Irwin, M. R. (2022). Hybrid delivery of mindfulness meditation and perceived stress in pediatric resident physicians: A randomized clinical trial of in-person and digital mindfulness meditation. *Journal of Clinical Psychology in Medical Settings, 30,* 425–434. https://doi.org/10.1007/s10880-022-09896-3

Purewal, R., Christley, R., Kordas, K., Joinson, C., Meints, K., Gee, N., & Westgarth, C. (2017). Companion animals and child/adolescent development: A systematic review of the evidence. *International Journal of Environmental Research and Public Health, 14*(3), 234. https://doi.org/10.3390/ijerph14030234

Purves, D., Augustine, G. J., Fitzpatrick, D., Hall, W. C., LaMantia, A.-S., Mooney, R. D., Platt, M. L., White, L. E. (2018). *Neuroscience* (6th ed.). Oxford University Press.

Ranapurwala, S. I., Casteel, C., & Peek-Asa, C. (2016). Volunteering in adolescence and young adulthood crime involvement: A longitudinal analysis from the add health study. *Injury Epidemiology, 3*(1), 26. https://doi.org/10.1186/s40621-016-0091-6

Rao, U., & Chen, L. A. (2009). Characteristics, correlates, and outcomes of childhood and adolescent depressive disorders. *Dialogues in Clinical Neuroscience 11*, 45–62. https://doi.org/10.31887/DCNS.2009.11.1/urao

Rapp, C., Bugra, H., Riecher-Roessler, A., Tamagni, C., & Borgwardt, S. (2012). Effects of cannabis use on human brain structure in psychosis: A systematic review combining in vivo structural neuroimaging and post mortem studies. *Current Pharmaceutical Design, 18*(32), 5070–5080. https://doi.org/10.2174/138161212802884861

Reyna, V., & Farley, F. (2006). Risk and rationality in adolescent decision making: Implications for theory, practice, and public policy. *Psychological Science in the Public Interest, 7*(1), 1–44. https://doi.org/10.1111/j.1529-1006.2006.00026.x

Rhoades, H., Winetrobe, H., & Rice, E. (2015). Pet ownership among homeless youth: Associations with mental health, service utilization and housing status. *Child Psychiatry and Human Development, 46*(2), 237–244. https://doi.org/10.1007/s10578-014-0463-5

Rogoff, B. (1990). *Apprenticeship in thinking: Cognitive development in social context.* Oxford University Press.

Rohde, P., Stice, E., Shaw, H., & Gau, J. M. (2015). Effectiveness trial of an indicated cognitive-behavioral group adolescent depression prevention program versus bibliotherapy and brochure control at 1- and 2-year follow-up. *Journal of Consulting and Clinical Psychology, 83*(4), 736–747. https://doi.org/10.1037/ccp0000022

Rohrer D., Dedrick R. F., & Burgess K. (2014) The benefit of interleaved mathematics practice is not limited to superficially similar kinds of problems. *Psychonomic Bulletin & Review, 21*(5), 1323–1330. https://doi.org/10.3758/s13423-014-0588-3

Rose, S. E., & Lomas, M. H. R. (2020). The potential of a mindfulness-based coloring intervention to reduce test anxiety in adolescents. *Mind, Brain and Education, 14*(4), 335–340. https://doi.org/10.1111/mbe.12255

Rosenburg, B. M., Kodish, T., Cohen, Z. D., Gong-Guy, E., & Craske, M. G. (2022). A novel peer-to-peer coaching program to support digital mental health: Design and implementation. *JMIR Mental Health, 9*(1), e32430–e32430. https://doi.org/10.2196/32430

Rueda, H. A., Yndo, M., Williams, L. R., & Shorey, R. C. (2021). Does Gottman's marital communication conceptualization inform teen dating violence? Communication skill deficits analyzed across three samples of diverse adolescents. *Journal of Interpersonal Violence, 36*(11-12), NP6411–NP6440. https://doi.org/10.1177/0886260518814267

Sacker, A., & Cable, N. (2006). Do adolescent leisure-time physical activities foster health and well-being in adulthood? Evidence from two British birth cohorts. *European Journal of Public Health, 16*(3), 331–335. https://doi.org/10.1093/eurpub/cki189

Sameroff, A. J. (1998). Environmental risk factors in infancy. *Pediatrics, 102*(5 Suppl. E),1287–1292.

Saxena, S., Thornicroft, G., Knapp, M., & Whiteford, H. (2007). Global mental health 2: Resources for mental health: Scarcity, inequity, and inefficiency. *The Lancet (British Edition), 370*(9590), 878. https://doi.org/10.1016/S0140-6736(07)61239-2

Scher, C. D., Forde, D. R., McQuaid, J. R., & Stein, M. B. (2004). Prevalence and demographic correlates of childhood maltreatment in an adult community sample. *Child Abuse & Neglect, 28*(2), 167–180. https://doi.org/10.1016/j.chiabu.2003.09.012

Schiefermeier-Mach, N., Egg, S., Erler, J., Hasenegger, V., Rust, P., König, J., Purtscher, A. E. (2020). Electrolyte intake and major food sources of sodium, potassium, calcium and magnesium among a population in western Austria. *Nutrients, 12*(7), 1956. DOI: 10.3390/nu12071956

Schmidt R.A., & Bjork R.A. (2017). New conceptualizations of practice: Common principles in three paradigms suggest new concepts for training. *Psychological Science, 3*(4):207–218. https://doi.org/10.1111/j.1467-9280.1992.tb00029.x

Schreier, H. M. C., Schonert-Reichl, K. A., & Chen, E. (2013). Effect of volunteering on risk factors for cardiovascular disease in adolescents: A randomized controlled trial. *JAMA Pediatrics, 167*(4), 1–6. https://doi.org/10.1001/jamapediatrics.2013.1100

Schwartz, C. E., Keyl, P. M., Marcum, J. P., & Bode, R. (2009). Helping others shows differential benefits on health and well-being for male and female teens. *Journal of Happiness Studies, 10*(4), 431–448. https://doi.org/10.1007/s10902-008-9098-1

Seewer, N., Skoko, A., Käll, A., Andersson, G., Luhmann, M., Berger, T., & Krieger, T. (2022). Evaluating the efficacy of a guided and unguided internet-based self-help intervention for chronic loneliness: Protocol for a 3-arm randomized controlled trial. *JMIR Research Protocols, 11*(7). https://doi.org/10.2196/36358

Selemon, L. D., & Zecevic, N. (2015). Schizophrenia: A tale of two critical periods for prefrontal cortical development. *Translational Psychiatry, 5*(8), e623–e623. https://doi.org/10.1038/tp.2015.115

Serrander, M., Bremander, A., Jarbin, H., & Larsson, I. (2021). Joy of living through exercise-a qualitative study of clinically referred adolescents' experiences of moderate to vigorous exercise as treatment for depression. *Nordic Journal of Psychiatry, 75*(8), 574–581. https://doi.org/10.1080/08039488.2021.1909128

Shapiro, S. L., Carlson, L. E., Astin, J. A., & Freedman, B. (2006). Mechanisms of mindfulness. *Journal of Clinical Psychology, 62*(3), 373–386. https://doi.org/10.1002/jclp.20237

Shatz, C. J. (1992). The developing brain. *Scientific American, 267*, 60–67. DOI: 10.1038/scientificamerican0992-60

Shinn, A. K., Bolton, K. W., Karmacharya, R., Lewandowski, K. E., Yuksel, C., Baker, J. T., Chouinard, V., Pingali, S. M., Bye, H., Cederbaum, K., & Öngür, D. (2017). McLean onTrack: A transdiagnostic program for early intervention in first-episode psychosis. *Early Intervention in Psychiatry, 11*(1), 83–90. https://doi.org/10.1111/eip.12299

Shirreffs, S. M. (2003). Markers of hydration status. *European Journal of Clinical Nutrition, 57* (Suppl. 2), S6–S9. https://doi.org/10.1038/sj.ejcn.1601895

Shvarts, A., & Bakker, A. (2019). The early history of the scaffolding metaphor: Bernstein, Luria, Vygotsky, and before. *Mind, Culture, and Activity, 26*(1), 4–23. https://doi.org/10.1080/10749039.2019.1574306

Siegler, R. S. (1992). The Other Alfred Binet. *Developmental Psychology, 28*(2), 179–190. https://doi.org/10.1037/0012-1649.28.2.179

Siegler, R., Saffron, J. R., Gershoff, E. T., Eisenberg, N., & Leaper, C. (2020). *How children develop* (6th ed.). Worth Publishers.

Simkin, D. R. (2019). Microbiome and mental health, specifically as it relates to adolescents. *Current Psychiatry Reports, 21*(9), 93–12. https://doi.org/10.1007/s11920-019-1075-3

Sinatra, S. T., Oschman, J. L., Chevalier, G., & Sinatra, D. (2017). Electric nutrition: The surprising health and healing benefits of biological grounding (Earthing). *Alternative Therapies in Health and Medicine, 23*(5), 8–16.

Singh, A. S., van den Berg, V., Uijtdewilligen, L., de Groot, R. H. M., Jolles, J., Andersen, L. B., Bailey, R., Chang, Y.-K., Diamond, A., Ericsson, I., Etnier, J. L., Fedewa, A. L., Hillman, C. H., McMorris, T., Pesce, C., Pühse, U., Tomporowski, P. D., & Chinapaw, M. J. M. (2019). Effects of physic combination of a systematic review and recommendations from an expert panel. *British Journal of Sports Medicine, 53*(10), 640–647. https://doi.org/10.1136/bjsports-2017-098136

Smith, S. M. (1984). A comparison of two techniques for reducing context-dependent forgetting. *Memory & Cognition, 12*(5), 477–482. https://doi.org/10.3758/BF03198309

Smolucha, L., & Smolucha, F. (2021). Vygotsky's theory in-play: early childhood education. *Early Child Development and Care, 191*(7-8), 1041–1055. https://doi.org/10.1080/03004430.2020.1843451

Spear, L. P. (2018). Effects of adolescent alcohol consumption on the brain and behaviour. *Nature Reviews. Neuroscience, 19*(4), 197–214. https://doi.org/10.1038/nrn.2018.10

Speed, L. J., & Majid, A. (2020). *Grounding language in the neglected senses of touch, taste, and smell.* https://doi.org/10.1080/02643294.2019.1623188

Sperling, J. (2021). *Find your fierce: How to put social anxiety in its place.* Magination Press.

Stapleton, B. (2009). Connecting with kids: Lending a helping hand. *Parenting for High Potential, 21.*

Steinberg, L. (2008). A social neuroscience perspective on adolescent risk-taking. *Developmental Review, 28*(1), 78–106. DOI: 10.1016/j.dr.2007.08.002

Ster, Caroline. (2011) *Face 2 Face: Navigating through cyberbullying, peer abuse, bullying.* Reflections Publishing.

Stillman, C. M., Cohen, J., Lehman, M. E., & Erickson, K. I. (2016). Mediators of physical activity on neurocognitive function: A review at multiple levels of Analysis. *Frontiers in Human Neuroscience, 10*, 626–626. https://doi.org/10.3389/fnhum.2016.00626

Straub, J., Metzger, C. D., Plener, P. L., Koelch, M. G., Groen, G., & Abler, B. (2016). Successful group psychotherapy of depression in adolescents alters fronto-limbic resting-state connectivity. *Journal of Affective Disorders, 209*, 135–139. https://doi.org/10.1016/j.jad.2016.11.024

Suhr, J. A., Patterson, S. M., Austin, A. W., Heffner, K. L. (2010). The relation of hydration status to declarative memory and working memory in older adults. *The Journal of Nutrition, Health & Aging, 14*, 840–843. https://doi.org/10.1007/s12603-010-0108-8

Szyf, M. (2014). Lamarck revisited: Epigenetic inheritance of ancestral odor fear conditioning. *Nature Neuroscience, 17(1)*, 2–4. DOI: 10.1038/nn.3603

Taylor, L., De Neve, J., DeBorst, L., & Khanna, D. (2022). *Well-being in education in childhood and adolescence*. International Baccalaureate Organization.

Teicher, M. H., & Samson, J. A. (2016). Annual research review: Enduring neurobiological effects of childhood abuse and neglect. *Journal of Child Psychology and Psychiatry, 57*(3), 241–266. https://doi.org/10.1111/jcpp.12507

Tesser, A. (1988). Toward a self-evaluation maintenance model of social behavior. *Advances in Experimental Social Psychology, 21*, 181–227. https://doi.org/10.1016/S0065-2601(08)60227-0

The Recovery Village. (2023). https://www.therecoveryvillage.com

Therrien, W. J. (2004). Fluency and comprehension gains as a result of repeated reading. *Remedial and Special Education, 25*(4), 252–261. https://doi.org/10.1177/07419325040250040801

Thomas, M. (2019). *TWO: Attention management problems undermine your success. In Attention Management* (Vol. 1). Sourcebooks, Incorporated.

Thomassin, K., Wilson, F., Vaughn-Coaxum, R., Campbell, W. K., Zeichner, A, & Miller, J. D. (2020). Development and validation of the praise, indulgence, and status parenting scale. *Journal of Personality Assessment, 102*(6), 804–816. DOI: 10.1080/00223891.2019.1639187

Tomoda, A., Sheu, Y. S., Rabi, K., Suzuki, H., Navalta, C. P., Polcari, A., & Teicher, M. H. (2011). Exposure to parental verbal abuse is associated with increased gray matter volume in superior temporal gyrus. *NeuroImage, 54*, S280–S286. https://doi.org/10.1016/j.neuroimage.2010.05.027

Tukel, Y. (2020). *The study of the relationships among participation in recreation activities, life satisfaction and happiness in university students. In international society for technology, education, and science*. International Society for Technology, Education, and Science.

Twenge, J. M., Joiner, T. E., Rogers, M. L., & Martin, G. N. (2018). Increases in depressive symptoms, suicide-related outcomes, and suicide rates among US adolescents after 2010 and links to increased new media screen time. *Clinical Psychological Science, 6*(1), 3–17. https://doi.org/10.1177/2167702617723376

Twenge, J. M., Martin, G. N., & Campbell, W. K. (2018). Decreases in psychological well-being among american adolescents after 2012 and links to screen time during the rise of smartphone technology. *Emotion (Washington, D.C.), 18*(6), 765–780. https://doi.org/10.1037/emo0000403

Tymofiyeva, O., Henje, E., Yuan, J. P., Huang, C.-Y., Connolly, C. G., Ho, T. C., Bhandari, S., Parks, K. C., Sipes, B. S., Yang, T. T., & Xu, D. (2021). Reduced anxiety and changes in amygdala network properties in adolescents with training for awareness, resilience, and action (TARA). *NeuroImage Clinical, 29*, 102521. https://doi.org/10.1016/j.nicl.2020.102521

Tymofiyeva, O., Sipes, B. S., Luks, T., Hamlat, E. J., Samson, T. E., Hoffmann, T. J., Glidden, D. V., Jakary, A., Li, Y., Ngan, T., Henje, E., & Yang, T. T. (2024). Interoceptive brain network mechanisms of mindfulness-based training in healthy adolescents. *Frontiers in Psychology, 15*, 1410319. https://doi.org/10.3389/fpsyg.2024.1410319

Tymofiyeva, O., Yuan, J. P., Huang, C.-Y., Connolly, C. G., Henje Blom, E., Xu, D., & Yang, T. T. (2019). Application of machine learning to structural connectome to predict symptom reduction in depressed adolescents with cognitive behavioral therapy (CBT). *NeuroImage Clinical, 23*, 101914–101914. https://doi.org/10.1016/j.nicl.2019.101914

Tymofiyeva, O., Zhou, V. X., Lee, C.-M., Xu, D., Hess, C. P., & Yang, T. T. (2020). MRI insights into adolescent neurocircuitry–A vision for the future. *Frontiers in Human Neuroscience, 14*(237) 1–27. https://doi.org/10.3389/fnhum.2020.00237

United Nations Office on Drugs and Crime (UNODC). (2015) World drug report.

Umberson, D., & Montez, J. K. (2010). Social relationships and health: A flashpoint for health policy. *Journal of Health and Social Behavior, 51*(Suppl. 1), S54–S66. https://doi.org/10.1177/0022146510383501

United States Preventive Services Task Force. (2022). Screening for depression and suicide risk in children and adolescents: U.S. Preventive Services Task Force recommendation statement. *JAMA, 328*(15), 1534–1542. DOI: 10.1001/jama.2022.16946

Van der Meulen, M., Veldhuis, J., Braams, B. R., Peters, S., Konijn, E. A., & Crone, E. A. (2017). Brain activation upon ideal-body media exposure and peer feedback in late adolescent girls. *Cognitive, Affective, & Behavioral Neuroscience, 17*(4), 712–723. https://doi.org/10.3758/s13415-017-0507-y

van Harmelen, A.-L. van, Kievit, R. A., Ioannidis, K., Neufeld, S., Jones, P. B., Bullmore, E., Dolan, R., Fonagy, P., & Goodyer, I. (2017). Adolescent friendships predict later resilient functioning across psychosocial domains in a healthy community cohort. *Psychological Medicine, 47*(13), 2312–2322. https://doi.org/10.1017/S0033291717000836

Velthorst, E., Zinberg, J., Addington, J., Cadenhead, K. S., Cannon, T. D., Carrion, R. E., Auther, A., Cornblatt, B. A., McGlashan, T. H., Mathalon, D. H., Perkins, D. O., Seidman, L. J., Tsuang, M. T., Walker, E. F., Woods, S. W., Reichenberg, A., & Bearden, C. E. (2018). Potentially important periods of change in the development of social and role functioning in youth at clinical high risk for psychosis. *Development and Psychopathology, 30*(1), 39–47. https://doi.org/10.1017/S0954579417000451

Vian, J., Pereira, C., Chavarria, V., Kohler, C., Stubbs, B., Quevedo, J., King, S. W., Carvalho, A. F., Berk, M., & Fernandes, B. S. (2017). The renin-angiotensin system: a possible new target for depression. *BMC Medicine, 15*(144). https://doi.org/10.1186/s12916-017-0916-3

Vigo, D., Thornicroft, G., & Atun, R. (2016). Estimating the true global burden of mental illness. *The Lancet. Psychiatry, 3*(2), 171–178. https://doi.org/10.1016/S2215-0366(15)00505-2

Villeneuve, J. C., Conner, J. O., Selby, S., & Pope, D. C. (2019). Easing the stress at pressure-cooker schools. *Phi Delta Kappan, 101*(3), 15–19. https://doi.org/10.1177/0031721719885910

Voelcker-Rehage, C. (2016). Exercise-induced changes in basal ganglia volume and their relation to cognitive performance. *Journal of Neurology and Neuromedicine, 1*(5), 19–24. https://doi.org/10.29245/2572.942X/2016/5.1044

Vygotsky, L. S. (1978). *Mind in society*. Harvard University Press.

Vygotsky, L. S. (1962). *Thought and language*. M.I.T. Press.

Waldinger, R. J. & Schulz, M. S. (2023). *The good life: Lessons from the world's longest scientific study of happiness*. Simon & Schuster.

Wang, Y., Zhao, T., Zhang, Y., Li, S., & Cong, X. (2021). Positive effects of kangaroo mother care on long-term breastfeeding rates, growth, and neurodevelopment in preterm infants. *Breastfeeding Medicine, 16*(4), 282–291. https://doi.org/10.1089/bfm.2020.0358

Wang, X., Cai, Z.-D., Jiang, W.-T., Fang, Y.-Y., Sun, W.-X., Wang, X. (2022). Systematic review and meta-analysis of the effects of exercise on depression in adolescents. *Child Adolescent Psychiatry Mental Health, 16*(16). https://doi.org/10.1186/s13034-022-00453-2

Ward, M. K., & Broniarczyk, S. M. (2011). It's not me, it's you: How gift giving creates giver identity threat as a function of social closeness. *The Journal of Consumer Research, 38*(1), 164–181. https://www.jstor.org/stable/10.1086/658166

Weinberg, R. S., & Gould, D. (2015). *Foundations of sport and exercise psychology*, (6th ed.). Human Kinetics.

Weng, P.-Y., & Chiang, Y.-C. (2014). Psychological restoration through indoor and outdoor leisure activities. *Journal of Leisure Research, 46*(2), 203–217. https://doi.org/10.1080/00222216.2014.11950320

Wester, K. L., Wachter Morris, C., & Williams, B. (2017). Nonsuicidal self-injury in the schools: A tiered prevention approach for reducing social contagion. *Professional School Counseling, 21*, 142–151. https://doi.org/10.5330/1096-2409-21.1.142

White, M. P., Alcock, I., Grellier, J., Wheeler, B. W., Hartig, T., Warber, S. L., Bone, A., Depledge, M. H., & Fleming, L. E. (2019). Spending at least 120 minutes a week in nature is associated with good health and wellbeing. *Scientific Reports, 9*(1), 7730–11. https://doi.org/10.1038/s41598-019-44097-3

Winsler, A., Fernyhough, C., & Montero, I. (2009). *Private speech, executive functioning, and the development of self-regulation*. Cambridge University Press.

Wyman, P. A., Pickering T, A., Pisani, A. R., Rulison, K., Schmeelk-Cone, K., Hartley, C., Gould, M., Caine, E. D., LoMurray, M., Brown, C. H., & Valente, T. W. (2019). Peer-adult network structure and suicide attempts in 38 high schools: Implications for network-informed suicide prevention. *The Journal of Child Psychology and Psychiatry, 60*(10), 1065–1075. DOI: 10.1111/jcpp.13102

Wood, A. M., Froh, J. J., & Geraghty, A. W. A. (2010). Gratitude and well-being: A review and theoretical integration. *Clinical Psychology Review, 30*(7), 890–905. https://doi.org/10.1016/j.cpr.2010.03.005

World Health Organization (2010). *Global Recommendations on Physical Activity for Health*. WHO Press.

Xia, T., Song, L., Wang, T. T., Tan, L., & Mo, L. (2016). Exploring the effect of red and blue on cognitive task performances. *Frontiers in Psychology, 7*, 784–784. https://doi.org/10.3389/fpsyg.2016.00784

Young, J. F., Mufson, L., & Schueler, C. M. (2016). *Preventing adolescent depression: Interpersonal psychotherapy–adolescent skills training*. Oxford University Press.

Zalesky, A., Solowij, N., Yucel, M., Lubman, D. I., Takagi, M., Harding, I. H., Lorenzetti, V., Wang, R., Searle, K., Pantelis, C., Seal, M. (2012). Effect of long-term cannabis use on axonal fibre connectivity. *Brain, 135* (Pt. 7), 2245–2255. https://doi.org/10.1093/brain/aws136

Zavaruieva, I., Bondarenko, L., & Fedko, O. (2022). The role of colour coding of educational materials when studying grammatical categories of the Ukrainian language by foreign students. *Review of Education, 10*, e3312. https://doi.org/10.1002/rev3.3312

Zehra, A., Burns, J., Liu, C., K., Manza, P., Wiers, C. E., Volkow, N. D., & Wang, G.-J. (2018). Cannabis addiction and the brain: A review. *Journal of Neuroimmune Pharmacology, 13*(4), 438–452. DOI: 10.1007/s11481-018-9782-9

Zhou, W., & McLellan, R. (2024). The effectiveness of taught, self-help mindfulness-based interventions on Chinese adolescents' well-being, mental health, prosocial and difficult behavior, and coping strategy. *Applied Psychology: Health and Well-Being, 16*(3), 1024–1045. https://doi.org/10.1111/aphw.12517

Zoogman, S., Goldberg, S. B., Hoyt, W. T., & Miller, L. (2015). Mindfulness interventions with youth: A meta-analysis. *Mindfulness, 6*(2), 290–302. https://doi.org/10.1007/s12671-013-0260-4

Zuromski, K. (2020, November 9). *Assessing and Intervening on Imminent Risk* [Lecture]. PSYC E-1247: The Psychology of Self-Harm, Harvard University, Boston, MA, United States.

Create-Your-Own Life Topic

- _____

- **Journal:**

• **Doodle or Draw:**

Your Favorite Inspirational Quote

_____

_____

CREATE-YOUR-OWN LIFE TOPIC

Brain Power

From what you have learned in *The Resilience Game Plan*, select your own life topic and write about how this life topic will affect your brain. Below, use the space to practice drawing an illustration of a brain, marking the parts of the brain as you go. Use **page 21** as a reference.

Cognitive Skills

Step #1: Expressive Writing to Overcome _____ (Write a "_____ Life Topic" causing you distress.)

#1 Stop and Acknowledge - What are you thinking/feeling?
_____
_____

#2 Question and Tweak - What facts back up these thoughts?
_____
_____

#3 Balance and Thrive - Change your negative thought to this positive thought:
_____
_____

#4 Create your "I Am Statement" in overcoming this obstacle.
_____

Cognitive Skills _____

(Write a "_____ Life Topic" causing you distress.)

INSTRUCTIONS for Steps #2 and #3:
On the line above, write the "_____ Life Topic" causing you stress. Next, On the "Feelings Thermometer," color up to the point of your distress (from 1 to 5) and write a phrase on the matching line describing how you are feeling about this topic. Now that you know how you feel, move to Step #3 and write ten steps to overcome this fear. You can find tips below with a "possible scenario" to get you started.

Step #2: Gauging Your Feelings

SUBJECTIVE UNITS OF DISTRESS SCALE (SUDS)
FEELINGS THERMOMETER

5. _____
4. _____
3. _____
2. _____
1. _____

Step #3: Overcoming Obstacles

FEAR AND AVOIDANCE HIERARCHY
WRITE EXPOSURES ON LADDER

10. _____
9. _____
8. _____
7. _____
6. _____
5. _____
4. _____
3. _____
2. _____
1. _____

Ideas on How You Feel About _____:
5. Extreme anxiety/distress; boiling over with emotions
4. High anxiety/distress; cannot concentrate; freaking out
3. Moderately anxious/distressed and upset
2. Mild anxiety/distress; concentrating well
1. No anxiety/no anxiety; distress

Possible Thoughts on Overcoming _____:
10. I am confident _____.
9. I will practice _____.
8. I will create _____.
7. I will do _____.
6. I will practice "I am" statements to _____.
5. I will work with a tutor to help _____.
4. I will join a study group and identify _____.
3. I will watch online videos with lessons about _____.
2. I will watch TikToks on _____.
1. I will listen to an upbeat song about _____.

Communication Skills

Mindfulness Skills

Mindfulness Exercise:
1.
2.
3.
4.

Well-Being Habit Tracker:

1. **Fill out each Well-Being Habit Tracker category below.**
2. **When completed, check the box and note your subjective well-being from 1-10.**

- ☐ **Sleep:** How many hours? _____ **Morning Light Exposure:** ☐ Well-Being Rating: _____
- ☐ **Exercise:** Length/Type? _____ Well-Being Rating: _____
- ☐ **Mindfulness:** Length/Type? _____ Well-Being Rating: _____
- ☐ **Nature:** Time spent/Activity outside? ____ / _____ Well-Being Rating: _____
- ☐ **Hydration:** I drank ☐☐☐☐☐☐☐☐ 8 oz. glasses of water. Well-Being Rating: _____
- ☐ **Nutrition:** Number of healthy meals or calories consumed? _____ Well-Being Rating: _____
- ☐ **Social Fitness:** Time spent/Activity? ____ / _____ Well-Being Rating: _____
- ☐ **Caring:** Act(s) of service? _____ Well-Being Rating: _____
- ☐ **Gratitude:** I am grateful for _____ Well-Being Rating: _____
- ☐ **Happiness:** _____ brought me joy! Well-Being Rating: _____
- ☐ **Laughter:** I laughed about _____
- ☐ **Smile:** I made someone smile by _____
- ☐ **Music:** I sang or listened to this song to motivate me and boost my mood and well-being: _____

© 2024 Reflections Publishing LLC. All rights reserved.

Anxiety-Buster To-Do List:

1 Big Task - Let's Go!

☐ _____

2 Medium Tasks - Let's Do This!

☐ _____

☐ _____

3 Small Tasks - You Got This!

☐ _____

☐ _____

☐ _____

© 2024 Reflections Publishing LLC. All rights reserved.

Space to download and process your thoughts:

Congratulations!

You have completed
The Resilience Game Plan curriculum.

This certifies you have acquired and developed
the necessary cognitive, communication,
and mindfulness life skills you need to
help you navigate challenging life scenarios.

You are on your way to
developing a growth mindset and
through your hard work, determination,
and positive attitude, you are creating a
foundation to ensure yourself a healthy
emotional, social, and physical well-being.

Date: **Facilitator:**

_____   _____

Go to www.ReflectionsPublishing.com

For Up-to-Date Information on:

- Upcoming Conferences
- *The Resilience Game Plan* Professional Development HyFlex Training
- Book Collections by Reflections Publishing LLC

www.ingramcontent.com/pod-product-compliance
Lightning Source LLC
Chambersburg PA
CBHW080735300426
44114CB00019B/2595